SO
MA

"*Soul Making* will leave you breathless. A winding, intense, and illuminating journey into the realms we can experience when we surrender to the infinite power within. This tantalizing, visceral, and strikingly personal book captures the profound experiences that await us as we delve deep into our being and open our minds to experiencing what we cannot yet imagine."

ISABEL UNRAVELED, WRITER, COACH, AND
CREATOR OF MIND MINE

"I commend Doug for his bravery in writing this book. It's unlike any other book I've read, covering his spiritual experiences from childhood to adulthood, from seeing spirits to exploring existential questions. These are conversations I often have with myself, and it's comforting to know others share similar experiences and questions."

DARRON BROWN, HOST OF *A PODCAST FOR MEN*

"Douglas M. Gillette offers a portrait of a universe that is loving, inclusive, broad, and deeply personal. He seamlessly weaves seemingly impossible theories together and gives the reader the encouragement to imagine what 'This Life' is all about. *Soul Making* is a tour of the Universe's personhood-making activities inviting you to become all that you already are in the dance of life."

DREW LITTLEJOHNS, PH.D. CANDIDATE, LECTURER FOR
ENTREPRENEURSHIP ACCELERATORS, AND OWNER OF VH NUTRITION

"The infinite and the finite, the ordinary and the divine are inexorably united within us. After a journey lasting a lifetime, the author reveals this final truth: there is an unending love at the core of our being."

WILLIAM R. MISTELE, AUTHOR OF *ENCOUNTERS WITH MERMAIDS*

SOUL MAKING

THE REALIZATION OF THE MYSTICAL LIFE

DOUGLAS M. GILLETTE,
M.A.R.S., M.Div.

Inner Traditions
Rochester, Vermont

Inner Traditions
One Park Street
Rochester, Vermont 05767
www.InnerTraditions.com

Cataloging-in-Publication Data for this title is available from the Library of Congress

ISBN 978-1-64411-895-5 (print)
ISBN 978-1-64411-896-2 (ebook)

Printed and bound in the United States by Lake Book Manufacturing, LLC

10 9 8 7 6 5 4 3 2 1

Text design and layout by Priscilla Harris Baker
This book was typeset in Garamond with Arno, Avenir, and Summa used as display typefaces

To send correspondence to the author of this book, mail a first-class letter to the author c/o Inner Traditions • Bear & Company, One Park Street, Rochester, VT 05767, and we will forward the communication, or contact the author directly at **gilletted@sbcglobal.net**.

Scan the QR code and save 25% at InnerTraditions.com. Browse over 2,000 titles on spirituality, the occult, ancient mysteries, new science, holistic health, and natural medicine.

For Kennedy

Contents

. . . .
Note on Capitalizations

In general, I've used capitalizations when I'm referring to God and God's Aspects, Attributes, and (sometimes) Actions. I also capitalize Divine pronouns: He/His/Him, She/Her/Hers, It/Its. In places I refer to the Divine simply as *He*; this is out of convenience, and not meant to signal that God is only, or in any ultimate sense, masculine or even gendered. To provide a fuller picture of the Divine Reality I'm describing, I also capitalize adjectives and sometimes adverbs that belong to God. I also capitalize Angels and Demons but not their pronouns and so forth because I consider them to be lower forms of Divine Self-disclosure as beings and as actions. Because I view Nature, in some way, as an Aspect of God, I also capitalize It, as well as some of Its pronouns, processes, and so on. Depending on the context, I also capitalize Good and Evil (as Aspects of the Divine). The same goes for Psyche, except that I use lower case to talk about more finite expressions of It. Often, I mean two or more levels of some aspect of Reality (which I also capitalize . . . because It is What God is and/or is a Product of what God does), as, for example, in psyche/Psyche, or multiplicity/Multiplicity. Furthermore, I've capitalized what I believe are the highest states of consciousness and being that we have access to because, for me, they are merged with, or are entering into the Presence of the Divine, and are examples of Divine Effects and Actions. So, in many places in the text there is an uppercase and lowercase mixing. I'm trying to show graphically the meshing of the Divine and human at our experiential level, or levels. In my view that meshing is *always* taking place—so, it's often difficult to *unmesh* these elements, although it is useful—even necessary—in conventional or daily-life contexts.

In some places where I'm using terms from other authors that I would capitalize, but they don't, I defer to their case usage.

I know this capitalization practice is unorthodox in modern secular writing. But I'm influenced by the Islamic tradition of honoring the Names of God. My intention has *not* been to write just another secular book about psychospiritual material but, rather, to convey something of the thrill of actually *entering into* the Sacred. An important way to do that, so far as I'm concerned, is to honor with capitalizations the Reality of the Divine and those ultimate and penultimate things that come near to or merge with or are expressed by It.

. . . .

Preface

This book is about our adventures of becoming within an Infinite Person. Those adventures, and in that Context, give us the gift of our identities as persons of Infinite, Eternal, and Absolute Worth. So, this book is about our experiences of the simultaneously Transcendent and Immanent Divine in and through the everyday ex-pressing ("pressing out from within") of our lives in the mediums and environments of Nature and of one another. It's about our becoming in the world(s) of matter, energy, space, and time what we always are in the Infinity and Eternity of the Divine Psyche. It's also about reflecting on these experiences.

My purpose in writing this book is to share with you experiences of Wonder, Awe, Dread, and Mystery—experiences of the Divine that, hopefully for all of us, also include Peace, Gratitude, and Love—and with these, an empowering sense of your own well-being in the here-and-now as well as at your All-embracing and Eternally Transcendent Core.

A secondary purpose, and one of the vehicles for actualizing this core purpose, is to bring together in an organic and unifying way a wide range of contrasting worldviews and contentious issues—worldviews and issues that are usually interpreted as polar opposites. I'll try to do this within an overall framework of merger between a theistic Neoplatonism and Panentheism. These worldviews are explained in rough form in the introduction and show up throughout the rest of the book. Within this framework, I try to integrate conflicting perspectives that come up in discussions about matter and mind (Mind), multiplicity and oneness (Multiplicity and Oneness), Nature and Supernature—and beyond That, *Supra*nature, the finite and the Infinite, the mortal and Immortal, time and Eternity, the question of Evil, evolution and Purpose, and others.

I can't guarantee that I'll be able to work out to your, or my, satisfaction the full integration of all of these controversies and issues. But I'll do my best. You'll have to be the judge of how well I've succeeded . . . for *you*.

But far more important, I want to bring you into awareness of the Infinite Presence—inner and outer—in which we live every picosecond of our lives, here and Elsewhere and Elsewhen!

Acknowledgments

As always in the process of writing a manuscript and publishing it as a book, I have many people to thank. First is John Loudon, my agent for this project. Second, the great team at Inner Traditions • Bear and Company: Jon Graham, acquisitions editor, whose enthusiasm did much to get the book proposal accepted; the publisher Ehud C. Sperling, who personally worked on the manuscript (a particular honor); Jeanie Levitan, VP and editor in chief; Courtney B. Jenkins, acquisitions and editorial assistant, who worked with me, especially in the early stages of creation; Meghan MacLean, senior editor and project manager for transforming the manuscript into book form; Erica Robinson, content director, who produced a wonderful catalog page which is the foundation for the publicity of the book; and then Kate Mueller, the copyeditor; Priscilla Baker the designer; the typesetters, and now the publicity crew, especially Mercedes Rojas and Ashley Kolesnik, my publicists!

In addition to all of that wonderful support, I want to thank my wife, who was happy to relieve me of my weekend obligations so that I could take that time to move the manuscript to completion. Also, our baby granddaughter for whom I was the primary daytime caregiver for a wonderful ten months (from three to thirteen months old). She was as patient as a baby can be, letting me write in the midst of all the things little babies need. We had a wee of a time together!

INTRODUCTION

Inklings of an Infinite and Intimate Presence

You say I'm talking as if there were a ghost
in the machine.
I say, there is a ghost in the machine.
I say, the ghost invented the machine, and
did so in order to inhabit it.
I say further that when the machine's exhausted
its usefulness, the ghost exits this,
drops it as disarticulated wreckage, according
to the second law of thermodynamics,
and returns to wherever ghosts go to recover
from their dreams of inhabiting machines!

DOUGLAS M. GILLETTE,
AT THE THRESHOLDS OF ELYSIUM

I was eleven or twelve. It was a hot summer night. The air was humid and close. I'd stormed out of our house after another violent argument with my mother. I was filled with frustration, anger, bewilderment, and despair. I stood there in our backyard trying to get a grip.

1

I looked up at the stars and the cold vacuum between them—vast, absolutely indifferent, and completely alien to the feverish upheavals of feeling that living things undergo—and, at that moment, me. I felt the literally unspeakable separation between my feelings and the schizoid feelinglessness of the universe above and around me. The disjunction between that vast lifelessness and my painful but intense aliveness conveyed a deep sense of dread to me, as if I could be swallowed up into that infinite deadness, leaving no trace of me, my joys and trials, my anger and my love, my identity, meaning of any kind and in any sense. I felt the excruciating contrast between that subhuman fathomlessness and personhood, persons, whether at peace within and among one another or in conflict.

Suddenly, from a point in the middle of my forehead, a little above my nose, I felt a pencil-thin ray of red light shoot out with enormous speed. Instantaneously, it pierced the farthest boundary of the universe and punched through and then merged with a far-flung Realm of complete Comfort, Peace, Kindness, and Light. My feelings turned on a dime, and I immediately felt awash in a Reality outside the cosmos in which I was loved unconditionally and in which my personhood with all its strengths and flaws, me specifically, was totally Validated and Affirmed. No matter what I was going through down here, I was at deep and unassailable Peace There. I was inside my Core, my earthly life transcended, yet somehow included.

I felt gratitude beyond words. I knew absolutely, not through reason or wishing, certainly not by willing, that I am Eternally Fulfilled—my life as the person I normally think of as me, the mess of my day-to-day existence, and the densely tangible and undeniable Tranquility of what I took to be my Eternal, or Immortal, Identity.

I knew I had to come down from that experience and re-engage in my daily life. But that experience changed my sense of who and what I am forever. Of course, I lose touch with it, sometimes for long stretches of time. But it's always there, indelibly stamped into the substance of my awareness—everything I am and do—and re-enterable through the memory of it, which makes it immediately present . . . in all of my presents.

The Limitations of Knowing . . .
at Least Mine

I don't know what Reality is. I don't know anyone who does. I deeply suspect that no finite creature no matter how gifted—in the past, present, or future—*can* know. Certainly, when it comes to daily life and its extension into the sciences, we can (and must) know enough to get by. In terms of extraordinary states of mind in which everyday consciousness is exceeded, some of us, I believe, get clues, glimpses maybe—felt or even visual—but I am much more than suspicious of that multitude of mutually conflicting maps of Heaven, minutely detailed and passed off as literalistic accounts of what's really There, above, below, or beyond our usual states of awareness. The same goes for pat explanations of what these usual states of awareness are.

But even if the experiences of alternative states of consciousness and their environments (or, for that matter, our spatial-temporal daily life consciousness and environments) are in some sense true (which I believe they are), they cannot be put adequately into words. Why not? Because 99.9999 percent of Reality (or something like that) is irremediably beyond our comprehension. And words and the neural architecture that makes them possible are, as the philosophers say, discursive—one after the other. Just as seriously, they are all shorthand, finite and consequently necessarily imprecise, not sufficiently layered or nuanced. They are temporal and more or less literalish, whereas What-This-Is-as-a-Whole, both usual and unusual, spatial-temporal and Infinite and Eternal, ultimately and immediately—"closer . . . than breathing, and nearer than hands and feet"[1]—is simultaneously one-after-another and All-at-Once, here and All-where/Nowhere, this and Everything. No matter how extraordinary, no state of consciousness is experienced as that simultaneity of specifics and Whole. Even if it could be, it could never be rendered fully in a mode of expression that is restricted to the finite. "The Tao that can be spoken is not the true Tao."[2]

That doesn't mean we're not right now living It, in It, *as* It. It does mean It is experienced by creatures who evolved within and as the ferociousness of a little corner of It, to address It from the immediate perspective of trying to survive and, where possible, to flourish . . . in and as the specific materialized forms that we are—paramecium, fungus, bat, human, octopus, extraterrestrial. That goes for un-, dis-, non-, or not fully incarnate psyches as well—what we generally call spirits.

Put simply, just try to describe the taste, sight, smell, texture of a really luscious plum! Any plum, for that matter.

I've had a lifetime of the usual, as most of us have. I've also had a lifetime of experiences of what I, along with a lot of us, would call the unusual. It's the unusual that leads me to experience that Whatever-This-Is goes from the Odd to the Weird to the Very Weird to the Awesome to the Terrifying (the Wonderful is in there too), then shoots clear off the charts into the Absolutely, Fantastically Unknowable! To experience that gradient and then its Climax is a thrill that dwarfs standing on the edge of the Grand Canyon or lying on your back in the Sinai Peninsula (as I have) at night and feeling like you're going to fall up, or out, into that black sky that is, astonishingly, more light than darkness. Stars and galaxies.

That brings me back to the story of that painful and wonderful summer night in our backyard in Rock Island, Illinois. First, I should say that when I had that experience, I'd never heard anything about a third eye or lasers. I'm not sure lasers had even been invented then.

The Experiential Fact and a Little Interpretation

No doubt endorphins saved me from the heat of my overwrought emotions and also from the terror of facing the subzero, totally unfeeling indifference of the vastness above me. Biochemistry to the rescue in the crazy making of both the emotional heat and the breath-stopping cold of an exceedingly more expansive environment . . . and their slamming-together juxtaposition!

And yet, I was not conscious of endorphins. I was conscious of the feelings they enabled and the vision they afforded. Endorphins—biochemistry—were the equipment, the agency that delivered me to Salvation. Not the cause. Well, the cause, yes, but themselves caused. By what? Ultimately, I believe, by the Lure on the far side of this localized expression of Reality we call the cosmos. That opened me and conveyed me to a Presence, a Loving and Validating and All-healing Presence—"a" Person of Unfathomable Magnitude Whom I perhaps somewhat colloquially call God.

So, there was me here in this beautiful and tortured world, and me There in a realm of utter Peace, Joy, Love.

The experience suggests at least three levels or aspects of that piece of Reality I underwent and, in effect, spanned in that jarring and soothing moment. (As you'll discover, I'm convinced that all of Reality—every aspect of It—is layered.) The first is the level of the (relatively) conscious and emotional human—the suffering of life in general raised to a fever pitch in the human in need of succor, safety, and reassurance. The second level is what I would call out as the mostly schizoid emotional deadness of the Soul, Spirit, or Psyche of Nature as a nameable entity of some kind. The third level, as I experienced It, is outside Nature, while at the same time infusing It (although incompletely). Again, as I experienced It, It was the Place where all existential or core needs, yearnings, and deepest wishes are completely fulfilled, and all conflicts at the first level are resolved.

That was the actual experience, the psychological fact, with a minimum of interpretation.

Two More Stories

Throughout my life, especially in moments of stress—but not always— I've had experiences like that. And with them has come the powerful sense that no matter what I undergo here, I am always also above my life in a Wondrous Peace in which God knows me, knows what we're going through together, and makes it all right, not always here, perhaps, but forever There.

First story:

I spent an entire summer when I was seven or eight years old at a place called Camp Hauberg on the Mississippi River not too far from Rock Island. I remember archery lessons, botanical excursions, algae scum (accompanied by a sharp, acrid, green stench) on the surface of the water in a little screened-in pen (where I taught myself how to swim), separated from the main flow of the mile-wide river, leeches, cicadas, crickets, plopping fish, and pungent oil slicks from the barges that chugged up and down the channel. Of course, there were camp songs and plastic models to build on rainy days, and the sweetly stinging smell of model glue. There were canoeing classes and every Friday evening exciting "war canoe" races for the older boys, their cabin counselors in the sterns calling out the strokes.

And then there was the "Indian" ceremony on the last night in a clearing deep in the woods. Each cabin had to thread through the forest separately to the clearing. It was pitch-black except for the flaring torch held aloft by our cabin counselor at the head of the line, barely visible through the dense vegetation. I was near or at the rear, mostly in the dark, feeling both exhilarated by the night adventure and claustrophobic from the looming trees, which pressed closely on either side.

It was hard to keep our footing and maintain an even pace, so we had to look down a lot, which didn't do much good because we couldn't see the ground. There was a certain amount of thrashing in the thick underbrush with leafy branches whipping across the sides of our heads.

In spite of this, I looked up from time to time, up, up toward the little bit of sky visible between the topmost branches of the trees. I suddenly felt like running, lifting, flying. It was a powerful, even over-whelming sensation—a soaring of spirit, almost as if I could levitate (which I couldn't). Something, I imagine, like what people feel in out-of-body experiences (I've never had one of those so far as I know). I felt this incredible sense of Expansiveness, and I wanted to lift my arms and embrace the whole universe! Hold It all, and, at the same time, become It, or evaporate into It, become one with It.

Second story:

I remember at two or three years old, every night before I went to bed, going from window to window looking for the moon. And when I saw it, I would feel that lifting, tranquility, and wonder beyond the bounds of the world. And always a vast Presence.

Interpretation of these.

These states of Expansiveness, Ecstasy I think, were experiences of being drawn into and losing myself (almost) in the All of the Soul of Nature. But what makes Nature-as-a-Whole so powerfully lifting and compelling is the Divine Person Who paradoxically is both hidden and revealed by It, Who shines through It, illuminates, irradiates It, and, at the same time, projects It as a Veil or Mask, by which It protects us from direct encounter with Its Infinite Fullness, which would annihilate us.

I want to stress that there are a few core things I believe I know—for example, that there is God; that God is Unity, or Oneness, expressed in multiple ways and at multiple levels, layers, or dimensions; that whatever else God may be, God is "a" Person, although of Unfathomable, ulti-mately of Infinite, Extent; that God makes everything—time, Eternity, space, Infinity, and all the manifestations and inhabitants thereof—and in some sense *is* them; that, known to them or not, finite persons are the most intimate and precious Expressions of God, of Infinite Worth and Immortal (in some way) because they are most directly and immediately parts of God's Substance, Essence, and Existence or Being, both in their individuality and in their identity with God; therefore, speaking temporally, personhood is the core and purpose of all that is, has been, or will be. I also want to be very clear that the rest of my interpretations are truly provisional, my evolving take on Reality, Its Structures and Dynamics. I am not trying to create a map of Reality (much less of Heaven) but, rather, to share my personal reflections on my own experience of living the usual and the unusual over the course of seventy-four years. With these things in mind, onward!

A Mythopoetic Prefiguration of the Book and More Interpretation

Unseen, yet felt from within, Psyche (capital *P*) blooms upward like thunderheads on summer afternoons, Self-manifesting from some invisible behind-the-world Place. It does so through and as the mist of matter, and forms it as It rises into dynamics and structures It can use to make Itself increasingly manifest in space and time. It makes Itself Present, though It never directly displays, as specific finite matter-souls, psychophysical beings who can touch, taste, smell, hear, see, and interact with one another. At Its highest, most noble, and most deeply and wholly satisfying, It forms Itself into persons who can love and be loved, ultimately without limit.

Some Aspect of Psyche, Infinite and Immortal, fogs out and diffuses to unconsciousness as It becomes expressed by the confining medium of energy fields and matter and is initiated into a process of inevitable and unstoppable change—body and soul: Psyche, now psyche, expressing as material body; body expressed as immaterial psyche. Yet, in my belief and life experience, the Core of personhood, collective and individual, remains serene, unperturbed, and unconfined . . . ultimately, Infinite and Immortal. At the same time, and inexplicably, that Core Identity is impregnated and filled with the creative experiences It has had in the realms of Its life or lives in the soul-and-matter constructions It was engaged in building for Itself while living within them, is building now, and will build.

The initial shock of materializing renders Psyche unconscious as It shifts from Its Infinite and Immortal condition to the process of informing the apparently finite worlds of matter, space, and time. Its recovery and unfolding within those dimensions are gradual, a process of emergence, evolution, projection, and complexification—in short, remembering, waking up. A central aspect of this recovery (of Its Original State) involves incremental maturing both in terms of individuals and in the grand sweep of cosmic and biological evolution. For human beings, this maturing may continue and even accelerate even as the material expression of the biological construction begins to deconstruct through illness and aging toward death. In that sense, and under certain circumstances, further psychic growth may actually be *enabled* by the decay of the physical medium and its final disintegration. When that is complete, psyche/Psyche separates from the matter that had enabled it to become and, one way or another, eventually returns to what It always is.

As this happens, room is made for new creative constructions of Psyche as psyche. Again, this is true at the level of individuals and also for the species-wide (kingdom, phylum, class, order, family, genus) psychobiological constructions and perhaps for all manifestations of energy and matter in space and time—the vast apparently progressive panorama of the evolution-emergence of this universe (and any others) and of living beings on this planet (and any others). Psyche to psyche-as-soul-body to free psyche en route to psyche-as-Psyche—sequential, but also ultimately and immediately One . . . one Present, one Presence, while remaining individual.

This "making room" is not a painless or obviously benevolent process. In Its novelty-seeking creations, Nature seems completely indifferent to the suffering and death that are evidently inherent to It. These are on a massive scale as well as being crushingly personal for individuals. According to the degrees of their awareness, all biological entities (at least them) do what they can to protect themselves from those aspects of the rest of Nature that are painful or lethal to them. The more sophisticated the matter-soul, the more devastating the sense of Nature's Alien-ness becomes.

For us, not only can Nature seem—and be—threatening, disorienting, even terrifying, Its Strangeness also becomes apparent, especially at the quantum, the cosmic, and the psychic levels. Add to this the subquantum glimpses we get of the underlying nonlocality of things, our investigations of time and the present (which turn out to be disturbingly Weird), and unsolvable questions about randomness, free will, and determinism. The overwhelming Strangeness of Nature can become more than we can sanely bear. On top of this, there is the issue of hallucination. How much of the Nature we experience is objectively out there and how much of It is in here, a projection of the perhaps inescapable subjectivity of our senses and the way our psyches are structured?

All of this Darkness and Mystery seem somewhat offset by the pleasures we experience in and as Nature—the healing and wholeness we can experience when we let ourselves be open to Nature's undeniable Beauty. Then we may realize that we really do live in the Shadowlands and are ourselves, at least in our body-souls, exactly that—Shadow and Light.

When Personhood came into the cosmos by means of an expressed oneness between psyche/Psyche and matter (energy, space, time), Immortality became manifested (albeit partially) in a transient and continuously changing realm. It did so according to those oddly fine-tuned rules of physics that we recognize as expressions of mathematics and geometry, themselves invisible, which define the dynamic patterns and shapes that govern the existence and behavior of all finite things. Persons come into being as labyrinthine psychophysical expressions of oneness and multiplicity—ultimately, Divine Oneness and Multiplicity. However complex the aspects of these multiple dwellers in our psychological "houses" become, they are always finite in their viewpoints and capacities, at least as normally experienced.

But then, like the approach to a black hole, an event horizon may be crossed, and Infinity encountered at the Center. It is here, where the structures and dynamics of our finite body-souls find themselves in the presence of the Infinite Psyche, that our God-images arise to guide us in our space-time creations and the remembrance of our Immortality.

I think it likely that persons experience themselves as Immortal only in the Presence of the Immortal Person, whether they do so consciously, semiconsciously, or unconsciously. When we touch or are touched by the Immortal while remaining ourselves, we experience our own Immortality in a way that is absolutely convincing and feels as real as our day-to-day lives. In those moments, we remember ourselves as we forever *are*—before (in a certain way) our journeys of becoming in space and time and after (in a certain way) those have come to an end.

For me, our experiences of Immortality can lead to two basic ways of thinking about the when and where of It. In the first way of thinking, our Immortality becomes realized, at least by us, after our biological deaths; in the second, It is realized right now, at a higher level of consciousness and being and above our current space-time experiences. Psyche above psyche, Mind above mind, Heart above heart.

Psyches as matter-souls strive. All projects, constructions, journeys, creations strive. Wherever there is striving, it is aiming at fulfillment. There is no striving without the purpose of reaching a goal. Striving would not occur at all if its goal did not already exist. In the case of human beings, no matter what the specific goal, and whether we're aware of it or not, we all strive ultimately for an Absolutely Fulfilled State of Consciousness and Being. We do so, I suspect, because we remember, however dimly, that we once enjoyed such a State (albeit perhaps in a different form from the one we are after in our earthly lives and beyond) and fell out of It. Our goal in striving is to regain It but in a more richly realized form, a form that makes our this-worldly journeys central. One way of stating this goal is *sat*, *chit*, *ananda*, as the Hindus refer to it, or Infinite Being, Knowledge, Bliss.[3]

If our and the rest of Nature's strivings do not reach this Fulfillment some-where, some-when, then all of this—us and everything else—is thwarted and finally without meaning or purpose. That seems perverse to me, even demonic.

My way of stating the Ultimate Goal (which undoubtedly includes sat, chit, ananda) is Pure Love. Absolute Meaningfulness is the Pure Love of persons (inclusively defined) for each other, at all levels of complexity and sophistication up to their capacity for such Love. The finite stages of this striving for ultimately All-inclusive Love are both symptoms of the already existing Goal and prerequisites for Its attainment. This is the actual person that becomes in space and time, yet always is . . . but transfigured, intensified, and remembering, and thus living its simultaneous individuality and Oneness with all that is, has been, or will be . . . and God. I believe this is made possible by the ever-present, if not always immediately obvious, Benevolent Infinite Person within Whom we ever are and Who is within us.

Of course, several crucial questions arise right at this point of affirmation. If a State of Bliss, or All-inclusive Love, was once ours—or is ours already and Forever—why do we have to go through these person-creating journeys? Why are we finite and mortal at all? Why do we have to strive for Something that is already ours? Why are we here instead of There?

Human beings have proposed many possible answers to these questions. We've tried to figure it out, to reason our way to the meaning of our struggles to reach, or remember, our Larger Identities and our Immortality—like amnesiacs, or like when there's a word or a thought on the tip of the tongue that just cannot be spoken. None of the proposed answers to these questions is completely satisfying to me.

This brings up another, and related, question. Why is there Evil? Why does Nature, including our own, seem to be an irresolvable combination of what we experience as Good and what we experience as Evil? Again, the attempts to answer these questions seem mostly unsatisfying to me, at the very least incomplete. I do feel that there is some truth in all of our explanations, but they only partially reveal the elusive answers, darting around from place to place in a hall of mirrors—something like the mathematical physicist Robert Laughlin's "deceitful turkey effect."[4] And so, we are delivered unto Mystery and, with it, to the philosopher Rudolf Otto's "the Holy" (1869–1937).[5]

I can't promise that I'll offer solutions to these and other apparently intractable problems in the pages that follow. But I will lay out the options. Then let's see where we go from there.

I do think Something falls out of that Mystery and makes Itself known, however indirectly. My own visceral acquaintance with life leads me to the conclusion that, whatever else is going on that I can't see or understand, I feel deeply, centrally that I at least am here to manifest personhood/Personhood and to experience Reality by means of it. What could be more valuable? What could be more validating? For me, nothing . . . and infinitely so.

A Sketch of the Framing of
My (Provisional) View of Reality

Here's a telescoped view of my general framing of that part of Reality to which I believe I've had access, particularly through the unusual experiences I've lived. I think the usual also provides clues to a world-view that is something like this. Although I readily admit that my interpretations of what I've experienced are in fact provisional and, as I've mentioned above, I definitely think words do not and cannot provide anything like an adequate way to express the deep intuitions that have led me to this specific perspective, I do believe there's something in my admittedly rather mythic, or mythopoetic, framing that is actually true on a level that is beyond my capacity to think it and certainly beyond my ability to express it. Feel free to reject my framing, of course. But it does represent a view—actually an amalgamated view—that I'd like you to at least consider. Anyway, I think it's only fair to show you up front where I'd like to take you, before we get into the nitty-gritty.

As I've mentioned, I believe in God and do so in the multitude of ways in which human beings express that realization of Transcendent yet also Immediately Knowable Presence. I'm eclectic in this, but I do have an anchoring God-image or a short series of these. That makes me a theist. I am also a Platonist. I'm a Platonist because I very much believe I've had experiences of a world—actually worlds—behind this one. I'm a Neoplatonist on two main counts. First, because Plotinus (204–270 CE), the founder of Neoplatonism, understood Reality to be made up of the One and Its "radiated" or "projected" (but within God as Self-complexification) and then congealed and configured Hypostases (Aspects, Expressions, or Levels), which makes more sense to me than any other explanation I've encountered, given my experience of Reality. Plotinus describes these radiations or projections of the One as including: the Intelligible Realm, where everything is itself and everything else; the World Soul (or Psyche of Nature), in which the individual things have largely forgotten that they are themselves and the All of Nature—ultimately, the One (they're somnambulant); and Matter, which permits individual things to become actualized physically by means of their uptake of form. I'm also including No-thingness, which is essential to the crafting of the boundaried thingness of things (see chapter 5). Under the aspect of Matter, we would talk today about energy and particle fields as well as space-time and gravity.

Second, I'm a Neoplatonist because, along with the later disciples of Plotinus, I believe there is some kind of correspondence among all of the aspects and expressions of the One at each higher Level and all of the individual things inhabiting and making up each lower Level. This is why all forms of psi (parapsychological and extrasensory phenomena), as well as how what we've envisioned becomes manifested in our lives with little or no overt effort on our parts, work. I should say that my inclusion of No-thingness, or the Void, in the manifestations of the One is not Plotinus's idea. I've imported it from the philosophers J. G. Fichte (1762–1814) and Friedrich Hegel (1770–1831) and from the medieval Kabbalist Isaac of Luria (1534–1572), as well as from modern physics and cosmology (see chapter 5).

I am a theistic Neoplatonist because, unlike Plotinus and his followers, my experience is that the One is an Infinite and Eternal Person, or Divine Psyche, Who is intentional about the manifestations of Its Aspects and their inhabitants. In this I agree with the Jewish, Christian, and Muslim theistic Neoplatonists of the Middle Ages. From my perspective, the Personhood of Ultimate Reality also means that, as the most direct Expressions of the One, finite persons (with the One at their Cores) are at least as valuable to the Divine Psyche as any of Its more general expressions—for instance, the World Soul, the Intelligible Realm, and even Its own Self-proposed Oneness. (Note: As you'll see, while I very much admire Plotinus for his understanding of the layered quality of All of Reality, I do find some aspects of his system inadequate.)

I agree with the ancient Egyptians that "He has made Himself into these millions" (a common theme in Ramesside era and later hymns).[6] In modern terms this comes out as some kind of Panentheism. My kind of Panentheism sees the manifested worlds as partial Expressions of the One Who is present in them, as them, but Who is unimaginably More than they, and so, for immediate or practical purposes, is outside them. In the total scheme of things, however, nothing is or can be outside the Infinite and Eternal Person.

Put theistic Neoplatonism together with Panentheism and you get the notion, intuited by mystics in many different spiritual traditions, that human beings, and perhaps all things, are indeed becoming in space and time what they always *are* in Infinity and Eternity.

Wonder, Mystery, Awe, Dread, Peace, Joy, Gratitude, Humaneness, and Love—person to person/Person. These are my foundational experiences of this beautiful and terrifying Reality "in which we live and move and have our being."[7]

Three Days and Nights of Ecstasy

I was working on my thesis for my master of divinity degree from Chicago Theological Seminary. At the time, I was living in a northwestern suburb of the city and commuting into the city several days a week. I'd recently been reading the sermons of Meister Eckhart (ca. 1260–1328), which convey the sense of the Immediate Presence of the Divine within us—living from within—and the conviction that Scripture is only meaningful in the context of the inner world of each individual; the mystical yet fully rational reflections of Giordano Bruno's (1548–1600) astounding visions of the universe and beyond, long before the James Webb telescope and modern cosmology. With Nicholas of Cusa's (1401–1464) idea of the insurmountable-by-finite-creatures Wall of Paradise, which encloses God's Unknowable Essence, I felt an exhilaration of clarity about my inability to finally penetrate the Divine Mystery that is Reality. I put on the music of Mascagni's *Cavalleria Rusticana* and Puccini's *Tosca* and, notes to the side, started typing.

Within minutes, half an hour at the most, without meditation, effort, or intention, I felt everything solid melt around me and within me, and I was ushered into a fantastic Magical World, an Alternative Dimension, a breath-catching, exhilarating Re-manifestation of my consciousness and being—a New Me, fresh, alive, "resurrected," light . . . and Light! I felt completely enveloped by what I can only describe as Exaltation, an Exalted and Exhilarating World that enfolded and enclosed me, or one I had simply inadvertently stepped into and immediately been engulfed by. I had the feeling that this Dimension of Consciousness and Being existed in the same space and time, the same location, as the one I usually inhabited, and that all that had had to happen was for a veil to be brushed aside, or perhaps a sideways glance on my part, peeking around a corner, or something like that.

In hindsight I can say that it seemed to me to have been a fuller, more unfolded rendition of that same Reality I had experienced that night in my backyard. While in that experience the Exalted Realm had appeared to be outside the universe, and I had been connected to It by a thin shaft of red light, and except for that, It had seemed very far away. This time, however, that Realm was right here. I was within It, and It had taken over my apartment.

This went on for three days and nights, as I wrote my thesis, the words of which just flowed, almost effortlessly, as if someone else was working with me to write them. I was so enraptured, I hardly paused to eat, and I didn't sleep at all. After a day or two, no doubt food and sleep deprivation enhanced the state of my ongoing Ecstasy.

As I gradually came down from that "High Place," and the magic bubble that had held me in that Paradisal World dissolved, there was one final surprise. I went out to the kitchen, which opened onto the living room, and there, in the middle of the living-room floor, stood a giant disk on edge, perhaps five or six feet in diameter! On its surface was some kind of extremely complex high-tech system—chips, diodes, connectors, channels, switches—everything flowing from the circumference to the center. I had the experience of knowing all things and the sense of the absolute harmony of all of Nature, Its underlying Oneness. The center itself seemed like what I've since called a "rabbit hole," a pin-prick-sized window to Whatever may lie behind and beyond the disk and everything in the physical world. As I stood gaping, the disk gradually faded. That fading signaled the end of this particular extra-dimensional experience.

Many years later, after having become familiar with the mathematician Max Tegmark's proposal that our universe and an inconceivable multiverse, of which ours is a miniscule part, are the products of what he thinks of as "a giant mathematical object"[8] that exists beyond the finite realm(s) and is Eternal,[9] I've wondered if the disk I glimpsed was Tegmark's extracosmic (yet also panentheistic) object, which organizes, informs, and manifests the universe we live in and of which we are a part.

I would say that in all of my extraordinary experiences, I am lifted up as I am, as myself, my usual identity, but somehow augmented, aligned, attuned to a more expansive Me—still me but somehow "additioned." Sometimes I'm conscious of alternative aspects of me that seem to stretch my identity in a direction where I can no longer quite feel me as myself. In any case, what does not change is my sense of personhood, however small or great, or my conviction that, beyond and above all the fireworks and displays of light and shadow, persons are of Infinite and Eternally Enduring Worth. And the meetings between them, especially when these are particularized as Love, are without equal in all of Reality. And I mean *all* of Reality!

Okay. My hope is that if you accompany me through these pages, the experiences I've had (and continue to have) may resonate with you, that we can share them, reflect upon them together, and companion each other through this Terrifying and Joyful Reality into which we've been thrown and become ourselves—persons/Persons of Infinite Worth and Immortal!

1
Likely Stories

There are many ways of loving God, in aspects actualized
and ethereal, finitized as incorporeal, within our grasp
and also past the sum of our capacities for abstraction.

I myself need double vision when it comes to Deity, and, I think,
God is more than happy to supply my aptitude for being—as well, my yearning for transcendence of it.

DOUGLAS M. GILLETTE,
AT THE THRESHOLDS OF ELYSIUM

When in his dialogues Plato (ca. 428–347 BCE) reached the end of his trying to solve a cosmic or psychological-spiritual question and could no longer use logic or argument to make his point, he moved into myth making—not the myths that were part of his Greek culture but his own myths. Sometimes his dialogue partner would say something like, "Do you really believe that?" And Plato would answer in effect, "Well, it's something like that." That happens in a number of his dialogues. The most famous example is in the *Timaeus*, where he lays out a mythical version of the creation of the universe but one he says is a "likely story."[1] That's the title of this chapter because while several stories I tell are personal, things that happened in my own history or life—and so are literal facts, as we would say—most of the stories are drawn from the myths of a number of different peoples and from majorly different eras.

Personal Stories

The following three stories are personal. They're not likely in the way that most of the stories in the rest of this chapter are. As is true for all personal stories, they are made up of actual people and events, psychological facts (in this case, my subjective perceptions and feelings), and interpretations based on the sense of levels or layers of Reality intuited to lie behind them. So:

Early in my wife's and my courtship, in social settings but especially when we were alone, I felt as if I'd entered a very small Region of Timelessness that enclosed only us, as if we'd stepped into the "holy of holies" of some ancient temple or church. In that close space I felt a transporting and inviolable quiet, a hushed atmosphere, perhaps laden with incense. As I approached her person—her body and her soul—I felt the presence of the Sacred, as if I were nearing the Divine in her, in her form, *as* her. I felt a worshipful tenderness and an almost paralyzing hesitancy to reach her, to touch her. And when our fingers met, at first only the tips, I felt an incomparably delicious whelming of Love for the whole of her, as if I had been given permission to enter a State of Intimacy with God.

In retrospect, I believe I was in communion with the *fact* of *her* Infinite Worth—of a person/Person whose Infinite Value in and of Itself was *fully embodied in finite form* right there, before me, and whose

Core Identity, above, beyond, within that finite person *as* her, transcended her soul-full embodiment without leaving any of the wonder of her earthly identity behind. In fact, her finite person *gave that Core its individual distinctness and Its very Divinity*: the earthward person I was in love with and her paradisal Essence were simultaneously two different aspects of her one single person, both aspects mutually informing each other, each one impossible without the other.

After an extremely hard, even toxic pregnancy for our daughter and an equally difficult gestation for the little person growing within her, the birth itself was fraught. Our daughter had caught Covid a few days before the delivery and was in the throes of it when she gave birth. She and our granddaughter literally fought for their lives, individually and together.

After that harrowing experience, our granddaughter was immediately whisked away to the neonatal ICU, and our daughter spent three days in a Covid isolation room, crying. But when they were reunited, the bond of Love between them, almost certainly made stronger for what they'd been through together, was wonderful, so powerfully beautiful that it was startling, arresting, a joy I can't adequately describe. As I told my wife, "They went through Hell together, and now they're in Heaven with each other . . . and they *know* it." When I saw our granddaughter on our daughter's chest, smiling in her sleep, loving her mommy, her mommy loving her, I knew there is absolutely nothing in all of Reality as precious, as meaningful, as Supreme in Value as this one "infinitesimal" event in the midst of an Infinite Reality—two persons loving each other, knowing it, and filled with grace and gratitude to be with each other. What is greater than that? Not the whole of Reality itself.

At seventy-four, most of my life is memories—wonderful memories, blah memories, and terrible ones. But for *all* of them—especially the wonderful ones—I sometimes feel the most irresistible sensation of being drawn back into them, as if a tractor beam from *Star Trek* had hold of me. And I am overwhelmed by nostalgia.

What *is* that . . . nostalgia, which most of us feel pretty regularly as we get older? I think, at least for me, it's the expression of what psychologists call "appreciative consciousness." In my case at least, it's very *deeply* appreciative consciousness. I'm aware that my moments—sometimes hours—of nostalgia carry the sense of the Infinite Worth of all those people, pets, homes, family cars, places we shared life together, events—often very small things we did together, even very brief moments, like snapshots of more inclusive and prolonged times than our memories are able to focus on. Sometimes these memories surface only many years later, but whenever they do, I'm struck to the heart and feel the tears welling in my eyes. I long to go back to each of those moments and stay in them, never moving out of them, for the duration-less span of Infinite Time. I feel those people, those events, "the way we were," as of Unfathomable Worth—a Worth that has no horizon, no end, that goes on and on, and finally disappears into a Mystery I can't even begin to imagine, cannot track, and, at least in my present state, cannot fully enter. For me, they disappear, not into some trumped-up No-thingness (or worse, just plain nothingness) but into some Infinite and Eternal Memory. Mine at a higher level of consciousness and being? God's? I hope both.

Likely Stories

The stories that follow are likely to *me* because they affirm (albeit in a variety of ways) what I have experienced in my own life as the Infinite Worth and the Immortality of persons. These stories have different emphases when it comes to Worth and/or Immortality issues. But the two seem to me to go together. Things of Infinite Worth *should* be Immortal, at least in *some* way. And things that are Immortal would seem, by definition, to be of Infinite Worth. Otherwise, why save Them in Eternity—the timeless version of Infinity?

For me, these stories are not literally true in the sense of history—history-history or personal histories. They're fiction, but fiction in the *mythic* sense as understood by depth psychologists and comparative religionists. The truths they communicate are in coded language because they are bigger and deeper than our daily lives, which, for the most part, are literalistic in their approach to Reality (paying almost exclusive attention, as they must, to what appear to be literal *things*) and therefore can only take in these supra-literalistic truths in a kind of disguised way. Nonetheless, daily life flows from them, draws its own significance from them, and points toward them. From one perspective, our day-to-day lives are rich and meaningful because they *are* those deep truths acted out and *lived* on the (mostly) literal (for us) level of Reality.

On the other hand, and paradoxically, the acting out of these truths is so rich and vivid, so felt, and with such fantastic detail and specificity that it equals and, I believe, surpasses the significance of the mythic, metaphorical, essential, or archetypal layers of Reality. I think that stories that are told from these deeper levels of Reality are likely in part *because* they reflect the patterns of *daily* life—certainly *psychological* life, the life of our psyches. At the same time, daily life is what it is because of the truths the stories tell us about the wider sweep, the mythic underpinnings, the Structures and Dynamics of the Reality in which, *as* which, we and all things become . . . and are. We can't have one or the other—literal or mythic. We are living *both*. Both are as true as anything gets.

Again, from my perspective, these likely stories are *only likely* because, as I mentioned, the deep truths they tell cannot be told as they actually are in themselves, at deep levels of psyche and Psyche, where they may be *literally* true at those deep levels. As they pass through the filter of our finiteness, where they become refracted and reshaped by our finite life experiences and imaginations, they become for us *only likely for us.* They can only be told through an intermediate realm—a realm of "translation"—a less direct, muffled, or seemingly other-than-literal medium like dreams, visions, poetry, art, and music, in forms that we can grasp as true for us in the states of mind in which we usually operate, while recognizing that they go beyond those usual states into Registers of a Truthfulness we can't fully or finally follow at all.

So, for me, the stories I'm about to tell you are both *very* likely . . . and *only* likely. See what you make of them.

Ancient Egyptian Accounts of the Infinite Worth and Immortality of Persons

There is such an incredible wealth of ancient Egyptian writings about the nature of the Divine, the manifestation or emergence of the world, the relationship of human beings to the Gods or God, and the Immortality of persons—much, but not all of it, in mythic language—that I've had to choose just a few texts to highlight the themes I want us to focus on. I've also had to minimize the mythology in order to make my major points. By way of introduction to this vast field, I think it's fair to say that most prominent Egyptologists for the most part agree (with different emphases and some controversy) that the Gods of Egypt were all ultimately manifestations of a single God, that often They were experienced as interchangeable with one another and with that God,[2] and that this Divine Being was usually addressed and thought of as a Person—Someone that humans could have personal relationships with. Also, the universe and, along with and beyond it, Reality have been manifested by that Ultimate Person in stages, stages that from a depth psychological point of view look very much like a gradual dawning of consciousness, like waking up or coming out of a coma.[3]

Most importantly for us right now are the beliefs that human beings are formed of the same Substance as God, that we are in effect His children and His special (but not exclusive) concern and that we become Immortal partly from living a kind, moral, ethical, and compassionate life and partly through what Christians would call Grace—in the case of the Egyptians, the Grace of magic, by which we can erase our faults during the Afterlife Judgment of Osiris, and the Grace of becoming, or coming to realize, that at the Core of each of us is God-as-us or us-as-God. On this last point, we become in time what we ever are in Eternity—in union or identity with the Divine while at the same time keeping our mortal identities. On top of this, that union allows us to enter the three kinds of Eternity—Kheper, Neheh, and Djet.[4] We'll look at these different versions of Eternity briefly below. They'll also show up again in later chapters.

The idea that persons are of Infinite Worth is affirmed either directly or indirectly in many Egyptian texts. It is certainly implied in all the texts that assert the union with God, both in this life and in the Life after Death. One of the most direct (or minimally mythical) of these texts in terms of the theme of the Infinite Worth of persons in *this* life (as well as beyond it) comes from the so-called Middle Kingdom period (2040–1674 BCE). It's called the *Teaching for King Merikare*. In the text, it is affirmed that human beings are the Images and Substance of God, Who cares for them intimately, feels their pain, and renders each one sacrosanct.[5]

Of the many mortuary texts in the Egyptian Book of the Dead, the *Papyrus of Ani*, by the Theban scribe Ani, dated to the New Kingdom period (ca. 1250 BCE for *Ani*; 1552–1069 BCE for the New Kingdom), is one that has been intensely analyzed. The whole papyrus addresses both the Infinite Worth of the person and, perhaps because of that Infinite Worth, his or her Immortality. In fact, the whole point of the text is to help Ani achieve his Eternal Life, again, partly by affirming his goodness in his earthly life, and where that failed him, by the magic of what are known as the "negative confessions"—a long litany of sins he erases by saying, with the help of magic, that he did not, for example, "cause anyone to weep" (a rather steep hill to climb!). The additional boost into a Blessed Immortality for him is his affirmed oneness or identification with Osiris, the Dead and Resurrected God, and ultimately with Re, in many respects, *the* God.[6]

Here, as elsewhere in the text, Ani is facing the rising sun, Re, the Creator, in His primary this-worldly guise. Ani is bathed in the miraculous light and Light of the Creator and prays that Re will see him as identical in Essence with the dying resurrecting Osiris so that Ani too—as himself-Osiris—may be resurrected like him. Ani's concern throughout the papyrus is not just about gaining Eternal Life but rather a Blissful Version of That. The alternative is unthinkable. So, Ani, like every Egyptian, is faced shortly after biological death with a Judgment presided over by Osiris. Ani's "heart" is weighed on a scale against the nearly weightless Feather of Truth. It is essential that the person (read "conscience") not be heavier than the Truth about him or her and his or her earthly life.[7]

An interesting sidebar to this involves the Egyptian idea that each of us is made up of a number of soul fragments or elements, for example: what we would call the ego; the *ba* (the ego's double, which continued after death to have the ability to move in and out of various dimensions or levels of Reality, including the earthly)[8]; the *ka* (which meant something like the life force, and the life-giving blessing)[9]; and the *akh* (the transfigured spirit, in effect, a part of the person that is granted a Blissful Immortality).[10] There is some ambiguity about the akh in the Egyptological community. Some scholars favor the idea that the akh comes into being at the moment of a favorable judgment in the Afterlife Court. Others believe that the akh has never left Heaven, and so, has nothing to do really with the fate of the other aspects of the person. In other words, the akh is our Eternal *Essence* detached from our mortal *existence*. Maybe both sides in the debate about the akh are right.[11]

A summary of the person-centered affirmations that the Egyptians make in the *Papyrus of Ani* and in other texts in the Book of the

Dead might go something like this: (1) God Self-discloses to human beings, as He does to all things, up to their capacity to perceive and process these revelations of the Infinite to the finite; (2) as that happens, persons (at whatever level) become disclosed to God both in their individuality and in their oneness with God through the Divine Gaze, which happens through God's Self-disclosure; (3) that identification of individual persons with the Divine Person—or the waking up to the fact that that identification was always present but is now disclosed—makes them become aware of their Infinite Worth and their Immortality; (4) that infinitizing and eternalizing happens in three modes—Kheper, or the Eternal Growing of the soul as a creative transformation and triumph over destruction, Neheh, or the Eternal Cycling of Reality, and Djet, the Eternal Momentless Now above time in which everything always is and is all-at-once. When all is said and done, the Egyptian belief that we become God *without losing our finite identities as persons* is, for me, a statement about the Infinite Worth of persons that is absolutely unsurpassed in all the assessments of human nature ever thought or written.

According to Egyptologists, throughout Egyptian religious literature we find the belief that the individual soul, or psyche, replicates in miniature the process of Divine Eternal Becoming, Kheper, that Ani is praying for. A part of this Eternal Becoming is a complex myth of descent into the Underworld and ascent into the Overworld—what I'm calling "the grand tour" of Reality. The descent is a fear-full process of psychic shrinking, almost to No-thingness, certainly to the state of death. The ascent involves the defeat of Demons that try to block the psyche's fight for what today we would call "expansive states of consciousness" or "Spiritual Experience." Theoretically, a successful ascent—ultimately to union with God—is not guaranteed.

Coffin Text 312 from the Middle Kingdom gives us an especially good example of the grand tour.[12] In this text a heavenly messenger is sent by Atum-Re in the guise of Horus, the Son of Osiris, to complete the resurrection of His Father by ascending through the many levels above the Earth plane (what we could think of as dimensions of consciousness and being) to the "Great Support" at the pinnacle of Reality. On His way upward, Horus must confront a whole series of murderous Monsters who attempt to destroy Him and so deprive Him (and through Him his Father) of Eternal Life with, in, and as God. Horus is only partially successful in defeating these Demons and is saved at the last minute only by the intervention of Atum-Re. In our terms we could say that, left to its own devices, the human psyche is not able to face and defeat its own Darkness, its own self-destructiveness, and is dependent for victory and full entrance into the Light by the saving Grace of God. The myth certainly seems to be reassuring us that that Divine help will come!

Ancient Maya Myths

The myths of the ancient Maya tend to be considerably darker than the ancient Egyptian accounts of the psyche's Worth and Immortality. But not entirely so. Avoiding most of the complexity of the Maya accounts, let's take a look.*

In ancient Maya mythology, the universe has been created at least three times and destroyed at least twice. In its present version it was birthed by First Father, who is also called "the Holy Thing," or "the First Father Holy Decapitated and Resurrected Creator Thing," often depicted as a singing skull. At any rate, as He resurrected from death, First Father raised the World Tree, which serves as the core support for the present cosmos. The World Tree is sometimes depicted in Maya stone carvings and paintings as the giant ceiba or, when an evolutionary process (remarkably similar to those of contemporary science) is envisioned, as a gigantic corn plant. In both cases the roots of these complex

---

*Everything in this subsection I've streamlined from my earlier book on ancient Maya mythology, *The Shaman's Secret: The Lost Resurrection Teachings of the Ancient Maya* (New York: Bantam Books, 1997).

symbolic representations of the cosmos are shown growing up from Xibalba, the Maya Underworld of decay, death, and fecundity. The upper reaches of these life-giving plants reach into the highest heavens, where earthly being is fulfilled in Metawil, the Eternal Paradise in which souls preexist before birth and to which they return after death.

The soul, or psyche, is pictured in Maya iconography and literature as a tiny white ceiba flower called the *sak-nik-nal*, "the white flower thing." It appears at both ends of a rod symbolizing the ecliptic cradled in the arms of the dead and festooning the ritual garb of Maya kings. This white flower thing was thought of as emerging in the upper branches of the cosmic ceiba at the moment of creation when First Father raised the tree to begin the manifestation of the world. This suggests that *all* souls have existed from the beginning of time and space, if not earlier. They come into full earthly existence through what the Maya called the 01 Portal in the far north of the sky in the midst of the Supracosmic Ocean, from Which they descend to the Earth plane. Fascinatingly, this cosmic 01 Portal was believed to be identical with every Maya woman's birth canal, which was the embodiment in the flesh of the structure of physical as well as spiritual Reality. There is an equally fascinating depiction of what the Maya believed happened at the end of the white flower thing's earthly existence. In Maya paintings it is shown reaching out from Metawil to pull the body that had housed it into Paradise with it, thereby implying that the body is a transient manifestation of the psyche rather than the other way around.

While still on Earth, the soul could enter Metawil through Ecstatic States of Consciousness. These were achieved by using drugs, by bloodletting (for example, piercing one's own lips, tongue, or penis and then passing a rope with thorns through these apertures), and by whirling dervish-like dances. Often so-called Vision Serpents would appear from the Otherworld in these ceremonies, bearing messages from the deified dead or from Goddesses and Gods. At the height of these rituals, Maya kings could show that they had themselves entered Metawil by climaxing their dances with what Maya scholars call the "toe-heel strut," a dance step that indicated that the king had triumphed over the forces of Xibalba and the "Lords of Death" and was now "walking on water," the Infinite Overworld Ocean.

Greek Myths and Philosophies

Throughout most of ancient Greek prehistory and history, people believed that souls inhabited animals and at least some plants as well as human beings. This was true of most if not all traditional forager societies. By the Archaic Period (ca. 800–480 BCE), as the Greek scholar Jan Bremmer emphasizes in his *Early Greek Concept of the Soul* (1983), the Greeks à la Homer thought of the human soul as divided into at least four and maybe five aspects or functions: the *thymos* and *phrenes*, which carried emotions in general;[13] the *menos*, which expressed rage, especially on the battlefield;[14] and the *noos*,[15] which housed the mind or thinking function. All of these soul fragments largely ceased to be at biological death. Bremmer calls them "body-souls."

Occasionally, a fifth component is mentioned in the early texts (mostly by Homer), the *psyche*, which survived the death of the body and lived on in a dismal Underworld, although sometimes the psyche, especially that of heroes, was granted the privilege of living forever on Olympus, on the Blessed Isles, or in Elysium. The psyche filled the role of what Bremmer calls "the free soul"—the soul that is free from biological death.[16] However, stripped of emotions and mind, I wonder really what the point of such survival would be. Presumably, the free souls that made it to the Bliss of Olympus, the Blessed Isles, or Elysium still had some emotions and, I would guess, their minds. From the perspective of modern parapsychology and its documentation of the experience of apparitions, a fascinating power of the Greek post mortem psyche was its ability to manifest the *eidolon* of the dead person—an image of him or her that could speak for the dead, albeit with a sort of buzzing sound. By the Classical period (ca. 500–336 BCE), the psyche had absorbed the soul fragments from the Archaic period and was increasingly believed to be what we today mean by the term *psyche*.[17]

We can find another plotline in the story of the development of ancient Greek mythology and philosophy about the Immortality of the soul, or psyche (and, presumably, its Infinite Worth), in what are called the Eleusinian mysteries. The mysteries promised a Blissful Eternal Life for individual persons who'd undergone initiation into them. But before we can take a look at the mysteries, we have to briefly backtrack to ancient Crete and its Minoan civilization because, according to scholars, Minoan spirituality lies behind the Greek mysteries.

It seems to me that Minoan civilization and its spirituality was one of the last hold-outs of what Lithuanian archaeologist Marija Gimbutas (1921–1994) called Old Europe (ca. 6000–3500 BCE). Old Europe was a Goddess-centered farming and livestock culture in southeastern Europe and much of the eastern Mediterranean, originally founded by immigrants from northern Syria and Anatolia. Most important for us is the fact that the central God-image of Minoan spirituality was a Goddess called Potnia[18] and that Minoan spirituality, as Rodney Castleden makes clear in his *Minoans: Life in Bronze Age Crete* (1990), was a spirituality of Ecstatic Altered States of Consciousness.[19] The Goddess and the way She was celebrated by ecstatic, even hallucinogenic, frames of mind (aided by ingesting poppy milk)[20] survived on the Greek mainland, mainly at Eleusis near Athens, even after the Mycenaeans or Achaeans with their mostly male God-images had come to dominate the Greek peninsula.

Potnia on Crete had several Aspects, one of which appears to have been the Goddess Who would become known at Eleusis as Demeter-Persephone[21]—Goddess of death and Eternal Life. What may be the earliest representation of Persephone comes from a cup found in the ruins of Phaistos on Crete,[22] dated to the Middle Minoan period (just after 2000 BCE). It seems possible that the cup once held the sacred poppy milk. Persephone's mother Demeter, Goddess of Grain and Grief, may also have been worshipped in Minoan spirituality.

Anyway, Persephone and Demeter were the central figures at Eleusis.[23] But they were accompanied by the male God-images of Hades-Dionysus[24] and the Son of Persephone and Hades, Eubouleus. Persephone is famous for her abduction by Hades to the Underworld and Her marriage to Him. *Per* Zeus's decree, She would have to spend three months of the year underground with Her Husband and the other nine months on Earth, helping to ensure the flourishing of all living things. But the Eleusinian mysteries, which lasted at least two thousand years and into which millions of people were initiated, were not mostly about grain or the fecundity of the earth. They were about death and resurrection into Elysium in Which all initiated persons could realize their own Immortality.[25]

According to comparative religionist Carl Kerenyi (1897–1973) in his *Eleusis: Archetypal Image of Mother and Daughter* (1967), Persephone and Demeter were ultimately a single composite Goddess,[26] while Hades, God of Death, and Dionysus, God of Ecstatic Life, were as well.[27] The name of their Son Eubouleus meant "Good Counsel."[28] And what was that good counsel? Ecstatic Eternal Life as the result of the "marriage" of death and earthly life[29]—and this, for *individual human persons* who identified with the Goddesses and Gods of Eleusis yet remained themselves, could take on—or realize in Ecstatic States right here and now—their resurrections into Bliss![30]

A number of schools of Greek philosophy agreed, most notably Plato's. Another school, the Pythagorean, affirmed the Immortality of the psyche but seemed to shift the emphasis away from the importance of the survival of specific individual *persons* to something more like a collective *Person*. This collective Person would remember persons (and perhaps they would remember themselves) but only to some degree—which is hard to determine exactly—as vehicles or agents of an All that was trying to remember Itself by means of their lives. Here, I want to use as a supplement to my own understanding of Pythagorean philosophy a few ideas from the contemporary philosopher James Luchte's beautifully thought and gorgeously written meditation and extension of the Pythagorean tradition, *Pythagoras and the Doctrine of Transmigration* (2009).

Luchte says that for the Pythagoreans the self—I would say the *person*—was not to be identified only with his or her present life, although every present life was a necessary aspect of the complete(d) person or Person. The Psyche was on its way through innumerable embodied lives to its Fullness as what Pythagoreans called the All. It could do this only by *remembering all* of its bodily expressions.[31] I would add that the Soul's projection of many life-forms (not only human) as it gradually wakes up and does this remembering is made possible by its crafting over eons of better and more adequate cellular structures and neural architecture for increasingly fuller Self-expression and Self-remembering through the medium of matter. All of this activity of the Psyche is to further its project of filling out to eventually recall Itself as the All. This, from the Pythagorean point of view, is the heart and the motivating force of evolution. The Psyche-as-psyches remembers Itself as all of them and so *becomes* what It always *is*. In this sense (and others), as Luchte says, the Soul, or Psyche, is older than the body . . . any body, all bodies. Furthermore, each individual combination of psyche and body has *intimations* of the All of Which it is a part and to Which it yearns to return fully.[32] Luchte says that for Pythagoreans as for the philosopher Parmenides, the All is *above* time, *is* time, but All at Once. In Luchte's view, each psyche, from within the Psyche of the All, will remember its (in my language) adventures of becoming. And it will do so as simultaneously itself and the All.[33]

The world—Nature Itself as the All—wishes to merge with, or disappear into, the Divine.[34] Still, while we have our hypotheses about why we're here, what we are, and so on—including the Pythagorean hypothesis—we ultimately come up against what Luchte rightly calls out as the Unknowable Purpose of the whole project.[35] When . . . and if . . . the All, what I'm calling the Psyche or Soul of Nature, is reached, we then see through the interstices of the things of this world a Reality beyond the All to Which we . . . and all of Nature . . . aspire.[36] That "Beyond" is the One, what I experience as the *Supra*cosmic Psyche beyond Nature—in other words, God.

Zoroastrian Myth and Theology

In ancient Zoroastrianism—basically the merger between what William Malandra in his *An Introduction to Ancient Iranian Religion* (1983) calls "the Old Iranian Religion"[37] and the reformed version of that proclaimed by the prophet Zarathustra (dates uncertain)—the All-encompassing God, Ahura Mazda, Expresses Himself as two opposed Person-like Entities. The first is Spenta Mainyu, a Good God-image Who creates a wholly good and beneficent creation. The second, Angra Mainyu, is an Evil God-image Who enters into the new creation to mar and deface it with His Evil. The task of the human soul is to decide which side of things it is on. Of course, despite the Divine Call to decide, made clear by Zarathustra, actual human beings are ambivalent, not to say confused, about what really is Good and what genuinely Evil. This ambivalence and confusion results in virtually all human lives being spent somewhere in the middle. Since this is the case, as in the Egyptian view, a Judgment after death is required to determine who gets to live an Afterlife of Eternal Bliss and who is condemned to an Eternity of unspeakable Pain.[38] I might add that, as again in the Egyptian worldview, the very *fact* of an Otherworldly Judgment could mean the Deity's perhaps Infinite Valuing of the human person and so the Infinite Importance to Him/Her/It of human decisions and behaviors. The same goes for the idea of an Eternal Life (of either Bliss or Pain). Although, on both counts, one might not want to be valued so highly!

An interesting feature of the person in Zoroastrian thought is that each individual one of us is a multiplicity—the *ahu* (life principle), the *baodhah* (consciousness), the *fravashi* (guardian spirit), the *urvan* (an individual's guiding moral faculty), and the *daena* (the individual's innermost earthward nature, personality, and temperament).[39] The fravashi, which perhaps had never left Ahura Mazda's Heaven, might be thought of as everyone's Immortal Essence, Which remains untouched by the thoughts, feelings, and behaviors of Its projections into the temporal world—that is, to one degree or another, all the other soul fragments. (We might want to ask, though, how much of the "us" we normally think of as ourselves such a detached Essence might include.) At any rate, of these assorted elements of the person, the one most vulnerable to post mortem Judgment is the urvan, which on the Chinvat Bridge between this life and the Next, is confronted by the daena. If a person is greeted by the daena as a beautiful maiden, it means that the Judgment of the person is favorable and he or she is ushered into Paradise. If the daena appears as an ugly hag, the urvan is in for a very rough time![40]

Apocatastasis Panton in Christianity and Islam

The fascinating doctrine that all persons—human and even demonic (past, present, and future)—are eventually saved for an Eternal Life of Bliss, perhaps after some time spent in Purgatory or "Hell for a spell," was first put forward in Christianity by the early Church Father Origen of Alexandria (ca. 185–253 CE). This teaching was called *apocatastasis panton* (universal salvation).[41] In proposing this idea, Origen relied on the partially biblical belief that God is Infinitely Loving and Merciful and that His Absolute Power to restore all things to their original Paradisal State—the State He had originally intended—cannot be thwarted. To accomplish this Universal Salvation, however, God created successive cycles of worlds in which individual souls could gradually evolve toward perfect Goodness—however many worlds in which they'd have to incarnate and however long it took. Apparently even the Devil would eventually be saved. A bit later, and in a related and question-begging way, Gregory of Nazianzus (ca. 329–390 CE) wondered how a Good and Loving God could impose Eternal Punishment on persons who had had only a finite time in which to have sinned. And, taking his cue from Origen, Gregory of Nyssa (ca. 335–395 CE) proposed a doctrine of Perfect Restoration for all persons, including Satan.[42]

The Islamic theologian Al-Ghazali (d. 1363 CE) in his *The Remembrance of Death and the Afterlife* (translated for the 1989 edition) told a similar likely story, supposedly handed down from an extra-Quranic saying of Muhammed. In this story God summons His Angels and tells them to descend into Hell and release anyone who has a dinar's weight of Good in their heart and bring them into Paradise. The Angels return with a huge crowd. Then God says to the Angels, "Okay, now go back into Hell, and bring to Me everyone who has a half-dinar's weight of Good in their hearts." The Angels come back with a truly vast number of souls. But God isn't finished. He tells the Angels to go back a third time and release all those who have even half an ant's weight of Good in their hearts. A final vast throng vacates Hell. But God is still not finished. He Himself reaches down into Hell and brings up all the rest of His creatures, those who had never done, felt, or thought any Good whatever. These souls are particularly grateful (as we might expect) and praise God for His Mercy. But God says, "I have something even better for you—My [Infinite and Eternal] Satisfaction with you!"[43]

The Anthropic Cosmological Principles

Closely related to Design arguments for the creation of the world and particularly human beings, there are four versions of what are called the anthropic cosmological principles, each of them proposed by scientists—physicists, mathematicians, and cosmologists. These four versions are what I would call myths (in the depth-psychological and comparative religious senses)—that is to say, likely stories, as in "*very* likely" and "*only* likely"—in the ways I've mentioned above.

First is the so-called weak anthropic principle or WAP.[44] This is the least controversial of the four. It states that our own existence—the fact that we're here and that we are as we are, especially in our intellectual capacities—means that this universe *had* to be as it is within vanishingly small parameters of the values we observe. Those measurable values include mathematics, geometry, physics, and all of their derivations (chemistry, forces, fields, topography, and so forth) and the fine-tuning necessary to have produced us . . . to, among other things, know them and measure them. Those measurements span the quantum level to the specifics of macro-objects and processes, like the specifications for forming planets, their positions in relationship to their stars, their compositions and processes, and the evolved characteristics of the life-forms that inhabit them—and so on to the necessary structures and dynamics of galaxies and beyond. In short, *everything, exactly as it is* (or very nearly so). This fine-tuning at *all* levels is required for our thinking this thought, right here, right now. In other words, our existence and our specific natures *require* these (nearly) exact cosmic conditions. Therefore, they *had* to occur as they did. In an extrapolated sense, *we* are *their* reason for being.

My take: Okay.

Which brings us to the second anthropic principle, called the strong anthropic principle or SAP.[45] Here, the universe is *required* to have all the values (and more) mentioned above *for the express purpose* of producing us (and any other intelligent beings at or beyond our level).

My take: Likely

The third anthropic principle is called the participatory anthropic principle or PAP.[46] In this version, as subjects-observers (without subjects nothing is observed), *we* are *necessary* for the manifestation of *any* universe *at all*. Of course, at least in *our* case, it *had* to be this one, for the reasons cited above. This view is tied to the hypothesis in quantum physics that only observers can collapse wave functions and thereby produce matter as we know it. It goes without saying that matter is essential for us to be, at least in our present forms. While some theorists suggest that any object larger than quantum-potential-objects-cum-materialized-objects (from quarks to universes) can, in effect, serve as observers and thus collapse wave functions, the reality is that all of these ideas (including that of such alternative observers) are subjectively produced—thought of—not by, for example, asteroids, but by conscious subjects. There is no higher court of appeal beyond our own subjectivity.

My take: Hmmmmm.

The fourth anthropic principle, the so-called final anthropic principle or FAP,[47] states that once intelligence has (necessarily) come to be by specifying the universe that must have all the values to make it not only possible, but actual, that intelligence will never cease to be, no matter what happens to that universe.

My take: Yes, okay, but in a nonmaterial way, and not at the moment of the hypothetical Big Crunch in which the universe collapses in on itself, as proponents of FAP argue.

If you're interested in exploring these anthropic principles in greater detail—and I mean *much* greater detail—I recommend wading (as I did) through John Barrow and Frank Tipler's *The Anthropic Cosmological Principle* (1986).

A Likely and Literal Story

I believe I remember my birth night. I was born in the morning on November 6, 1948, at what many years ago was St. Anthony's Hospital in Rock Island, Illinois. I don't remember my actual birth or the rest of that day. But I think I do remember that night. It feels like a memory. It's way too vivid and coherent to have been a dream. How did it come to me? As a waking vision or in that twilight time between sleeping and waking? I don't know. But I remember the first time I told anyone about it. I was standing in the kitchen by our blue Formica-topped table, about fourteen years old. I told my mother, who, as I recall, had her usual reaction to reports of the more than commonsensical—"Douglas, that's impossible!"

Infant amnesia is a usual phenomenon, generally accepted by psychologists and neuroscientists. Supposedly, we forget most everything that we experienced before the age of two or three. Actually, though, I remember quite a bit. I remember the blue Pacific Ocean and the beach in Southern California, which my mother, father, and I visited when we lived in Bakersfield. I remember teaching myself to walk—actually, run—from one chair to another, my carpet-burned knees when I fell and then crawled to the chair across the room, hauled myself up in tears, frustration, and rage, and launched again. I remember my mother's seamed nylons. I remember our blinds and the hot California sun making light stripes on the walls. I remember unrolling a whole roll of toilet paper all over the bathroom floor . . . and my mother's anger when she saw what I'd done. I remember when my father would come home from work in his yellow convertible. I remember how I'd toddle out to meet him—how he'd lift me up above his head . . . how we'd smile and laugh.

I don't remember my mother leaving him when I was two and moving with me and my one-year-old brother into her parents' upstairs apartment in Rock Island. But I remember that house, the cold winters. And I remember that every night before I went to bed, I'd go from window to window looking for the Moon. I remember the sense of Wonder, Awe, and Mystery I felt when I saw it!

So, I'm not so sure about infant amnesia. It seems to me I have about the same amount of amnesia about much of the rest of my life. Anyway, my birth night.

I'm lying in a glass bassinet in a row of these, facing the viewing window. The hall on the other side of the window is dark. I think there are one or two other babies in the bassinets farther down the row. They're quiet though. I can barely move my head a little from side to side. But mostly I'm looking up at those old white hospital ceiling tiles with the soundproofing holes in them. There's a dim light somewhere in the room behind me. The room seems cavernous, though I can't see it. Someone is back there, probably a nurse, making noise as if she's stacking metal pots and pans of some kind.

I remember the blankets under and over me feel a combination of soft and rough. I feel so heavy—basically paralyzed—and a little cold. I have the thought, "What is this place . . . this 'world' or mode of being? I'm so heavy. I can't move, and it's cold." Then I have a vision of the Place I'd come from. There were lots of very soft balls of light gently moving around in a kind of illuminated fog or a cloud. I was inside one of those balls, and I knew there were others in all the rest. I felt a warm togetherness with them. I felt light and free. Then I thought, "I'm going to forget all that . . . Where I was before I came here."

And at that instant, I do. I become a baby.

Okay. So newborn babies probably don't think in English (or any other known language). But animals clearly think, evaluate, even strategize . . . without words. I certainly have translated what I was thinking that night into English. Right. But I remember that I was thinking.

Impossible?

I don't think so. Many spiritual traditions affirm our preexistence as souls (as we've seen above), and sometimes as scattered sparks or balls of light. Jewish mysticism claims that all souls were born at the same time, at the very beginning of things, and dwell in a kind of Storehouse until it's their turn to incarnate. That suggests something very close to Immortality. So does the intuition, I'll call it, that there never was a beginning as a moment of time. The "beginning" is *above* time, *outside* time. That too suggests Immortality. Since there was a *kind* of time in the light ball cloud, I . . . we . . . were already falling out of timelessness—for that matter, spacelessness. Moving out of the Storehouse toward incarnation?

I don't know. My memory of the memory of my birth night and before (?) is a *psychological* fact. The rest is speculation, as I'm sure you're aware. If my story is literal truth (it actually happened), my interpretation of it is, I freely admit, either a "likely story" or an "only likely story." Or both. In any case, a truth, I suspect, that was masquerading as those or that. A truth that can't be told literally at *our* level of literalism but may be literally true in some way in its own Realm.

2
Psyche:
The Multitude

*Many who've heard Narcissus' tale have
condemned him as a self-ensorcelled
fool.*

. . . .

*But what I think Narcissus saw was the face he
wore before his fall into the world of space and
matter.
Which one of us, confronted by our Higher Selves,
would not go suddenly still as death and waste
away, enchanted?*

DOUGLAS M. GILLETTE,
AT THE THRESHOLDS OF ELYSIUM

First is Psyche—Infinite Psyche—because the Psyche of Nature, finite persons (and Nature as Person, persons, and things) are Its Envisagements. The Infinite Psyche of the Infinite Person Expresses the structures and dynamics of the Psyche of Nature and individual psyches, however incompletely. However incompletely, these manifest at their own levels the Structures and Dynamics of the Psyche of the Infinite Person.

43

Also, psyche/Psyche is first because It's the first thing we know.

It's also only by psyche/Psyche that we know *anything*.

A Mirror Experience

Sometime around the age of eleven or twelve, I had a particularly eerie experience. I was standing in front of our upstairs bathroom mirror and was unexpectedly drawn to look into my eyes reflected in the mirror. I realized something odd was about to occur if I held my gaze and didn't look away, even for a split second. So, I decided to play this game and see what would happen. As I looked, I seemed to see layers and layers of identities, or presences, fall away—gradually less and less me and more and more something, or someone, else. I'd been reading about human evolution, and so I imagined that the increasingly alien eyes were "me" at earlier stages of evolution—earlier versions of humans, then ancestral apes, the first mammals, reptiles, and so on. That was my imagination . . . probably . . . but there was certainly a peeling away of *some* kind, which revealed progressively less conscious beings or aspects of myself, which, as I watched, were invested somehow with my very present and very focused consciousness in that moment. And then I hit a wall. The peeling away stopped, and what I saw looking back at me from the mirror was a pair of eyes observing me with complete, blank indifference. That was a gripping and chilling discovery! A Presence—and it *was* a Presence—"within" me, completely alien to my personhood, utterly detached, much like that night sky after the fight I'd had with my mother, before the laser shot out and connected me with the Paradise of Love beyond the indifference of the cosmos.

What *was* that? Over the years since the mirror experience, I've tried various explanations for that schizoid, personalityless awareness-of-me *personish* Thing. I've thought of Carl Jung's Self (with a capital *S*), which he sometimes equated with the Hindu Atman. I've tried the multiple centers of consciousness theorist John O. Beahrs's hidden observer. I've tried the Atman directly (with and without Ken Wilber's interpretations), Adam Kadmon of medieval mystical traditions, and so forth. I've tried the Neoplatonist Plotinus's Soul of Nature. Perhaps that's it: Nature, with Its obvious Indifference to the fate, not only of individual creatures, but, from the looks of the evolutionary record, Its Indifference to life itself. At the same time, though, Nature *has* manifested self-aware beings like ourselves, who in effect serve as Nature's *Own* Self-awareness. So maybe that doesn't quite work either. All of the above? The Buddhists' Void? But this Thing in the mirror, while apparently empty of feeling, I had the strong intuition was, as I've said, at least Person*ish* but really more like a kind of detached Person. The Void isn't supposed to be a Person, right?

I want to think more about this in later chapters. For now, let's move on.

Discerning Structure: Models and Analogies

It's clear to me from my own life experience and that of many other people—friends, colleagues, students, clients, the stories told by people I've never known, and, really, the nightly news—that the identities we usually think of as us are being pretty regularly "invaded" by what seem like psyches that are not us. These often-unwelcome visitors find their way to the surface of our psyches all the time but especially in moments when we are stressed or otherwise vulnerable and maybe too open to outside influences. Sometimes, our visitors *are* welcome, though, because they bring with them expressions of breath-catching beauty, flashes of insight (some of these profound), greater knowledge, wisdom, and feelings of Goodness and Love.

But also, the darker sort make their appearance. They bring with them a desperate narcissism, cruelty, and moral and ethical Evil, at times too awful to contemplate. The invaders—Good and Evil, or less starkly, creation and destruction—reveal other realms, dimensions of dazzling Light and terrifying Darkness. Sometimes we can sense the Presence of Something or Someone Else behind them, beyond them—Someone, say, Who is hugely Remote from us, yet also always unimaginably Intimate, Who is the Source of both Light and Darkness in ways that we can speculate about but never understand, and Who is both the complexity and the unity of our psychophysical persons. Let's take a brief look at how three of the most thoughtful psychologists (in my view) have tried to discern the structures and dynamics of the astoundingly complex human psyche, which, as I say, houses not only us and us-like psyches (and partial psyches) within, but also plays host to our visitors—both the benevolent and the malevolent kinds and perhaps everything in between.

F. W. H. Myers: Layers of Light and Darkness

First up, the early British depth psychologist F. W. H. Myers (1843–1901), who proposed a model of the psyche that went beyond those of his immediate forbears and, in some ways, I think, beyond even Carl Jung's (1875–1961). Let me say up front that, from my perspective, *no* model of the psyche and, for that matter, no analogies for *any*-thing are completely accurate or adequate. None represent the nuances and complexities of the things they're trying to model. That's because models are "blocky," and analogies are incomplete (because, in the case of analogies, Reality is always More than we can think). By blocky I mean they don't—and can't—flow organically, keeping the whole in view while looking closely at the parts. A little bit like the Copenhagen view of quantum physics—actually, *all* the interpretations of quantum physics. And yet, for me, Myers's model analogy is the best attempted description of the structure and dynamics of the human psyche certainly and probably for at least some major portion of *the* Psyche, at least as That has played out in the guise of Nature (as in "evolution").

As far as it goes (and I don't think it goes quite far enough), I think Myers's perspective is the most directly tied to what I've *actually experienced* of my psyche/Psyche . . . and what it looks to me like others have experienced too. What I mean is, it most closely tracks what philosophers call the *phenomena*—the experiences as they present themselves, as we *have* them. In that sense, it is the most realistic.

To describe our actual experience of the psyche/Psyche, Myers used the analogy of the electromagnetic spectrum, from infrared to ultraviolet.[1] Along this spectrum we normally see a very short range—what we call visible light. In Myers's map of the psyche/Psyche, visible light stands for our usual states of consciousness, our feelings and moods, and our (hopefully) growing knowledge, even maturity and wisdom. In the actual electromagnetic span, each band of light is distinct at its purest but fades into its neighboring bands to create a mixed (and so partially smoothed-out continuum), yet also a semi-granular or defined set of "colors." Myers's view of the psyche/Psyche shows similar characteristics.

Myers stood this spectrum on end, so that the infrared is below our usual experiences and the ultraviolet is above. He proposed that the *below* part of the psyche is made up of instincts, action patterns, and autonomic functions, yet also of a host of sub-personal entities, varying from somewhat mechanical to fully developed persons who are and are not us as we normally think of ourselves.[2] With our knowledge of the quantum world today, we can theoretically go much further down into the infrared part of the psychic spectrum. Some researchers in the field of philosophy of mind are currently searching for evidence of the material foundations of psyche in quantum fluctuations within neurons.[3] In the *above* area of the psyche/Psyche are layers and layers of ever more comprehensive aspects of consciousness and the persons that support them there.[4]

Myers suggested that our usual states of consciousness are bounded by a lower and a higher *limen* or threshold. Experiences at the lower threshold he called "subliminal"[5] and experiences at the upper he called "supernormal" or "superconscious."[6] Here, I'm going to agree with the psychiatrist Edward Kelly that Myers is a bit confusing in his terminology because he used *subliminal* to mean *both* infrared and ultraviolet—in other words, to describe both what lies below and above our normal daily life consciousness (which Myers called "supraliminal") as subliminal.[7] In any case, these thresholds are porous to some extent in all of us—some more than others—so that they let into our usual identities, states of mind, feelings, moods, and even entire alternative centers of consciousness.[8]

I'm going to summarize in the following discussion some of the major observations about Myers's system in *Irreducible Mind: Toward a Psychology for the 21st Century* (2007), edited and contributed to by Kelly, because they are scattered all over the place, and the book is a tome. So, onward. These "invasions" of our usual identities are often felt as just drips or trickles—vague hints or clues that there's more to us than we tend to be aware of. But sometimes we experience them as floods of various degrees of intensity, some of them overwhelming. Some of these alternative states of consciousness are more or less fully developed persons with their own ways of thinking, dispositions, memory chains, even medical conditions. Some are only fragments of persons, not fully formed. Others are only person*ish*. Others feel more like *non*personal drives and urges (which we may still feel are somehow "ours"). Still others may not be experienceable as us at all but instead may be felt and known as markedly alien presences—in my terms, Angels, Demons, the dead, Gods, Goddesses, and, yes, extraterrestrials! Here, we're no longer talking about psyche, but Psyche—both a Unity and a thriving Collectivity of more or less individual psyches. And we have no idea how far *that* goes below and above us. As they enter our awareness, or in extreme cases actually take over our psychic functions, in the process shoving us offstage completely (rendering us unconscious of ourselves as such), their effect can be exhilarating (if they come from above) or devastating (if they come from below).

Myers's research into subliminal and superconscious characters, and his theorizing about the sources of intuitive flashes, strokes of genius, sudden inspirations, and what today we call the darker (more infrared) world of parapsychology dovetails rather well with the work of hypnotherapist John O. Beahrs and colleagues in their analyses and therapeutic approaches to multiple personalities, and Carl Jung's therapeutic practice and theorizing about the structures and dynamics of what he called the "objective psyche."[9] At the same time, from my perspective, Beahrs's (et al.) and Jung's ways of thinking about psyche, and Psyche, while the most comprehensive of the current theoretical and therapeutic schools of psychology—hence, most adequate and effective in terms of conception and treatment—are still only pieces of the bigger puzzle that Myers was trying to see and communicate. A brief look at Beahrs's and Jung's maps of the psyche/Psyche at this point might be helpful. I should say that I've made the call to include these two systems based on my own experience as an analysand (for eight years) and as a life guide and teacher (for many more).

Beahrs's Labyrinth: Others within and Layers of Light and Darkness

In his book *Unity and Multiplicity: Multilevel Consciousness of Self* (1982), Beahrs has developed a complex system of discernment of various inner entities and their relationships to one another and to us. I'm not going to summarize his system in detail, but I think some general features of his work are really important for understanding *our* psyches. These features also have implications for our understanding of the Structures and Dynamics of *the* Psyche. Beahrs sees a fairly sizable population within each of us of fully developed alter personalities as well as a host of only partially developed, what he calls "mental units."[10] The personalities and mental units show complicated interactions that in large part are the result of two basic kinds of repression barriers between them and our egos (plural), which he terms

Selves—for example Self 1 and Self 2.[11] (Repression barriers are walls between psychic entities that are generally formed semiconsciously or unconsciously.) Some of these repression barriers are horizontal, with less-developed mental units and personalities below them in a hierarchical arrangement.[12] Depending on the nature of these horizontal barriers—whether they are, in effect, one- or two-way mirrors or windows—these characters are or are not aware of one another in ascending or descending order.[13] That includes being aware or not of our ego(s). In addition, Beahrs sees vertical repression barriers.[14] These personalities and mental units are at similar levels of development, and separated from one another by repression barriers or walls side by side.

Beahrs and his colleagues use many different names for the members of several overall classes of these entities. These different names serve to highlight different functions that these members serve within their classes. The classes themselves include executives or conductors of the orchestra,[15] rescuers,[16] persecutors,[17] hidden observers,[18] and a central monitor.[19] The most interesting class for me is the persecutors. These include negative aspects of the parental introjects,[20] tyrants,[21] and demons.[22] The rescuers are generally Pollyannaish or naive[23] but could also be thought of as including more mature and wiser entities that we might call Angels. Indeed, Beahrs suggests that as we move outward in this labyrinth of inner actors we come into contact with fewer and fewer of these that we can identify in any way as aspects of ourselves[24] but instead begin to feel to us like alien intruders into our psyches—some, majorly benevolent, or Divine,[25] and others catastrophically malicious: Demons.[26] I wonder if hidden observers and/or a central monitor might serve the purpose in spiritual terms of higher-level Angels or even of God-images. I'm not really sure about this, though, since these aspects of the psyche/Psyche in Beahrs's system seem largely indifferent, something like what I encountered in my mirror experience. For me, whatever That was, It was *not* God.

Jung's Maze

Jung's map of the psyche/Psyche is just as complicated as Beahrs's but perhaps more comprehensive. I could actually see ways to fit Beahrs's system into Jung's. I'm not going to do that here because it would take us too far into technicalities than either you, probably, and I, certainly, want to go. So, for present purposes, a quick flyby of Jung's system will have to do.

Admittedly way oversimplified, I'm going to present Jung's account of the complexities of the human psyche-person as built on a variety of opposites—psychic elements, whether persons (including and also other than the ego), and person*ish* entities, or "instincts," that express apposition and/or opposition to one another and to the ego. The goal of Jungian analysis is to force these opposites into a series of mergers that will result in, as Jung calls it, the "transcendent function," a third element appearing that reconciles the appositions and oppositions and so leads to wholeness.[27] Wholeness produces "stasis," a balanced peacefulness within the psyche and/or Psyche. It also produces an immensely *sharper and more intentional reflective self-awareness*—what Jung termed "individuation."[28] I'm going to list and then very briefly discuss these sets of opposites[29] but not unpack Jung's system in detail: there is a lot more to it than the inner opposites I'm going to lay out here. Explaining in detail would take an entire library! And it's certainly not our main purpose in this book.

First, there is the division between the ego and what Jung calls the unconscious.[30] Second, the division in the unconscious between the personal unconscious[31] and the collective unconscious.[32] Third, this division is marked by the division between the archetypes[33] in the collective unconscious[34] and the complexes in the personal unconscious.[35] Fourth, there's the division between the ego and the shadow.[36] (Jung usually defined the shadow as a character in the personal unconscious in opposition to the ego but bearing the same gender identity as the ego.) Fifth, there is the division between the ego and opposite-gendered psychic elements; in the case of a female-gendered ego, the animus (expressed as a male, or masculine, identity) and, in the case of a male-gendered ego, the appositional or oppositional anima (a female, or feminine, identity).[37] Finally, there is the apposition and opposition between the ego and what Jung called the Self (capital *S*).[38]

A few definitions (with which many readers may already be familiar). The ego is, again, the person we normally think of ourselves as being. The unconscious is the potentially unlimited, perhaps even infinite aspect(s) of the psyche/Psyche that the ego is unconscious of. Jung makes the point that to call this area of the psyche/Psyche "unconscious" means that it is largely unconscious *to us*.[39] It Itself, as a whole and in many of its parts, is at least as conscious as we are. The personal unconscious, which contains the personal aspects of the archetypes in the form of the more personal complexes (for example, the famous Oedipal complex, but many more) shades off into the collective unconscious, in which are found the sub- or transpersonal archetypes (the basic dynamics and structures that pattern the psyche/Psyche as a whole and give rise to many of the more personal elements of our identities).[40] Within the collective unconscious we also find the subpersonal aspects of the shadow and the animus and anima, which, again, give rise to the personal aspects of these as they interrelate (however poorly or adequately) with the ego. At the center of the psyche and the Psyche, usually located within the unconscious—like everything else in the psyche/Psyche until the ego becomes conscious of it—is the Self. This is the Core of all the psyche's and Psyche's expressions and manifests in both personal and transpersonal ways—perhaps what Narcissus saw when he went "still as death and wasted[ed]/away, enchanted."

As complicated as all of this may sound, there is more. For example, the animus presents itself to the ego as multifaceted, as does the anima, and, really, everything else that makes up the psyche/Psyche. So, there are multitudes upon multitudes within. Jung recommended integrating as much of the personal expressions of the psyche/Psyche into ego-consciousness as possible—under the combined auspices of a more comprehensive and wiser ego in partnership with the Self.[41] I would say the rest, especially the more collective aspects of the psyche/Psyche—in particular the darker manifestations of the shadow, the anima or animus, and the archetypes—needs to be, in effect, "exorcised" beyond a reinforced repression barrier that can now be marshaled as the definitive boundary of the greatly complexified and more comprehensive *person*.[42] Two main reasons for adopting this exclusion strategy are, first, that these transpersonal psychic elements are far too big and powerful for any human ego to embrace and make integrated aspects of itself, and second, because, as dark as personal aspects of the shadow, anima, animus, and archetypes are, their darkness at deeper levels of the collective unconscious is stygian, abyssal, and so utterly destructive of personal identity.

That stygian Darkness is also the source of *Evil*, which seeps upward within the psyche/Psyche like a toxic fog and, even with our best efforts, infects our personal identities. In my view, integrating what we can of It and exorcising what we can't is the only way to maximize Goodness in the dangerous maze that is the human psyche—*us*, you and me. I strongly urge such an approach because there are elements of Evil that really are that—malevolent, cosmos swallowing, creation killing—that we can't ever be "friends" with. These must be excluded in no uncertain terms from our personal self-definitions and identities. My own experience as an analysand for eight years and my life-guide practice confirm for me the significant accuracy of the structures and dynamics—the maps—of the human psyche that both Beahrs and Jung have discerned, as well as the effectiveness of their therapeutic techniques. In my view both of their systems fit rather well within F. W. H. Myers's overall framework.

Fracturing, Repression Barriers, and Layers

The three models of the human psyche we just looked at all see that psyche as fractured, fragmented, and/or naturally layered. The

fragmenting and isolation behind repression barriers, whether horizontal or vertical, of different persons or person*ish* mental units, is
usually explained as the result of trauma of one kind or another, usually occurring in childhood.[43] This is a dominant feature in Beahrs's
and Jung's models (although they also make allowance for some natural layering).[44] Natural layering is more prominent in Myers's model.
Here, the layering happens in response to the Psyche's process of
incarnation. In that process, Psyche becomes specific finite psyches as
It crafts the neural architecture immediately available for Its project
of Expressing Itself through matter. In that case, a whole variety of Its
once unified characteristics are fragmented, sifted out, and stratified
like layers of sediment in a lake. That layering can be imagined as a
filtering in descent from above or as an ascent from below—in that
case, like the formation of a planet, where the lighter elements rise to
form liquids and, above these, gases, increasingly ethereal as they rise
higher in the planet's gravity well.

My own view is that both traumatic fracturing and natural layering
are dynamic factors wherever complex psyches manifest, at least in the
world of matter as we know it. And these processes are present not only
in humans. Actually, quite a few animals also show signs of fracturing
(maybe layering too). I have known at least two certifiably psychotic
robins! As I'll suggest further on, fracturing and layering might also
be a feature of *non*incarnate psyches as well as Psyche(s) *on a very much
larger scale.*

It looks to me like this fracturing and layering are necessary and
good, on the one hand, and tragic, on the other. Good, because they
are *essential* for the formation of *persons*, persons who can become
richly complex and nuanced and who can meet each other. These
meetings can further individual enrichment and, under the best of
circumstances, actualize Love. But the fracturing and layering are
also tragic because they create alternative—and all too frequently
oppositional—"I's." This gives rise to enmity and conflict within and

between the consequent finite individuals and groups—and so, to the full emergence of Evil, both natural and moral-ethical. More on this later.

The Collective Psyche:
Who Are We? What Is Inner, What Is Outer?

The discovery of a Collective Psyche by Myers, Beahrs, and Jung (as well as others) and, from a different angle (that of quantum physics), the corroboration of collective nonlocality opens the door to the plausibility of psi, which assumes a behind-the-scenes Unity of all mental units, individual persons, subpersons, and so forth—to some extent, even across taxonomic lines (in biological terms). Many of these manifestations of the Collective Psyche are incarnate—what we call "alive." Others may be, we could say, disincarnate or nonincarnate, or incarnate in a medium other than that of matter as we know it.

Some of the following stories, including those about apparitions, are similar to stories that I'll present in chapter 6. Here, the purpose of these stories is to show evidence that what we normally think of as psyche—that is, *our* psyche—is a tiny concentration of Psyche-as-psyche that extends upward, downward, outward, and that is part of a Collective Psyche, the limits of which are unknowable. These stories, both here and in chapter 6, also raise the question of what (if anything) is inner—inside us—and what (if anything) is outer? If Myers, Beahrs, Jung, and others are right, we live within a Psychic Medium that connects us telepathically with other people but also with animals and, as well, dis- or nonincarnate psyches. It also manifests communion across time, as suggested by the phenomenon of precognition, and across the barrier—whatever it is—between the so-called living and the equally so-called dead. These are all part of the Multitude that we are and that we are connected with, which, as we explore further and further "out," don't seem like "us" anymore.

Others Within

My college major was in theater and communications. I played many characters throughout my college career and then in community theater. I pretty quickly came to realize that the characters I was creating were a mixture of what the playwright had almost certainly intended and what my personality and imagination brought to the table. The odd thing was that the particular character I was playing eventually began to amalgamate, almost but not quite independently of me—my ego. On stage performing I became aware that, while my ego was monitoring the character and making little adjustments—timing, tone of voice, and so on—it wasn't as if the character was a puppet and I the puppeteer. It felt more like a cooperative relationship in which I exercised ultimate control . . . but over an almost-person that had formed inside my psyche. I remember that in the play *Marat-Sade* one of the minor characters actually "possessed" the actor playing that role—so much so that the actor had to be pulled from the play and spend some time in a psych ward! Remember the comedian Jonathan Winters—the actor who forgot who he was?

Human beings seem to have an almost unlimited capacity to simulate and then to not only play "as if" but to come to believe so completely in their simulations that they *become* them or, in the case of worldviews (whatever worldviews), become immune to any—and I mean *any*—evidence that contradicts their point of view. Here read: fundamentalism, literalism, rigidity, combativeness, and so forth. This capacity obviously has rather immense implications. How well can we trust our own or anyone else's claims about Reality? Fortunately, there are some checks on the road to outright hallucination, but the ambiguity remains.

I first experienced full-fledged others within—complete, or nearly so, alternative personalities—through a therapeutic exercise in the course of my depth-psychological analysis called *active imagination dialogue*. In this exercise (which was enormously helpful in reuniting repressed aspects of myself), you get completely alone in a quiet, dimly lit environment, with a tablet and pen. You start by writing an invitation to a rejected part of yourself—and, because rejected, usually an angry part who, you suspect, is sabotaging your life in general and/or a particular ego-driven project. You make your mind receptive, and if at first there is no response from the alternative person, you pause and again invite this alter-person to communicate with you. Eventually, a response does appear on the page. It's not "you" because it begins to write itself—as in something like automatic writing. You can tell immediately if it's you acting "as if," or if it's really the alter-person (also usually ultimately you) speaking. Acting "as if" takes energy (to compose) and feels artificial or forced. The real deal feels spontaneous. Then your conversation about mending bridges begins.

What is this stuff, and where does it come from?

One really cold winter morning in the Quad Cities (in Illinois) long ago, snow and ice everywhere, I was driving my Volkswagen Beetle and came to a slippery stop at the top of a very steep and high hill. Way down at the bottom of the hill, I saw a car stopped at a stop sign at the intersection of the street (32nd Street, I think) with John Deere Road. A little apprehensively, I drove forward down the hill toward that distant stop sign. Suddenly, I hit a patch of ice, and my VW began uncontrollably rocketing down the hill. It was obvious that I was going to rear-end the car at the bottom—and this, at a rapidly increasing speed. Brakes were completely useless, as steering seemed to be. Seeing the inevitability of what was about to happen, all of a sudden, a very calm feeling came over me. I seemed to switch gears (pardon the pun), and it no longer felt as if I were in charge. Something or Someone deep inside (I guess) took over. Everything went into slow motion, and this calm Presence (it did actually feel like a person) showed me, perhaps because we now had time for this, exactly how and the exact moment to direct the car to the right into a snowbank.

Who *was* that?

I think it was a number of years after the event that my brother told me about an absolutely eerie thing that happened to him in fifth grade at Lincoln Elementary School. He said that he'd been called upon to answer a question but that when he opened his mouth to speak, a different voice with inflection patterns that were not his, and using a vocabulary he had yet to encounter in his school career or reading, answered in his place! He said he had (understandably) been rattled as he experienced "someone else" answering for him, and that he still felt weirded out every time he thought of it. I get that! He later became a psychiatrist specializing in multiple personality disorder and dissociation.

Telepathy with Animals

Still thinking of a Collective Psyche in Which not only a multitude of incarnate and nonincarnate psyches dwell, but also one that might include the psyches of animals, I want to relate four stories about what I suspect were telepathic interspecies communication between myself and birds—a flock of blackbirds and two robins—and then, a very strange encounter with a gigantic snake.

When I was probably five or six years old, sometime in autumn, probably in October, when the trees still had leaves, mostly green, but it was cold, sad, and the sky was a dull gray, I stood under a very large tree in our backyard—don't remember the species—and began to hum a mournful Celtic-like tune. I was making it up as I went along and expressing the sense of sadness and loneliness I felt in that moment. Blackbirds began assembling in the branches of the tree above me. As I hummed, more and more of them came to the tree until it was full of them! They didn't make a sound, something rare for blackbirds when they come together in such a horde. It was as if they came to listen to the music I was making, were picking up on the mood of the music, which expressed what they themselves were feeling. I felt that we were communing across not only species boundaries but even biological classes, that we were somehow realizing ourselves as one. Of course, this last bit is my interpretation—imaginary, you might say. *Yes*, to the interpretation part; a cautious *maybe* to the imaginary bit. Whatever happened that cold autumn day, it was . . . is . . . a psychological and historical *fact*.

The first robin conversation took place on a summer afternoon when I was taking a work break from building a grape arbor over our back patio in Palatine, Illinois. I'd just dug a four-foot-deep post hole and was resting in a lawn chair. Suddenly, out of the side of the post hole popped a huge worm, probably a nightcrawler. It must have been at least ten inches long. Instead of continuing on its way and burrowing into the opposite side of the post hole, it climbed out of the hole and up onto the patio. I thought, "Uh-oh," and sure enough, a robin spotted it immediately and flew down within about three feet of me. I decided not to intervene in what was about to happen and remained motionless. The robin looked at me . . . looking at him . . . then looking longingly at the gigantic worm . . . then up at me . . . then the worm . . . me, worm, me, worm. That went on for probably one or two minutes. Finally— evidently reassured that I wasn't going to do anything about the horror he was about to perpetrate—he bent down and cut off a piece of worm with his beak, flew to his nest, and returned several times to carve off another piece, until there was nothing left of the worm but about an inch of its tough head area, now lying quite still on the hot bricks.

I have no doubt that we had had a conversation: from my side, moral-ethical revulsion but acquiescence in the relentlessness of Nature's feeding-machine setup; from his side, an urgent desire to feed his young, however repulsive I might have found his actions (if not his motives). And then our agreement that he proceed. All of this took place, you might say, telepathically—mind to mind. Not a sound was uttered by either one of us.

Second robin story.

This one was highly verbal and strongly emotional on both our parts. In fact, it was a very noisy business of yelling at each other. The question was where he and his mate were going to build their nest. I was standing on the inside of our garden room. He was perched on the narrow ledge of the transom, outside, of course, eyeing that space for a nest attempt. I knew that was what was going on because a pair of robins had tried to do just that several years before. Maybe he was even one of that earlier pair. At any rate, I shouted through the glass something like, "It's not going to work! It's too narrow! I'm telling you, I know from experience! Other robins have tried, and it's just not stable enough, not enough room!" Or words to that effect. He responded to my words, hollering and screaming at me on his side of the glass. I finally said in a more reasonable voice, "Look, you're no less of a 'man' because I won't let you build your nest here. You can depart, rightly, with your dignity intact." Oddly, he immediately quieted down, looked at me carefully, lingering a few moments, and then flew off to find a different nesting site . . . never to return to the transom. Okay. Vocalizations and body language were used in that argument. But I also think there was more than a little telepathy. Otherwise, really, how could he have known that I was angry about the proposed nest site specifically, and why did he calm down and look at me so carefully when I dropped my voice and tried to "reason" with him?

I mentioned earlier a couple of experiences I had with psychotic robins. But there was no getting through to them about their compulsive behavior, so I guess, no communication, telepathic or otherwise, took place.

Unquestionably, the most dramatic, and certainly the most eerie, of what I believe to be my telepathic communion with animals was my "sideways" meeting with a huge black snake outside the parsonage of my last church, in southern Illinois. The parsonage had two front doors— one opening into the living room and the other to my study.

It was a summer evening. I had just pulled into the driveway from a meeting of some kind and started for my study door, when I noticed a dark, tube-like form standing about two and a half feet high, rising from the bushes to the left of the low cement landing in front of the door. I looked closer. Whatever it was, it had a head—a snake's head! It was staring at the door, flicking its tongue, but otherwise completely motionless. Now I could see that it was black with the outline of tan diamonds on its back. I peered at the landing and the door. As far as I could see, there was nothing there that would be of interest to a snake.

Then I remembered that in the study, on the desk that faced the outside wall, was a pile of papers on which I'd been writing a series of poems to the ancient Egyptian serpents that guarded the gates of the Underworld. The snake outside the door remained absolutely motionless, as if it were concentrating very hard, transfixed really. In the absence of any potential edibles that I could see, the thought struck me that the psychic energy I had been generating with those laudatory poems about divine serpents might have attracted what appeared to be a quite sizeable reptile. Was it that atmosphere favorable to snakes that I had created just on the other side of the study wall that had been conveyed to it? If so, how? My guess was, and is, telepathically through the Psychic Medium in Which I have come to believe we all live, dream, die, and live again.

Still, I had to get into my study. The only thing I could think of was to unroll the garden hose and blast the snake with a strong jet of water. It didn't move a muscle as I unrolled the hose and turned on the spigot. Only when the water began beating on its head and flank did it slowly withdraw and equally slowly slither off around the house to our backyard. Now I could see its full dimensions. The snake must have been at least ten or twelve feet long!

I did, in fact, gain the study door. But I felt, and still do, that I had unceremoniously broken the spell, severed the connection that we'd had, and ended most ignobly what felt like a sacred moment of communion between two very different species. I was ashamed of myself for my fear of the snake and for my degrading treatment of it, although the snake had retreated from my onslaught apparently with dignity intact.

Telepathy between Human Beings

Many years ago, when I was a theater student at Augustana College in Rock Island, I had a friend, Peter, who was a Wiccan. One night we were sitting across from each other—again, at my mother's blue Formica kitchen table. We were talking about psychic phenomena, and I was playing the skeptic. He asked me if I was willing to entertain a little demonstration. I said okay. He said we'd need a deck of playing cards and lower lighting. I got the cards and used the rheostat to dim the light over the table. He shuffled the cards for a few minutes, and then asked me to relax and just let things happen. I did that and eased into a receptive mode, ready to let anything that was going to happen, or not, happen . . . or not. Peter picked a card from the deck so that I couldn't see its face. Then he looked down at the card, then up into my eyes. His face was expressionless. He said, "Get the color first, then the suit, then the denomination." He looked back down at the card. I immediately "saw" the card. I said, "Black, clubs, Jack of Clubs." He showed me the face of the card. It was indeed the Jack of Clubs!

Now I was interested! We did this for probably a half an hour or so. Sometimes I "saw" the color. Sometimes, the color and the suit, and sometimes all three—color, suit, denomination. Sometimes I saw nothing. Once I actually saw the card on the wall, enlarged, looking as if it were being beamed there by a slide projector. The important thing is that I knew when I knew, knew when I was struggling, and knew when I was just guessing. I'm not sure if at the end of our telepathic exchange we had exceeded the degree of chance or randomness according to statistics, which, of course, is an objective measurement. What I *am* sure of is my *subjective experience*—of knowing, partially knowing, and guessing.

After we called it quits, I felt mentally exhausted, completely drained. It dawned on me that, while I'd been "relaxed," I'd spent an enormous amount of focused energy. It was also obvious to me that minds can communicate, directly and immediately, without words, body language, or almost imperceptible movements of the mouth.

A few years later, I tried card projection with a girlfriend. It didn't work at all. So I switched to just trying to "send" a color. We were in a completely dark tent in the middle of the woods at night . . . so she would be unable to see my mouth move if I inadvertently moved my lips as I thought the color. After a few minutes of trying to send her the color black and her not getting it, I shouted it three times (in my mind) with as much psychic force as I could muster. She immediately said, "Black!" I asked her how she knew. She said, "I heard you shouting black, black, black!"

Another time I tried color projection with my grown daughter. I was downstairs and she was upstairs in her bedroom with the door closed. I tried to project once again the color black. After a minute or so, she called down, "Red." I said, "No." She asked me what I'd been trying to send. I said, "Black." She said, "That's what I was going to say, but then I second-guessed myself."

And right there is the learned distrust of our intuitions!

Precognition

According to much of the literature, many if not most precognitions seem to involve catastrophic events. Some may forecast life-and-death events for loved ones, while many also seem to "see"—often in great detail—traumatic occurrences for people the precogs have never known. It also seems as though most of the foreseen events will happen in the very near future—minutes, hours, or days later. Also, some writers, like Eric Wargo in his *Time Loops: Precognition, Retrocausation, and the Unconscious* (2018) and Jeffrey Kripal in a number of his books, claim that the events precogs foresee "retroject" from *their* specific futures to their presents things they will soon personally learn about—from newspaper articles, television news reports, phone calls, and so on. From what I've read, many precogs are deeply distressed by what they see and would readily give back this "gift that keeps on giving."

So far, I haven't experienced the future in quite these terms, but I would still classify my own experiences of it as precognitive. The same applies to some friends and loved ones whose precog reports I absolutely trust as true. Also, precogs I and my wife have known, so far as we can determine, never found out whether their foreseeing of *our* futures came true or not. So, their predictions were not based on events they would personally learn about. There may be a time loop effect going on, though I wouldn't put it in quite those terms, but it shouldn't be as narrowly defined as Wargo and Kripal frame it. Still, no matter how you look at it, the psychological *fact* of precognition really does suggest that, at least in some sense, the future already exists.

I have foreseen quite a few events in my life, things that I would, in fact, find out about later, and also have had others make predictions about my future that came true but that, again, the prognosticators would never know about. Another thing: most of these future events came to pass months or even years later, and while they happened to me in a sense, I was also engaged in bringing them about—which might mean that our own creative participation is already baked into the future we will experience, at least in certain types of precognition scenarios. Following are four stories about precognitive experiences in my and my wife's lives.

When I was five or six years old, my mother took my brother and me to what was then known as the Davenport Public Museum in Iowa. There I saw an Egyptian mummy case, caramel colored as I remember, and finely worked in relief with intricate symbols, pictures, and writing. It had an unwrapped mummy still inside, and the mummy case was, of course, housed in a glass display case. I had already begun to fall in love with ancient Egypt, although I don't think I'd quite gotten to the point of wanting to become an Egyptologist: I arrived at that point around the age of twelve. In any case, as I gazed at the mummy case, I had the passing wish to someday open it and unwrap the mummy. It was just a flicker of a wish, not a fervent desire, and it diffused and vanished shortly after it'd come to me. But my love of ancient Egypt and my developing passion for all ancient civilizations continued and grew. So, as a summer job between my junior and senior years of high school, I volunteered to work at the museum. As it happened, the curators (a husband-and-wife team) wanted me to clean and catalog the ancient Egyptian collection. I was dumbfounded. But more was to come!

Toward the end of the summer, the curators announced that they were going to unwrap a mummy in the museum basement and invite the press and public to attend the event. As it turned out, the mummy in question was *the very mummy* I'd been transiently fascinated with as a kid ten years earlier. It was to be unwrapped by the curators and a team of experts. I was in the audience as the unwrapping began. The room was instantly filled with the delicious aroma of the oils and spices with which the mummy had been embalmed and coated. After the first few layers of linen bandages had been removed, the lead curator paused the project and looked up and asked, "Is Doug Gillette here?" I raised my hand and stood up. *He asked me to come forward and help with the unwrapping!* Specifically, he wanted me to support the mummy's head, which had been completely exposed by then. Needless to say, I hurriedly came forward and, when in position, gingerly cupped her head in my hands.

The first thing I noticed was the stubble that had grown a bit on her shaved scalp, almost certainly after her death. It was, as stubble is, spiky yet soft. Then I noticed her delicate eyelashes, still completely intact. Of course, the eyes beneath her lids were sunken, and her nose was shriveled back and collapsed up to the nasal bone. Then, something wonderful! Her neck was almost completely mobile. As I shifted my weight, it moved—no rigor mortis—as if she had fallen asleep and been out for three thousand years. As the hands were unwrapped, I could see the wrinkles around her knuckles and her still perfectly trimmed nails. Then I noticed her cheekbones and the structure of her face, and I knew that she'd been beautiful.

The experts present judged that she'd died in her early twenties. She'd been a songstress in a temple of Isis. For the first time in three thousand years, her name was read out: Isis Neferit (Isis Is Beautiful). In my eyes, she was still beautiful. As was the totally unexpected and fantastic fulfillment of a passing childhood wish!

A number of precognitive events heralded the eventual and unlikely, even improbable, appearance of my third and present wife—indeed, the love of my life. First was a dream in which I was standing in a cavernous warehouse at the top of an entrance ramp to an expressway. I looked down and saw that the ramp had crumbled to rubble. At the bottom of the ruined ramp a young Mexican woman was kneeling and looking up at me. No words were spoken, but I felt that she was telling me that she would help me to rebuild the on ramp.

Next was Cheryl. She was a parishioner in my first church in Evanston, Illinois. Cheryl was a psychic. One Sunday after the service, she told me that, while I'd been preaching, she'd seen a young Mexican woman standing at my side in the pulpit. At the time, I was dating two Mexican women—in an increasingly painful lover's triangle—trying to decide which one to marry . . . and I was getting nowhere. I asked Cheryl if it was either of them. She said, "No." Of course, I asked her to describe the woman she'd seen. She said that she was short, somewhat dark skinned, with long black hair, but that she couldn't quite make out her face. This was about five years before I met my present wife, who indeed fits what Cheryl was able to see. Shortly after Cheryl's vision, I moved to a different church, and I never saw Cheryl again. During this time interval, I heard that Cheryl had died. And I still hadn't resolved the love triangle. I finally broke off both those relationships.

About three months before I met my present wife, my mother became incapacitated with double pneumonia and dementia. I made the decision to take her in to live with me in my apartment in Chicago. I was forty-six years old and extremely busy with book tours and guest lecturing across the United States and Canada. I quickly realized that

I was going to need someone to come in once a week to clean and cook dinners for my mother and me for the following week and also, on occasion, to caretake my mother while I was out of town. I had a connection to a Latino church and asked my connection if she knew of anyone in the congregation that might be interested in that kind of job. She found two young women. Before I could interview them, two strange things happened. First, out of nowhere I heard a voice (in my head) say, "I'm going to marry the woman I hire." Okay. That was odd. Then when I was entering the downstairs lobby to my apartment building, I saw a magazine lying on the low stone bench where the mailman left magazines, circulars, and packages. On the cover was a picture of a young Maya woman, dressed in Maya ritual garb and wearing a headdress of giant banana leaves. I looked more carefully at the face and suddenly knew that her features were the features of the woman I would marry. I said to myself with a combination of certainty and startle, "That's her!" I took the magazine, copied the cover, and put the magazine back.

A month or so later, I did the interviews with the women my contact had come up with. I immediately recognized those Maya features in the second woman I interviewed, not the same woman that was on the magazine cover but remarkably similar. She was also, even without that consideration, the obvious candidate for me to hire. The only problem was that she was already married. I hired her anyway and dismissed that precognitive voice in my head. Skipping the details, as it turned out, I did eventually marry her, and we've been happily married ever since. The last part of this series of precognitive events surrounding the arrival of the love of my life, as I found out later, is that, before she'd left Mexico for the United States with her then husband, she'd consulted a psychic, more or less on a whim. The psychic had told her that the man she'd married was not the man she would spend the rest of her life with; there was another man whom she'd meet in the United States. This man, the psychic told her, lived "in the north," far beyond her original destination of Houston, Texas. (In fact, my future wife and her then-husband did move from Houston to Chicago, where we met.) There's one more detail, not exactly precognitive, but something. My wife told me that when she'd first heard my voice on the phone (to set up the interview), she'd felt strongly that it was strangely familiar and that she'd heard that voice "long before."

Okay, Wargo's thesis that all precognitive events are due to our unconsciously projecting ourselves into *our own personal* futures, or our future selves are retrojecting themselves and their states of knowledge back in time to *our own personal* present, may be right about the kinds of precognitive events he's focused on. However, as I've mentioned, that others can precognize our futures—others who will never know the outcomes of our lives—seems to suggest that the time loops proposal is limited in its scope and that, in fact, we're not confined in our presentiments to things we will know in *our own* futures. It seems more reasonable to me that we are all connected in something like Jung's collective unconscious—a Universal Mind, the Akashic records, whatever you want to call it—to which some individual psyches are more closely connected than others. This Psychic Medium, whatever it is, spans all space and time instantaneously as well as in a whole variety of space-time modes, possibly but not necessarily infinite in number.

Apparitions

The jury is still out on what exactly apparitions are. I think those who study these things can't agree, really, because apparitions present a fairly wide range of evidence for what they might be. Are they whole persons who have lived and died and want to communicate? Are they (sometimes) whole persons who are communicating at the moment of death or shortly after? Are they images or fragments of dead persons (including pets) being used by the dead as, in effect, puppets—I mean, with intention? Are they whole persons or fragments thereof who are *unin-*

tentionally "stuck" between dimensions? Or are they mindless "psychic residues" left behind in this world by persons who have, in fact, moved on? *Or*, are at least some of them persons who have *never* been incarnate in the medium of matter that we're familiar with? Depending on the circumstances, I suspect they are probably any of the above.

Whatever they are, they do seem to manifest at the border between disembodied psyche and matter. They may register their *presence* just beneath or behind our visual capacities. Some of them *can* create visual effects. Some seem able to manipulate matter, so that objects move and the noise of moving objects is heard (sometimes even if the objects we associate with such noises do not actually move). Here are six short stories about my own experiences of apparitions and similar accounts by people who are close to me and whose reporting I trust. Most of the following stories are about what are called *incipient apparitions*[45]—that is, apparitions that give signs of their presence but that don't fully manifest or appear. Three are the real deal.

My wife and I have a housekeeping business. A few years ago, in a client's house in which the old father had recently died, my wife went up to the carpeted upstairs hallway to vacuum. At the top of the stairs she was stopped cold. Impressed into the carpet were fresh footprints, evidently wet, leading from the bathroom to about halfway down the hall to a bedroom. *Halfway* . . . and then they just stopped! This was the same house in which our client, the daughter of the recently deceased man, had reported to my wife that someone was playing with the light switches in random parts of the house—an event my wife and her coworker also witnessed—which our client believed was her dead father.

One evening in the parsonage in southern Illinois, where I was serving as pastor, I was reading on the sofa in the living room when I heard a rhythmic banging on the underside of the floor, coming from the basement. The sound seemed to move across the floor, from one end of the house to the other. It sounded like a metal pipe turned on end and slammed against the wood of the basement ceiling. When I say "rhythmic," I mean a repeated *bang, bang, bang, bang*—nothing fancy. It wasn't pipes expanding and contracting, like hot water or steam pipes do, and there was no water softener or other piped appliance in the house. This happened only once. My immediate impression was that "someone" in the basement wanted to let me know he or she was there. Of course, I went down and checked out the basement. Nobody. I wasn't alarmed. Actually, I've learned to just accept most odd events as a matter of course, like the slippered footsteps on the hard-tiled floor of our house in Miami shortly before the day my mother died in her bedroom there.

Now things get a little more real. Two or three days after my mother's death, sometime in the late morning, our daughter, about a year and a half, came running down the hallway from her bedroom to ours, pointing back toward her bedroom, excitedly saying, "Gamma, Gamma!" We rushed to her room and, perhaps predictably, did not see my mother.

When I was a young man, I drove with Elise, my brother's now ex-mother-in-law, to her parents' town house in Milwaukee to pick up some furniture my brother and his wife wanted. Elise did most of the driving. We spent the night there. Elise's father had died a number of months before. She and her mother slept in the main bedroom, and I took the living-room sofa.

About three o'clock in the morning, I woke up because of the strong sense of an angry presence in the middle of the living room staring at me. I knew somehow that it was a little old man. I peered through the semidarkness to see if I could make him out. I couldn't. The angry stare continued. Eventually I went back to sleep. But the experience was so vivid I told Elise about it the next morning. She said, "That's interesting. My father was here last night. He came into the bedroom. I woke up and said to him with some surprise but no alarm—these kinds of thing happen to me all the time—'Dad!' He smiled and disappeared." I remembered then that Elise was somewhat psychic. She asked me, "Do you want to know how he died?" I said, "Sure." She said, "They were in the basement doing the laundry and were coming up the stairs, when she heard him stumbling behind her. She helped him up, and they got to the living room. He died in her arms on the sofa." I said something like "Wow!" She said, "Every night ever since except for last night, she's slept on the sofa because that's where she felt him closest." It didn't have to be said why he'd come to the living room the night before, looking for her, and found me instead. That's why the anger. Did he feel she was being disloyal or that she was cheating on him? Was he just angry at the break in continuity? I don't know. But I *do* know he was there and very upset with me.

Many years ago, a friend of mine was staying the night in an old house of a couple he knew—somewhere in Iowa, I think. Frank was a business-man, hardheaded and straightforward. And yet, as he later told me, that night in the couple's house was anything but a straightforward experi-ence. He was reading in bed about 11:00 p.m. when suddenly the figure of a boy, probably five or six years old appeared standing expressionless in a corner of the bedroom, looking directly at Frank. He seemed to have his own illumination in that dark corner, as apparitions frequently do. Frank just looked him in the eye (or whatever it was!). The boy was dressed in what Frank described as "old-fashioned clothes"—knickers, long stockings, and so on. Frank couldn't remember how long this mutual staring went on, but he guessed maybe twenty minutes or so. He finally went to sleep.

The next morning at breakfast he told his friends about it. They said they'd never seen the boy. Frank had heard the stories we've all heard about apparitions haunting the places where something violent has occurred to them, often murder. So, he was curious enough to go to the public library to search the microfiche for old newspaper articles about the murder of a boy at that address—he guessed, early twentieth century as a time frame. After several hours of searching, he did find an article about the murder of a boy at that house, and in the very bedroom he'd stayed in. And the photo of the boy that accompanied the article was, not surprisingly, identical to the figure he'd seen.

This next story took place at what seems like a wholly different level of whatever is going on in the Collective Psyche. And, among other things, it raises the question of what is inner and what is outer with some urgency. And how does one become the other? It also raises the question of Evil within the Collective Psychic Medium.

My wife, daughter, and I were living in Oak Park, Illinois, in the mansion-like parsonage of Oak Park United Church of Christ, where I was serving as pastor. It was a late-summer, early autumn night in 2002. The windows were closed and the heat and air conditioning were off. I was sleeping in the master bedroom; my wife and daughter (who was about three years old) were in a bedroom to the right and down the hall. I was having a really terrible nightmare (which I don't remember). What I do remember is becoming aware of the sensation of a human-like thing inside my nightmare and inside my physical body, lying in the bed *within* me! I felt it as a kind of weight. In my nightmare, it seemed to be emaciated and black, as if it had been burned to a crisp in a fire. Suddenly, I felt it "sit up," pull itself up out of my chest, double over, and streak out of the room through the open door to the hallway. It sounded like a rushing wind. Indeed, it blew to the right outside my door, turned left, flew down the hall, and blew open the closed door to my wife and daughter's bedroom, where it . . . what? Dissipated? Entered my wife or daughter?

With its escape from my chest, I startled awake and so experienced its flight down the hall (though I couldn't see it) and its blowing open of their bedroom door. I jumped out of bed and ran after it. When I got to the bedroom, I found my wife wide awake and sitting up in bed with a terrified look in her eyes. In a stunned and hushed voice, she said, "What the hell?!" Our daughter was still sound asleep.

Okay. This happened. It is a *psychological* fact—on both my wife's and my part—and it is a historical fact; it took place in space and time. But what on earth can begin in an imaginal (not imaginary) psychological medium, and then transition into a material or quasi-material entity or force, have physical effects, both auditory and kinetic, and then disappear into . . . I'm guessing . . . a psychic plane, dimension, medium, what have you? It seems to have had a purpose, but what was it? I don't think it invaded my wife's psyche or mine. Did it inject itself into our daughter? Did it just want us to notice it, and, I have the impression, its profound unhappiness? Does psychic energy sometimes reach such a peak of "charge" that it materializes, expends its charge that way, and then vanishes? And, if it did have some kind of consciousness, *who* was it? A Demon? The dead pastor who'd had the congregation build this parsonage for him? If the latter, why did he seem so angry? Was it because I was the pastor who succeeded him in his position and *in his own house*? Did he object to my theology, which admittedly was a little unorthodox? Had he himself become possessed, "demonized"?

As I thought about it afterward, I entertained the demon hypothesis for a while. I'd been intensely studying the writings of Ibn 'Arabi (1165–1240 CE), the greatest sheikh of medieval Sufi Islam—writings of great beauty and wisdom, so far as I'm concerned, and absolutely radiant with spiritual Light. I remembered that Jung had said something like, "Where the light is brightest, the shadow is deepest." Had my "enlightenment" triggered a violent reaction from my own or, perhaps, a deeper shadow?

UFO Experiences

Some researchers and commentators in the field of UFOs and their occupants have proposed that both show the capacity to express a psychical *and* a material aspect—the one changing seamlessly into the other (like the demonic Oak Park "dream" figure and apparitions—the latter both incipient and fully manifested).[46] My own handful of UFO experiences suggests to me that this is right, at least in certain cases.

After my first ex-wife's and my UFO encounter (coming up), I remembered what I'd thought was a dream (and probably was) in which I was in an open field at night. Out of the sky a vast glowing disk descended in front of me and hovered inches above the ground. It almost completely filled my field of vision. What I remember of my feelings was a mixture of awe, wonder, and dread—also, a sense of the cosmic, of mystery, and of presence, of an intelligence of some kind within or behind the light show. Many years later, after my ex-wife's and my encounter, I began a series of paintings that attempted to depict my feelings from that childhood or early adolescent dream. Most of these depicted a giant disk or elongated orb, glowing brightly (but not blindingly) from within. Right through the middle of the object was a black split or wedge that ran the length of it. While the light expressed the awe and wonder, the black wedge was a way of showing the dread and the sense of cosmic mystery.

The experience my ex-wife and I had I later recalled in detail under hypnosis—and, in the telling of it in that state, my ability to reproduce her voice with her exact intonations—goes like this. It was a September evening (I don't remember the date or the year). The sky was clear except for one small cloud up high and just beginning to shade into twilight. We were facing west in our third-floor apartment in Moline, Illinois. I was sitting in my overstuffed chair. She was sitting on the floor beside me. I was talking (as usual). I didn't notice at first, but she got up with an extremely focused look on her face and walked to the windows that ran the length of the western living-room wall. She just stood there, staring out into the sky. She didn't move or shift her gaze. It was then I noticed that she was disconnected from our conversation and, it struck me, in an almost trancelike state.

I said, "Honey, what are you looking at?" She answered, "There's something weird out here." I said, "What?" She said, "It's a disk with lights flashing around the rim, and it stays in one position without moving at all, then shoots over to another part of the sky and stops, then shoots off to another part." I said, "My God, that's a UFO!" I ran to the window and looked where she was pointing. I couldn't see anything. I said, "Where? Where?" She said, "It's right over the telephone pole. Can't you see it?" I said, "No!" Then she said, "Now it just flew behind that cloud." I could certainly see the cloud, and we watched for a while to see if it would come out again. It didn't. Afterward, I grilled her about its appearance—how many lights, what colors, their sequence, and so on. I saw that she was extremely reluctant to talk about it, as if she were still a little entranced. She did say, "When I first saw it, I asked myself, 'Is that a plane? No. A helicopter? No. A blimp? No. I don't know what that is.'" I immediately called a friend, who gave me the phone number of the Center for UFO Studies in Evanston. I got ahold of J. Allen Hynek (the former Project Blue Book official). He told me that a number of reports had come in. People in Moline, like us, had seen it in the western sky, while people in Rock Island had seen it in the eastern sky . . . which pinpointed it as an *object in space*.

The eeriest part of the whole experience was that my wife could see it and I couldn't. What it felt like was that "they" had the power to get inside our minds and manipulate either our eyes or our brain's capacity to receive and process input from them. Either way, they had power over us—a power, I thought in that moment, only God could or *should* have. The emotional takeaway for me was that, as I told everyone who'd listen, "I felt like cattle!" Devastating . . . a completely devastating feeling of having been invaded and violated in *my own* psyche, in my *person*. I have since read many accounts of UFO encounters, and one of the main feelings people express afterward is exactly that—a sense of violation. Indifference to persons, to the whole experience of personhood, like my eyes in the mirror, like that starlit night sky in our backyard in Rock Island, like Nature itself. Creepy, awful, schizoid . . . demonic.

Demons and Angels

Dreams are probably many things. They may be ways our Unconscious has of reacting to events of the past day or days, trying to make sense of and order them. They may be attempted communications of deep insights to the ego-consciousness from the personal unconscious or layers of the unconscious that subtly shade off from the personal to the collective. They may occasionally be prophetic. In the majority of cases, they may be, as Jung believed, the psyche-as-a-whole's efforts to create a balance of attitudes or orientations between the conscious ego and at least aspects of the personal unconscious. He also suggested that the essentially timeless archetypes in the collective unconscious try through dreams to get the ego into a subordinate relationship to the Self. I think probably all of the above, depending. I also think, though, that, in accomplishing these various tasks, dreams additionally may open communications with disincarnate and nonincarnate conscious or semiconscious entities that are neither aspects of the personal unconscious per se nor as grand as archetypes or, for that matter, God-images. These are characters I believe I've experienced in dreams as demonic or angelic.

While neither as dramatic or malevolent as the Oak Park parsonage Demon that physicalized and rushed down our hallway, blowing open the bedroom door, the demonic figures that often come up in my recurrent dreams of being lost in a city, trying to find my car or my wife and daughter, are most decidedly tricksterish—I would say, Evil, but not in a deeply malevolent way. They appear as people supposedly trying to help me find my car or my loved ones, but whom I always discover are either misdirecting me or confused themselves.

Angels appear in other dreams—almost never the Christmas-card types but, rather, beings of Light, self-illuminated—who are genuinely trying to help me, for example, find my car or my wife or my daughter, or support me on a particular creative path I'm on. I'm thinking here, for instance, of the three fuzzy feminine light-forms in humanlike aspect who were co-owners of a beautiful and magical downtown combination boutique and coffee bar. In the dream, I went to them *with* my wife and daughter to meet with a Higher Angel in charge of some kind of evaluation of my life. He left me with his "business card," which was like cardstock, folded in the middle, in the center of which was a complex mandala figure. After the meeting, my wife, my daughter, and I went straight to our car. In this case, the Angels seemed to be counteracting and neutralizing the trickster Demons of my lost-in-a-city quasi-nightmares.

I've had many experiences of what I take to be the sense of angelic presences and even once in a while have "heard" angelic voices addressing me in moments of crisis.

The only time I can say that I "saw" Angels was in one of those twilight zones between waking and sleeping. I was either just about to fall asleep or I was in the process of waking up—I'm not sure which. But lying in bed I looked up as if through a wide and very long vertical tube—wide enough to encompass my bed and tall enough to reach far above my head, simultaneously a couple hundred feet and untold "millions of miles." Looking up, at the far end of the tube, was an oculus, or brightly lit disk area, surrounded by a rim or circular balcony. Peering over the edge of the rim and looking down at me were three figures spaced evenly around the opening, silhouetted against the light above them. I could see the upper parts of their bodies and their faces and what looked like the tops of their folded wings. They looked exactly like Eastern Orthodox Christian icons of Angels. And I heard one of them say to the others, "This one is marked for the Light." Meaning me, I supposed (and continue to hope!).

Rabbit Holes

So, from my lived experience, the human psyche/Psyche is vast in scope, maybe ultimately Infinite. It is crammed with mental units of dizzying variety and proportions and, it seems to me, dwelling in and as multiple layers. Those layers have boundaries and barriers, but they're also leaky, porous enough to allow some intermingling between the dimensions or zones. The question about what is inside the psyche and what outside is a tricky one. In one sense, everything that we don't readily identify as us is outside—that is, outside our current self-definition. On the other hand, everything that we come to know or experience, as we come to know it, is now inside, part of our expanded self-definition. Was it ever anywhere else? Is there anything other than the psyche/Psyche? As we'll see further on, that seems doubtful. And what about the fact that the boundary between psyche/Psyche and matter can, under certain circumstances at least, not only blur but disappear completely?

At the very center of all this bustle and thriving is, I think, what I call a "rabbit hole," an opening that drops down or out to the Infinite. I think the universe is full of these, like the holes in Swiss cheese, only worse: they're absolutely everywhere! Look closely and watch your step! We'll be looking for these as we move through the rest of the book. We'll find some in the next chapter. For now, let me just say, I'm not sure I've experienced any of these, including the one inside me, directly. On the other hand, I did write . . . and seemed to know what I was feeling at the moment of writing:

> I am the rim of a well that drops down forever.
> Sometimes when I look down I see nothing but light.
> Sometimes I only see blackness. Either way, I'm blinded.

DOUGLAS M. GILLETTE,
AT THE THRESHOLDS OF ELYSIUM

And then there is, again, the question of a Higher Self. Is that *beyond* the bottom of the well (if there *is* a bottom), Infinity, on the other side of it? *Is* it Infinity *Itself* in a person-like way? Is it us represented at a different register? Can it be identified as any of the figures mentioned above—Jung's Self, Beahrs's hidden observer, Nature, the Face Narcissus saw, the Eyes I saw looking back at me in the mirror, the Hindu Atman, Adam Kadmon? Is it God? The following chapters will try to answer this and other questions.

Before all that, I want you to know *something that I really do know*: There are worlds all around us, within us . . . right here, right now, where we say we *are*. They are inhabited. And we are not alone!

3
Nature:
A Beautiful Terror

Sharks, horses, dragonflies, grubs, trees, tachyons,
carnivores and caprids, serpents come . . . everted . . .
from some matrix of fecundity, some exultation of
of binding brightness of which I am inescapably
ignorant.

DOUGLAS M. GILLETTE,
AT THE THRESHOLDS OF ELYSIUM

Psyche, as It expresses Itself as and through Nature, is troubling to me—unspeakably Beautiful certainly . . . and utterly Terrifying. As am I. Yet, God Expresses the Beautiful Terror of Nature in order to make persons with whom to commune through that specific medium. *For us as we are*, there was no alternative.

The Terror

Planetary

Not too long ago, I saw a young female paleontologist being interviewed for a PBS special. She was in the dinosaur hall at the Natural History Museum, London. As she talked about past mass extinctions in the long history of life on Earth, her eyes took on a sparkle of what I'd describe as fascinated horror and on her face was an expression of, it seemed to me, a pleasurable terror. In this apparent frame of mind, she said with a mixture of wonder and dread, "There is so much death!"

That comment speaks directly to my own sense of Nature's profoundly disturbing Darkness, shall we call it. For me, that Darkness includes not only the unfathomably massive scale of *death* throughout evolutionary history, but equally unsettling, the sheer magnitude of *suffering*, at least for anything with a nervous system. The great mass extinctions inflicted extreme pain on innumerable organisms before they killed them through burning alive, suffocation in poisonous gases, crushing, disease, starvation and dehydration, drowning, and just about anything else you can think of. I mean, by the millions, even billions. Each one individually.

Along with this continually unfolding story of the destruction of living things is the powerful sense of the *transience* of those individuals and of their species, genera, families, orders, in some cases, classes, even phyla—ultimately, of the whole of life itself. Accompanying these realizations is my recoil from the immense cruelty of it all, whether intentional or unintentional, or some of both.

I know the following sections might seem like a lot of science for those who don't particularly like science. But all the facts and figures can have the cumulative effect of alerting us to *the thoroughly alien Strangeness of Reality in Its this-worldly form*. And that's exactly what I'm seeking to communicate.

Earth is an exceedingly violent and ferocious planet. More so than the roaring winds of Jupiter, Saturn, and Neptune, which are only wind. More than Io, which is merely a hot blob with massive volcanic eruptions. No, Earth is far more violent. It is made of a menagerie of solids, liquids, and gases (and things in intermediate states). It has roaring winds and volcanoes. But it also has far more varied dynamism. It is constantly growing and obliterating continents of basalt bedrock, which casts up floating granite masses, rolling, bouncing, and to-ing and fro-ing. It is constantly rearranging the continents, shifting them around—crashing them together and tearing them apart. Earth wobbles as it spins drunkenly on its half-knocked-over axis. It orbits its star irregularly—sometimes in an ellipse, sometimes near circular. At intervals it erupts in continent-sheathing flood basalts, sometimes for tens of millions of years, far more consequential than volcanos. These spew sulfur dioxide, carbon dioxide, and other toxic materials into the atmosphere, which, when combined with yet other elements, cause massive discharges of chlorine gas, sulfuric acid, carbonic acid, and hydrofluoric acid. These result in acid rain and "methane burps" (from the heating and release into the atmosphere of frozen methane bubbles sequestered in the ocean crusts).[1] Earth's magnetic field wanders, pulses, and flips, and the planet runs through cycles of planet-wide freezing and runaway greenhouses.

All of this and more is very hard on life but is evidently also essential for life's generation and evolution. And life itself has caused, and is continuing to cause, some of this chronically violent upheaval—a true child of its parent planet and rather thoroughly integrated into and expressive of its churning systems.

Living

Life. I do think there is such a thing—I mean, as a whole coherent entity, not just as a jostling conglomeration of individual living beings. Life is the violent, ferocious, and frenetic furtherance of the processes of the planet from which it springs. From a materialist perspective, life can be minimally defined as a fantastic acceleration of and frenzied self-catalyzing emergence from the natural chemical processes of its molecularly sumptuous world. It is also organized—self-organized—in a mind-boggling complexity of molecular processes that far surpass anything else in Nature (that we know of). It also reproduces with a vengeance. None of the paths of these molecular processes—for example, protein formation and folding—is itself alive (with the possible exception of RNA, at least according to the advocates of the so-called RNA world as a model for how life began on Earth).[2] But when combined in the startling and unexpected manifestation of even a single primitive cell, somehow, some way, the "lights come on," and life ignites. The differences between such a cell and the matter that surrounds it are so stark that they lead any thoughtful observer directly into a state of shock, wonder, and utter bafflement.

Life is tenacious, fiercely determined, undeterrably aggressive. Left to its own devices, it doesn't know when to stop. It is voraciously energy consuming and information gathering and integrating. It learns and grows rapaciously. From this perspective, life is the most sophisticated expression (that we know of) of the relentless processes of metabolization that is this universe. But life is also suicidal. Of the ten or so global mass extinctions, life has caused or had a major hand in at least five (counting the Snowball Earths).[3] What counts as a global mass extinction is controversial, depending on the researchers.[4] Partly, this is not settled because the fossil record is incomplete, and the dividing lines between the periods are usually fuzzy.[5]

The five (or more) mass extinctions caused or contributed to by life include the several Snowball Earth events, ranging from about 2.35 billion years ago to 635 million years ago[6] and accompanied by the catastrophic Great Oxidation Event, which culminated around 2.3 billion years ago.[7] The culprit? Mostly photosynthetic cyanobacteria in vast sheets and mats (including stromatolites). These sucked enormous amounts of carbon dioxide out of the atmosphere, so much so that the planet was nearly completely covered in snow and ice. Of course, this killed most of the cyanobacteria. These cycles of Snowball Earths were followed by runaway greenhouse effects, mostly due to volcanos replenishing the carbon dioxide over very long periods of time[8] but initially because there were insufficient photosynthesizing bacteria to bring the carbon dioxide down to comfortable levels for life. When enough bacteria had reproduced, generally over the course of millions of years, the next Snowball Earth began. Gathering information about the causes of this over-and-over-again extinction scenario, life "invented" the animal-like grazers known as Ediacaran fauna, which flourished between 635 and 540 million years ago.[9] The solution? They ate the cyanobacteria, however, not efficiently enough. So, true animals came online around 540 million years ago.[10] This seems to have stopped the Snowballs. Here, we have a little lesson about life not knowing when to stop—in other words, greed—but also life learning how to ensure its survival as a whole, regardless of the excesses of individual species.

Another instance of the same can be dated to the Carboniferous period—between 359 and 299 million years ago.[11] Again, the culprit was plants. Earth was warm and covered with vast forests, like an Amazon rainforest that went on and on forever, essentially covering all the continents. Once more, too much carbon dioxide was removed from the atmosphere, and a deep freeze began. I've joked with my classes that, if we'd been around during the Carboniferous, Arbor Day would *not* have meant, "Go out and plant a tree" but "Cut down as many as you can!"

The last of the life-caused global mass extinctions is the one some experts say we ourselves have started. The jury's still out on this. But assuming things continue the way they're going, between the burning of all those Carboniferous trees (and other things) and consequently shoving the carbon dioxide they had sequestered into the atmosphere pretty much all at the same time, a runaway greenhouse climate seems all but assured. Most of the other causes of mass extinctions are things no living thing could do anything about. We might be able to do something about really big incoming asteroids and comets (for example, the dinosaur killer of sixty-six million years ago), but we could do nothing about the most important other extinguishers of life—continent-devouring flood basalts—more of our planet's (probably) mindless violence.

In addition to catastrophes, I'm aware of what to me is the horrifying fact that Nature, whatever else It may be, and in Its business-as-usual mode, is a gigantic feeding machine. As such It is completely indifferent to the often-horrific fates of Its creatures. This is certainly true of the biological part of Nature. But it also may be true of the non-biologic aspects of Nature, whether they can feel or not. (There is ongoing debate about this.) I'm thinking here, for example, of the biologist Lyall Watson's (1939–2008) account in his *Beyond Supernature: A New Natural History of the Supernatural* (1987)[12] of inexperienced young lions eating their prey haunch-by-shoulder as it stands there trembling, experiencing its life ebbing as it vanishes in excruciating pain . . . in pieces. There are the wasps that lay their eggs inside living caterpillars, which when they hatch, eat the caterpillar alive. Indeed, many animals are eaten alive. Think of the prey of spiders, alive as their body's juices are sucked out. There are parasites, funguses, bacteria, and viruses, most of these life-forms killing their hosts slowly and painfully. I think too of the bears who, I remember reading somewhere, frequently suffer from temporomandibular joint dysfunction, from which many human beings suffer as well. The difference is that humans can get treatment for the unrelenting pain that comes with it, whereas bears cannot. They're frequently driven mad, with no hope of a cure, ever, except for death. This, of course, is just the tip of the iceberg.

Most of these natural horrors (and many more) never come to our attention, or we read about them, or maybe see carefully edited depictions of them on TV in Nature shows. We may shudder, but most of us will never be forced to witness them. Not so if you have a sizable backyard, some of it at least given over to Nature. We have such a yard. It's certainly beautiful from a distance. But if you look closer and more frequently, if you spend time with it, you'll see the little horrors in abundance—sometimes in process, sometimes their aftermaths. It goes without saying that they're not "little" for the participants.

One day it rained mice from the roof. Undoubtedly, these were inhabitants of the attic. They fell all over the patio, mostly dead before they hit. One lived a while. We gave it a lid filled with water. It took a few sips, and it too died. The whole thing was a complete mystery, until we discovered a nest of yellow jackets around one of the roof fittings. It looks like the mice had either blundered into it or come too close.

Who hasn't seen ants swarming around a living worm, each one taking tiny little bites out of it, watching in fascinated horror as the worm writhes in agony. It would take hours for it to die. We've seen confrontations between squirrels and eagles in the boughs of our redbud tree. We've seen hordes of blackbirds bullying robins en masse. We've watched coyotes go from statues to a rush of rabid predators, mostly chasing rabbits into the bushes. What happened next, we couldn't see. But the next day we have seen the remains—a still fluffy rabbit tail and bits of fur, just lying there in the grass, the rabbit to which these belonged utterly absent. And similarly, we've seen tangled piles of feathers on the lawn, certainly not from molting. We've gotten up in the morning to see our downspout extensions ripped apart and wondered if whoever had run inside for cover had made it out alive. We've watched as an eagle devoured a chipmunk, head first, its hind legs still kicking, its tail twitching, swallowed whole (or almost). I can imagine the last feelings of the chipmunk, the sharp beak digging into your spinal column, the stare into the eagle's maw—blackness and death, when a moment before it had been a perfect summer afternoon. Then utter and total extinguishment. We've seen dragonflies pack-hunting mosquitos in the tree beards of our big maple tree. One summer night, while I was enjoying the lightning bug display, I caught sight of one of these caught in a spider's web on the side of the house, the spider making its fast approach, wrapping the lightning bug round and round with its inescapable strands. I saw the lightning bug thrashing and frantically flashing its chemical light until the spider bit it and rendered it immobile.

One of the most bloodcurdling scenes I've seen in the backyard was a huge azure-blue butterfly of a species I'd never seen before and have never seen again, beautifully sailing through the summer afternoon air. Suddenly and completely unexpectedly, startling and horrifically, out of nowhere came an amazingly large blue hornet, oddly enough exactly the same color as the butterfly. The hornet made a beeline (no pun intended) for the butterfly, its twin in color but in nothing else. The hornet drove the butterfly into the ground and instantly began the process of shredding and eating it. That took, I would guess, less than thirty seconds. All that was left of that magnificent beauty was a wing tip in the grass, gently flapping in the breeze.

Pain in animals is not limited to the physical; there's also obvious psychological pain—not only from being hunted and eaten alive, but also evidently from enduring previous emotional trauma. I mentioned before my experiences with psychotic robins. Here are their stories.

Two springs ago, a pair of robins built a nest in our grape arbor, and the female laid her eggs. It was a really hot spring, so much so that the female couldn't and, I think, knew she shouldn't sit on the eggs. In the soaring temperatures, they were already too hot. We watched and waited for the eggs to hatch. They never did. But tragically, the female remained in the area. And when she saw a small bird or a chipmunk approach the nest, possibly to try to eat the dead eggs, she flew into the arbor and took up a rigid and aggressive pose in the branches a few feet away. She allowed the bird and the chipmunk to come up to the nest, but she didn't attack them. It was as if she was frozen in a pose of despairing rage. It was painful to see.

Another summer a robin stationed herself on our front porch and over and over again attacked our doorbell. The doorbell was a round white button in a dark brown setting. She kept leaping up and pecking the doorbell with force and, I would say, a look of obsessive madness in her eyes. She repeated this behavior until I painted the button the same brown as the setting. Of course, I don't know what that was about, but it sure looked as though she was interpreting the white button as an eye, the eye of some animal she hated and was determined to blind.

An even more alarming display of robin psychosis took place on our patio at the back of our house. We have a glass wall the length of the patio. Inside, in the garden room, I created a little paradise of foliage and some of my sculptures. On the back wall of the garden room, I painted a reproduction of an ancient Roman orchard scene. Suspended from the ceiling is a three-dimensional blackbird, adapted from a Roman painting of the same. Outside on the patio is a very large ceramic reproduction of a Minoan-style storage jar, about four feet tall. One day, from inside the house, I heard a bird aggressively and repeatedly hitting the glass. I went into the garden room and saw a robin launching from the Minoan storage jar and hitting the glass hard with its beak right where it could see the model blackbird hanging. This went on for days, and the storage jar on the patio gradually became half covered in white robin feces.

There was a very angry and very aggressive and, in that sense, somewhat frightening cast to this repetitive behavior. I finally decided to wrap a white cloth around the blackbird so that none of it would be visible. As I did this, from its perch on the storage jar, the robin watched me. I know this may sound like overinterpretation on my part, but I am sure she was giving me a smirky knowing look, like, "You can't fool me! Now I know you're in cahoots with the blackbird!" It was chilling to see a bird look at me like that. Not only was the evident intelligence unnerving, but that psychotic misinterpretation of what I was trying to do—the ascription to me of being in league with what to her was a sworn life-or-death enemy—felt exactly like those human interactions in which I'd been similarly misunderstood. With no recourse. No way to convince the other that I was not, in fact, intending harm. Helpless, at the receiving end of someone else's unjustified hatred. In any case, "knowing" that I was trying to defend the blackbird from her attacks and apparently understanding the perfidy of what I had done— the blackbird was still there inside the cloth—the robin continued her attacks on the window for the rest of the season.

I'm convinced that many animals are far more intelligent than we give them credit for. They are also psychologically vulnerable to mental illness. Just ask the owners of dogs and cats that have been previously abused. Or just take a good look at your backyard.

Human

Human behavior is, with few exceptions, animal behavior, especially as this has come down to us through our primate lineage, more specifically from the common ancestor of chimpanzees, bonobos, and us. We've gotten all the good stuff, like mutual caring, empathy, kindness, curiosity, thinking rationally (and calculatingly), learning, teaching, creativity, cooperation, and so on. However, we've also gotten the bad stuff, like aggression, cruelty, murder (including infanticide), genocide, war, manipulation, hatred, bullying, deception, domination, persecution, and cannibalism. We must also add tribalism (us against them), selfishness, laziness, and also a marked tendency toward psychological splitting—consequently, neurosis, psychosis, projection, and blaming. We also see the stirrings of conscience and self-loathing in our animal relatives, raised to a very high and complicated level in us. Additionally, we probably surpass other species in both cross-species empathy as well as in intentional cross-species cruelty (with the possible exception of cats).

I'm not going to list examples. We all know them. Needless to say, our suffering is immense—both at the hands of natural disasters, disease of one kind or another, aging, and at the hands of one another. And I'm not just talking about major events or things that make the headlines. I'm also talking about the many mini-atrocities, psychological and physical, that we inflict upon one another within our relationships and our families.

Evil

Which brings us to the problem of Evil. In his *Dark Nature: A Natural History of Evil* (1995), the biologist Lyall Watson suggests that Evil is an inherent part of Nature, an essential ingredient in Its ecology, one that is utterly pervasive.[13] I would add, actually inescapable at our level of Reality.

The problem of Evil is traditionally divided into two parts—natural Evil and moral-ethical Evil. It's always seemed to me that moral-ethical Evil is a subset of natural Evil but with some further ingredients. While natural Evil—such as natural catastrophes, disease, and death or, for that matter, the collapse of stars or, worse yet, the end of the stelliforous (star-formation) period of the universe's history, which will spell the end of life—may be thought of as a kind of neutral Evil, one without the added quality of malevolence, moral-ethical Evil seems clearly intentional and malevolent. Indeed, natural Evil, like the global mass extinctions, does appear to lead to life becoming stronger and smarter—something good, right? And the collapse of stars, at least the ones that lead to novas and supernovas, seed the universe with a richer and richer broth of heavy elements—exactly the ones needed for the emergence of life. And so on.

But moral-ethical Evil? The deliberate destruction of other sentient creatures' well-being? That seems as though a step has been taken beyond the neutral Evil of the (maybe) intentionless destruction of others—gravity versus intrastellar fusion and radiation, for instance. A step has been taken, yes. But I still think the step from natural Evil to moral-ethical Evil, whether or not intentional or conscious, involves a continuity from a perhaps more vague form of Evil to a more focused one and doesn't represent a *radical* break or disjunction. I would go on to say that Evil is inherent to the makeup of this universe—It has cosmic roots—and this particular universe would not exist without It. The feeding machine metaphor for what's going on in both the inanimate and animate spheres seems apt to me. I would go still further and suggest that, if Evil is inherent to the universe, It has its origin in Whatever or Whoever made and continues to make it. Since I am a theist, that means Some*one*—that is, the Divine, or God. I think there's no way around that one. We'll come back to this part of the problem of Evil in chapters 5 and 7 and a bit in 8. But first, I want to propose a specific transition point where natural Evil becomes transformed into moral-ethical Evil.

From my perspective, that transition point comes with the emergence of life. Actually, the chemistry that led to life. So, in that sense, *moral-ethical Evil is an emergent property of life*, emergent like the wetness of water when enough H_2O molecules have been assembled. In his *The Story of Earth: The First 4.5 Billion Years, from Stardust to Livig Planet* (2012), the mineralogist Robert Hazen makes a strong case for the emergence of moral-ethical Evil at the point at which complex molecules on early Earth—probably RNA—began to predate other molecules in order to reproduce themselves and, perhaps, actively sought to destroy rival complex molecules that were trying to do the same thing. Hazen doesn't use the word *Evil*, but he does paint a picture of life-or-death competition and predation at the molecular level, and he suggests that those RNA molecules were in some sense alive.[14] Of course, without nerves and certainly not brains, at the molecular level "nobody gets hurt," just as in stellar collapse, gases, planets, and stars being "eaten" by a black hole, eruptions of flood basalts on lifeless planets, and so forth.

On the other hand, it seems to me that the competition and, yes, predation between lifeless natural objects and forces and the slide from there into molecular competition and predation—"Darwinian," as Hazen calls it[15]—is a relatively smooth one. At some point in this natural progression, however, moral-ethical Evil shows up in the form of identity. Identity means "I"-ness, however vague or relatively unconscious. Indeed, long before the cellular or even the molecular level of complex identities, the quarks that make up protons and neutrons show a kind of "I" intentionality; they strive mightily to escape the strong nuclear force that keeps them within their respective atomic identities. Those atomic identities show an "I"-ness will to maintain their being as themselves by forcing the quarks to stay within their proton-ness or neutron-ness. Without the enforced subservience of the quarks, the protons and neutrons would cease to be. The mathematician-philosopher Alfred North Whitehead (1861–1947) put forward the idea that whenever there's an event of any kind—an "occasion," as he called it—something is *felt* by the participants, even at the subatomic level.[16] Biologists know that even multicellular organisms with neurons but no brains as central processors certainly feel, probably even pleasure and pain.[17] Eating and being eaten feel *very* different!

Taking a page from Richard Dawkins, Watson affirms the "selfishness" of the genes and proposes that that selfishness is the source of moral-ethical Evil.[18] As I've just suggested, the selfishness, so defined, of the genes has a long ancestry that goes back to the selfishness of RNA molecules, which, in turn, have an equally long ancestry in the selfishness of protons and neutrons and the quarks they're made of . . . and so, maybe on and on, beyond our horizon to investigate (at least in terms of matter). So, from a biological perspective, while there is continuity between natural Evil as *indifference* and the *selfishness* of moral-ethical Evil, nonetheless, once life has emerged, *Evil proper* has arrived, perhaps "innocently" and "unconsciously," but I'm not so sure. I do think, though, that the kind of consciousness and intentionality that gets expressed at its maximum of clarity in big brains, complexly wired, experiences and expresses Evil with a unique and fulsome vengeance!

What Dawkins and Watson call "selfishness," I would call "malignant narcissism." What is that, and why does it show up? We see it in animal behavior, our own included, around aggression, sex, and territoriality, especially where resources like food and sexual partners are in short supply in our environment—either natural or social (the particular ways our societies are constructed). The conflicts that follow become over the top to the extent that the situation is perceived to be a matter of life or death. Within that atmosphere, our "I"-ness, our narcissism, becomes malignant. It does so because we—consciously, semiconsciously, or unconsciously—fear a final and absolute loss of our identities, our complete cessation, our irremediable erasure, an "as if we'd never been." To try to cancel that terror, we murder and wage war. We project our fear of our own meaninglessness onto others, and we make sure they carry it by zeroing out their lives. As Watson suggests, it may be easier to do that kind of projection or handing off than to accept the horrifying realization that, for *all* of us, *our own only escape* from the Evil inherent to the world is death, itself the ultimate Evil.[19] Or so we think.

Here's a short version of my psycho-philosophical-theological take on all (or much) of this—the viciousness, the malignancy and the almost imperceptible slide from natural Evil to moral-ethical Evil. Evil, of the moral-ethical variety at least, arises and is expressed whenever the Self-finitized aspects of the One still want to claim that they *are* the One—the Absolute, Infinite, and Eternal—while *in relationship* with other Self-finitized versions of the Infinite-Eternal-Absolute One. *In relationship* should be a clue that, *as* the One Self-*finitized*, there can be no claim to Absoluteness at that level. There can and should be the awareness that we and all finitized forms of the One are precisely that—and so, of Infinite Worth and Immortal (at least in some sense)—*but at our Cores, not* in our this-worldly multiplicity! There is the fear that giving up the claim to Absoluteness at the relational level of Reality will mean that we can't make that claim at *any* level. If that were the case, then, indeed, the abyss would open beneath our feet, and we would fall into Forever/No-thingness. That feeling is intolerable to at least most sentient creatures. Hence, the malignancy—the desperation of the narcissism. Those who deny our claims at the finite level are our enemies. It is *they* who must be consigned to oblivion, so that *we* can be Absolute. It's an all-or-nothing misperception of what and who we are—the fact that we are Infinite and Eternal but not here and not now (to speak temporally).

Let me go back to the eyes I saw in the mirror. I suspect, in fact, that they expressed a level of Evil deeper than human, or even life's malignancy. I've seen those eyes, that look, that Other once more (so far) in my life, when I answered a persistent knocking on our front door at the height of the coronavirus pandemic. I put on my mask and, extremely irritated that someone—I presumed a salesman of some kind—would be trying to do the door-to-door thing at eight at night in the middle of a plague, I shouted, "I'm not going to answer the door!" But the knock continued. So, I did go to the door. I opened the inner door but demanded that the "salesman" not open the outer door. What I saw was a man in a dark business suit with a very large black briefcase. I shrugged my shoulders as if to say, "Well?" The look I got back was shark's eyes, cold killer eyes, perhaps a readiness to kill *me* with no remorse at all, characterless indifference to whether I lived or died—schizoid, detached, disassociated. After a long stare, he finally said, "I'm looking for . . . ," and he spoke the name of our neighbor, next house to the north. I pointed him in the right direction. Somewhat confused, he turned away from the door, said, "Sorry to have disturbed you," and disappeared into the night. As I closed the front door with some relief, I thought, "*That* is Evil. That was once a human being, and now it's been possessed by . . . what? Something beyond narcissism . . . asteroids, the unimaginable wastes of nothingness between them . . . Nature? Its Soulless Intelligence?" That walking horror in human form was decidedly *not* a salesman.

The Weirdness

The Weirdness of Nature is part of Its Terror!

I was probably seven or eight, and I had a terrifying dream. I was in some sort of spaceship, sitting on a kind of bay window seat. The window was a large, clear, hemispheric glass bubble. I was staring out into space—cold, black, yet absolutely flooded with stars. Somewhere in that uncountable multitude was the sun, my home star. But I'd lost track of it. I had no way to find it. I was cast out into the cosmos, utterly and totally with no way to locate Earth—no way to go home. Ever.

Along with feeling lost and cast out forever into a terrifying vastness, far beyond my power to imagine, I felt abandonment, absolute aloneness, overpowering anxiety and desperation—something worse than hopelessness. What I saw was infinite blank deadness, personlessness—a smothering, overwhelming meaninglessness, the total indifference of that unfathomable vastness. Even less than indifference. A cancellation, a zeroing. Something that was more featureless even than those eyes at the bottom of the well of eyes I would see in my bathroom mirror several years later. Now I was feeling, and traveling through, an endless schizoid vacuum. Nature without character or caring . . . not even the whisper of a thought, a single syllable. Bizarre . . . with a bizarreness like nothing I'd ever encountered and can't find the words to describe . . . mind annihilating. A totally nonresponding reality in which persons had never been imagined . . . couldn't be . . . for all Eternity.

Cosmic Weirdness

I have very few stories of personal experience in this section because most of what I'm about to talk about is not directly accessible to our daily life or even our extraordinary states of consciousness. So, there's a lot of straight-line exposition here. What I hope, though, is that the cumulative effect, the sheer magnitude and strangeness of this material internalized, *will lead you* to experience feelings of Awe, Wonder, and Dread—perhaps a kind of Rapture, even Gratitude for the Mystery.

As I said a moment ago, the Weirdness of Nature is a part of Its Terror. But there's so much of It that It deserves Its own look. The first thing necessary for our approach to Nature's Weirdness is our acknowledgment that no matter how much we've come to "know" about It, we're up against aspects of It—also aspects of Its stupendously unknown context—that dwarf almost to insignificance what we *do* know. For instance, we have no good idea whether our universe is alone, the only one, or whether it's set within a finite or infinite number of other universes—a multiverse. Researchers throw mathematics at any one (or more) of these possibilities but without achieving a consensus. The answers to these questions might have profound implications, not just in cosmology and physics, but also in our individual self-concepts.

When it comes to our universe specifically (without considering its context), it is stunning to realize that somewhere around 69 to 90-plus percent of what it is made of, as well as its forces and dynamics, are still mysterious.[20] I'm talking about so-called dark matter and dark energy. But it's worse than that! We say the universe is made of particles, yet there is no agreement about what particles *are* or even *that* they are.[21] And then there's the Big Bang. It was actually not big (less than the diameter of a proton when it began), and there was no bang—not even a pop. Excluding God, there was no one and nothing that could have heard it. Even if there had been, its "sound" would have been beneath the physically possible minimum of any neuronal capacity to detect it. Its temperature can only be conjectured because it was magnitudes beyond what any physical apparatus could create or tolerate.

And there were—and continue to be—extraordinary numbers that hint at a primordial unity that is still with us, just beneath the surface of the commonsense universe that we *can* experience.[22] Cosmologists and physicists have run into these numbers, which seem somehow to be correlated among many different phenomena and between both immense and submicroscopic scales. Apart from the number pi and the Fibonacci numerical progression (which are everywhere in the cosmos), in 1923, the astronomer Arthur Eddington (1882–1944) noticed a curious relationship among such things as the gravitational constant, the Planck constant, the speed of light, and proton mass. He combined these constants, factorized and neutralized them (mathematical terms), and got a "pure *dimensionless* number"—that is, one single number without expression as a dimension. He found that this number was a ratio. Within a factor of ten, he discovered that it was the square root of the number of protons in the universe. The quantum physicist

Paul Dirac (1902–1984) found a similar linkage of the electrical force between protons and neutrons, the gravitational force between them, the age of the universe, and the time it takes light to cross the width of an average atom. In his *Paradigms Lost: Images of Man in the Mirror of Science* (1989), the mathematician John Casti comments that if these numbers are coincidences, they are very strange![23]

In Lyall Watson's *Beyond Supernature*, he cites the well-known extremely delicate balance between gravity and electromagnetism. Based on the figures provided by cosmologists, he also mentions that the number of stars in a typical galaxy equals the number of galaxies in the known universe and that the age of the universe in nuclear units (calculated from our particular perspective within it) equals the number of charged particles. Then he says that, astoundingly, these and other measurements all approximate one core mathematical value—ten to the power of forty.[24] One possible explanation for these and other odd correlations may be due to the universe having once been in a state of Absolute Unity—in terms of so-called fields, forces, particles, and temperature.

There's more, of course, in terms of fantastic numbers. There are three fundamental forces that we know about: the *strong nuclear force*, which holds the quarks together (although they powerfully resist that togetherness), which make up protons and neutrons (the building blocks of matter that has mass); the *weak nuclear force*, which governs the radioactive decay of atoms; and the *electromagnetic force*, which holds all small- to medium-sized clumps of atoms together (for instance, us) by the interlacing of (massless) electron orbitals.[25] And, of course, gravity, which, although it acts like a force, is *not* that but is instead the *shape* of space and time.[26] It is thought that these forces were once one and indistinguishable, but that as the temperature of the then tiny universe dropped, it caused what physicists call "phase transitions," at the boundaries of which the three forces crystalized out, one after another.[27] The force that I'm fascinated with is the

electromagnetic one, which seems to have been arrested in its separation in mid-division. It was "supposed" to separate into the electrical
and the magnetic forces but only made it halfway, such that the two
forces remain stuck imperfectly together and can be illustrated as jut-
ting out from each other at right angles.

One of the most astounding things about all of this is the often-
remarked fact of the fine-tuning of these forces (and the math and
geometries behind them) that were (and are) necessary to have realized
our universe . . . and, consequently, us.[28] Had the forces been even min-
isculey different, matter itself could not have formed or, once formed,
would have immediately evaporated (if electromagnetism, the strong
nuclear force, or gravity had been even a tiny bit weaker). Or, if these
forces and the geometry of gravity had been just a little stronger, collapsed, perhaps infinitely so . . . into a singularity. I'm not going to go
over the astounding numerical values of these forces or the fields and
the particles that congealed out of these. If you're interested in the
mind-blowing specifics of these, you can find books that address these
and related issues in the bibliography.

I do want to mention several more Weirdnesses about the cosmos
as a whole, and then turn to a little closer look at what we call matter on a smaller subatomic scale, which itself is Weird and, because of
that, Terrifying. First, let's consider the shape of the universe, on which
there is still no conclusive agreement.[29] It's generally assumed that the
universe began at some unlocatable point, which then expanded into a
sphere. However, cosmogonists tell us that the point at which the universe started is *everywhere within it* and that, if the universe is a sphere,
it is a type of sphere that we can't possibly imagine. In addition, this
"sphere" may not be curved or have a circumference or limit. Instead, it
may be what cosmologists call "flat."[30]

Whether curved or flat, space isn't the only odd aspect of the universe; time is another. A related oddity is that, when we look out at
the universe—at least as far as we can detect it—we seem to be for-

ever at the center and in the *present*, whereas the rest of the universe seems to be rapidly receding from us . . . and in the *past*! As if *we*, right here at our location, were generating and radiating time. Of course, any other observers in any other part of the universe would experience *themselves* at the center, and in the present, and us in *their* past. There's another strange thing: we have detected the first moment in the early universe (perhaps 380,000 years after the Big Bang) when atoms had formed in sufficient numbers that radiation energy broke through the "fog" of primordial fields and formed matter in, among other things, the form of visible light—what's termed *microwave background radiation*.[31] That original light is now invisible because the light waves have been stretched with the expansion of the universe to become microwaves. The odd thing about this microwave background radiation is that it surrounds us. *We're still inside it.* As is the whole universe, both what we can see and what lies beyond our horizon of detection. It is the oldest thing we can see; everything else is younger. How can that be? Shouldn't it be physically in our past, as all the textbooks show it? Something we've left behind. Again, presumably, any other observers in any other part of the universe will have exactly the same experience. I'm reminded of the ancient saying attributed to Empedocles: "God is a circle whose center is everywhere, and whose circumference is nowhere." Another incomprehensible Weirdness.

Here's something that is truly terrifying. According to quantum physicist and philosopher David Bohm (1917–1992) and others, space is not in any sense empty. In fact, every cubic centimeter of it is packed with more mass-energy than the whole of the known universe combined.[32] This unimaginable power of "empty" space makes the rest of the universe look like a dust plume or vapor. The interesting thing about space, though, is that its "surface," the barrier that keeps all that inconceivable annihilating power from erupting into our world and instantaneously destroying it, seems to just slide out of the way as material objects (however large or small, of mass or massless) move across it. Furthermore, the surface of space, which is everywhere, intermeshed with our forces, fields, and matter, radiates a mist of apparently massless subatomic particles and their opposites which mutually annihilate each other.[33] The result is that space itself has a burned electrical smell! This is sometimes encountered by astronauts after docking maneuvers when they open the hatches . . . as if a tiny whiff of space has been caught between the vehicles by their docking collars and then released into the spacecrafts' cabins. Also, as mathematical physicist Robert Laughlin says in his *A Different Universe: Reinventing Physics from the Bottom Down* (2005), if we hit this surface of space hard enough (for instance, with a gamma ray blast), it shines back at us like a sheet of glass.[34]

Like the electromagnetic force, space and time—the products of gravity, or perhaps gravity itself *in the guise of* space and time—are incompletely separated. They seem to be different things, yet they are closely interrelated, so that any changes to one immediately result in changes to the other. It's a complicated relationship because, as the physicist Brian Greene makes clear, some aspect of this relationship is not in sync.[35] Specifically, the relationship in this aspect seems to be complementary. For instance, as he says, the more space you use, the less time elapses, and the more time you use, the less space is consumed. Among other things, this has the very bizarre effect of making the age of the universe a matter of perspective, if, for example, different areas of the universe have expanded at different rates. There is a strong indication that they have.[36]

That brings us to Einstein's relativity theories. First up, the special theory of relativity. Albert Einstein (1879–1955) created the special theory of relativity in 1905. He called it "special" because it involved the consequences of all motions except those induced by gravity.[37] Basically, the theory is about all sub-light-speed moving objects traveling in straight lines at constant speeds *relative* to one another. There are several basic premises.

First, all moving objects are always moving relative to one another so that no frame of reference or perspective on things (of any kind) is "privileged," or absolute in terms of truth or correctness. In other words, there is no one correct space-time perspective. Different observers—all of them moving (whether they know it or not)—will experience others' space-time perspectives as different from theirs and, in that sense, "incorrect." This is an illusion, because all frames of reference are correct for objects and observers within them. There's no way to ask the question "Who is moving?" because *all* are moving relative to one another. Thus, there is no ultimate or universal system *inside the universe* that is *not* relativistic. That qualification, "inside the universe," is important, as we'll see shortly.

Second, space and time, while not quite the same thing, are intimately inter-related, often in an inverse way (as we saw above).

Third, the only constant in the special theory is the speed of light in a vacuum—roughly 186,000 miles per second. According to some physicists and cosmologists, this suggests that light is tied to some element of Reality that is, after all, Absolute, Universal, and Objective.[38] Assuming the normal speed of light in a vacuum, consider the following bizarre consequence: Two cars, each going thirty-five miles an hour, crash head-on. We calculate their combined speeds at seventy miles per hour—so, the degree of damage to the cars and their occupants is twice that of one car hitting a lamppost at thirty-five miles an hour. But if you're moving at thirty-five miles an hour toward an oncoming ray of light, the combined speed of the collision is 186,000 miles per second. Likewise, if you're chasing a photon of light, even if you're going 99.99 percent the speed of light, when you measure your progress in catching up with it, you will still measure it receding from you at 186,000 miles per second. You never get any closer![39]

Fourth, special relativity requires *locality*.[40] It requires that objects are local—that is, *separate* from one another in space and time. This is what gives them their relativity to one another. Only two or more objects—local, or located—can relate, that is have different perspectives, send signals to one another, and communicate. It takes space and time for objects to relate, to be *relative* to one another. If there were no space or time, there would be no relative objects—actually, no universe. As we'll see shortly, various experiments have now confirmed that beneath, above, or behind our relativistic world of objects moving in space and time, *there is, in fact, nonlocality—no space, no time.* There is, though, a strange ambiguity about whether there still are objects "at" nonlocality.

One more thing. While this no-space no-time state would seem to negate Einstein's notions of relativity, it might oddly transpire that even though every perspective on *now*—the present—is different for each observer in Einstein's relativistic world, they nevertheless all experience *now*. It is an objective constant in every frame of reference (as is the speed of light in a vacuum). There is always a now, regardless of the fact that in our relativistic universe no "nows" coincide. Nonlocality suggests that outside our relativistic experiences of multiple nows, a singular Now always *is*, just experienced at different "times." Indeed, in his *Nature Loves to Hide: Quantum Physics and the Nature of Reality, a Western Perspective* (2001), the theoretical physicist Shimon Malin proposes that relativity itself is pointing to an Absolute, Universal, and Objective background.[41]

Einstein published his *general* theory of relativity in 1915.[42] His original insight was the equivalence between our experiences of accelerated motion and gravity, on the one hand, and the equivalence of our experience of no motion (stationary floating) and the absence of gravity (weightlessness), on the other. He called these equivalences the "equivalence principle," meaning that these pairs of experience are not the same thing; floating is not the same thing as weightlessness, and acceleration is not the same thing as gravity. Not exactly . . . but they *feel* the same, or have the same effects. This is the first claim of Einstein's general theory. The second is that space is curved rather than flat. The third, as in the case of special relativity, general relativity requires that our relativistic universe is what's called *background independent.* That means that, *within* this universe, there is no Absolute, Universal, or Ultimate Background against which motion (or not) can be measured. Fourth, as with special relativity, this requires that there be *locality*—locations in space and time that are moving relative to each other, using different frames of reference, which cannot be calculated against a background, but whose motions can only be measured against *each other's* motions.

Fifth, general relativity suggests that gravity is not a force like the other three so-called fundamental forces, but rather the *shape* of space-time, which is shaped, in part at least, by objects with mass embedded in it.[43] These objects (however massive) create gravity wells, curved regions that converge on the center of mass of these objects. These curved converging gravity wells can be graphed (imperfectly) by using a grid of lines that become increasingly distorted the further down the well they go—the closer they get to the center of mass of the object. In the presence of extremely massive objects like black holes, the gravity field the lines describe becomes perhaps (there's some argument about this) infinitely curved, so that matter and energy within that region of space-time are driven into a dimensionless point . . . and vanish completely!

Both of Einstein's theories of relativity have a lot of really bizarre corollaries, all of which have been demonstrated by experiments to be true. I'm not going to go into them here. Again, for interested readers, I'll refer you to the bibliography. I just want to note that it is almost impossible to exaggerate the shock and intellectual, as well as emotional, disorientation Einstein's theories have caused anyone who's tried to come to grips with them. They are profoundly counterintuitive, at least as much as Copernicus's (1473–1543) heliocentric hypothesis, which knocked Earth out of the center of the solar system . . . and the universe. More importantly . . . us! Actually, much if not all of the disorientation in contemporary philosophy and the humanities, often referred to as *deconstruction* and *postmodernity*, not to mention a kind of ultimate nihilism, is the result of our decoupling from an absolute background and then reeling into a relativistic universe where nothing is as it seems.

However, there are questions about the ultimate adequacy of the relativities for understanding reality raised by the discovery of nonlocality and other issues that suggest *the relativizing of relativity*. In his *Quantum Non-Locality and Relativity: Metaphysical Intimations of Modern Physics* (2011), the philosopher Tim Maudlin suggests that the speed of light in a vacuum, (mostly) invariant, might be an indicator of a higher order structure that we have not been able to identify.[44] Several questions come up for me around this search for an objective structure. For example, could the speed of light have crystallized out of a higher dimensional space-time order as a very early partial embodiment of that order in the form of a limit-setting parameter for the universe as it unfolded (and continues to unfold)? How might this hint (or not) at David Bohm's hypothesis of an "implicate order" of "undivided wholeness"—that is, Absolute, Universal, and Ultimate Reality—that only *partially* becomes embodied in this universe (and/or any others), in what he calls the "explicate order"? (To fully understand Bohm's system, I suggest you read his *Wholeness and the Implicate Order* (1980) in its entirety.)[45]

Maudlin himself questions the ultimacy of the relativities on several grounds. First is the apparently Absolute and probably Universal Unity implied by nonlocality. Second, various quantum experiments point to a single direction for cause and effect. Even though mathematical equations can work forward or backward, in our slice of Reality at any rate, causes always precede effects, even when the effects are caused by causes in the futures of the effects (as in at least some precognitive events). Maudlin claims that the cause-effect through line holds in all frames of reference, regardless of their relativistic relationship to each other. Einstein's theories of relativity, on the other hand, demand that there be no universality to through lines. As Maudlin suggests, Einstein's relativities may, from a broader perspective, be illusory[46]—I would suggest the word *provincial*.

There are many other clues that there is an Absolute, Universal, and Objective Background "beneath" or "behind" our relativistic version of Reality. I'll discuss these when we come to a fuller account of my rabbit holes.

The Weirdness of Matter

There is no way to experience the Weirdness of matter without taking an excursion into the quantum world. I'll make our excursion as brief as possible, just long enough to communicate the extreme strangeness of the origins and behavior of the matter we take for granted in what's known as the macroworld—the bit of what we could call the matter spectrum, the part of this which we are conscious of interacting with and which we *are* in our physical beings. We don't know if there's anything smaller than the Planck length, named after physicist Max Planck (1858–1947), which is calculated to be a billionth of a billionth of a billionth of a centimeter.[47] The researchers in this area—especially the string theorists, M-theorists, and loop quantum gravity theorists—believe there is something smaller, as does the mathematician Benoit Mandelbrot (1924–2010), famous for his fractal theory and coastline paradox. In the coastline paradox, Mandelbrot suggested that *all finite objects are actually made of infinity* . . . crafted, we might say, shaped by particular configurations of infinity with surfaces that, while functionally finite, go down forever in fractal fashion. A fractal measurement of the coastline of, for example, Great Britain, would repeat in ever-smaller fractal increments until the measurement reached the infinitesimal, increasing the overall length of the island's coastline to infinity.[48] A wild idea, but not any more far out than the idea that all subatomic particles are "surrounded" by infinities of force or energy, or that the singularities at the centers of black holes are infinitesimal—infinitely "smaller" than space and time. The idea is that everything is Infinity, or we could say, Infinity is Infinitely Closer than we think!

Okay. So, a few words about field theory where many quantum

physicists and quantum cosmologists begin their "conjuring" of matter. In field theory, all subatomic particles (for example, quarks, muons, gluons, electrons—and many, many more) and all forces (electromagnetism, the strong and weak forces, and, in this sense, gravity) are all originally manifested as so-called fields of indeterminate extent. All emerged in the Big Bang, separated out, almost certainly through phase transitions (probably initiated by rapidly falling temperatures) and immediately began to interact. Before their interactions, all were massless.[49] As they interacted, subatomic particles were formed. Some of these acquired mass, while others didn't. We have no real idea how interacting massless fields dragging through one another could have resulted in particles with mass. It's thought that acceleration and drag had something to do with it, a kind of friction in which a number of fields experienced resistance as they ran through others—probably particularly through the Higgs field(s) and strong-force, or gluon, fields, or space-time itself.[50] The particles that were created in this way have wildly varying masses (also unexplained), while others, such as photons, have none (ditto). It is theorized that particles (both massive and massless) became, as physicists call it, "excited" and thereby became defined. One very odd characteristic of these particles, though, is that they aren't particles in a simple way. They're some kind of combination of wave and particle, what I call "wavicles." This fact was referred to as *wave-particle duality* by Danish quantum physicist Niels Bohr (1885–1962) and his followers, who developed the so-called Copenhagen interpretation of quantum physics.[51]

Imagine an immense concert hall, completely empty of performers and audience. In the center of this cavernous room, suspended in midair, is an indistinct, fuzzy ball the size of a pea. The walls, floor, and ceiling of the hall are a more or less thin and wavering spherical shell, also fuzzy. And those are the proportions and appearance to us of an atom. (I've lost the written reference to this analogy, but it was reproduced in a PBS *Nova* series, which I've also lost track of.) The tiny ball in the center is the atomic nucleus, and the wavering shell, of which there may be just one or many, like the outer layers of an onion or the outermost set of Russian dolls, is (are) the electron orbitals. Orbitals rather than orbits because the electrons are wavicles, wave-particles until the wave function collapses into a particle. If an electron shell around a nucleus gains in energy, it instantaneously expands. If it loses energy, it instantaneously shrinks. *That's instantaneously!* It doesn't seem to traverse any space or take any time: it's in one orbital, vanishes, and reappears in another, as if there were a shortcut that skips space and time completely.[52] From my perspective, that counts as a rabbit hole.

The simplest atom is the hydrogen atom, made up of one proton and an orbital electron. The proton carries a positive electric charge, while the electron carries a negative charge. That makes all intact atoms electrically neutral. This neutrality is maintained no matter how many protons an atom may have, from the single proton of hydrogen to the multiple protons of various forms of uranium. The number of protons is always balanced by the number of electrons. The reason protons can stay together in an atomic nucleus is the extreme binding power of what are known as gluons, particles or quanta that create a force field that both holds the three quarks that make up protons together and also "leaks out" of the protons enough to bind proton to proton. This is the strong nuclear force, of which gluons are the so-called messenger particles. Though itself massless, it accounts for 99 percent of the mass of quarks![53]

Neutrons are found in the nuclei of many atoms. They're stepsisters of protons. Both are made up of three quarks, the smallest parts of protons and neutrons that are known. Quarks come in a number of varieties (actually, more are being found even as I write). Protons are made of what are called two up quarks and one down quark, and neutrons are made of one up quark and two down quarks.[54] Unlike protons, neutrons are highly unstable. A free neutron—one outside an atomic nucleus—can only last about eighteen minutes, at which point it decays into a proton while ejecting a tiny particle.[55] Many quantum physicists believe that protons and neutrons are the *same particle* under two different modes or guises.[56]

Electrons. So, what are we seeing when we photograph an atom? Some physicists believe we're seeing not an electron shell per se—the outermost—but the probability wave of the outer electron's orbital. The probability wave indicates where the electron probably is and where it probably isn't. But what does that *mean*? Probability waves are, supposedly, mathematical constructs that exist in what's called *configurational space*, which is not our familiar space but imaginal, mental, abstract, mathematical space. How could we possibly photograph math? Indeed, as we'll soon see, quantum physicists debate whether the wavelike characteristics of subatomic particles are math or matter or something in between.

Here's another Weird thing about electrons. At least when they're in a lattice structure, when one moves, it leaves a "hole." The hole has actually been found to be a particle, a positively charged electron called a positron.[57] These holes move too, leaving behind . . . what? An electron?

The quantum physicist Werner Heisenberg (1901–1976) established what became known as his indeterminacy principle, more popularly, his uncertainty principle. The uncertainty principle says that you can't measure, or determine, a particle's location and its momentum at the same time.[58] You have to design your measurement experiment to measure only one thing at a time. You can locate a particle, but at the price of losing any way to discover how fast it was moving.[59] Heisenberg originally believed that this was because of the necessary clumsiness of our measuring methods—namely, blasting the particle with, for example, a gamma ray photon barrage. In doing that, the particle you're looking for will go careening off at an unpredictable velocity.[60]

With prodding from Niels Bohr and others, Heisenberg came to believe that, while his earlier hypothesis about disturbing the particle by measuring it was correct up to a point, the deeper and more important truth was that the indeterminacy of all of a particle's properties was an inherent part of the so-called wave-particle duality of the target parti-cle.[61] Enter Erwin Schrodinger (1887–1961) with his mathematical equa-tion for calculating how the wave aspect of a particle will evolve over time.[62] This exercise in math indicated to Heisenberg and others that, while the equation was ostensibly deterministic as its math showed, what it was really determining was not inevitabilities but *probabilities*—the probability that a particle could be "condensed" out of its wave function at such and such a "place" in the (mathematical) wave function.[63] The apparent fact of these probabilities (rather than certainties) added fuel to the fire of the uncertainty principle. The quantum world was seeming Weirder and Weirder. Researchers tried to get a fix on what was really happening at the quantum level of physical reality. They called the crux of the matter "the measurement problem."[64] I would rather frame it as "the hypothetical constraints on quantum behavior problem."

For a hundred years now, theoretical physicists have been trying to understand how, when, and why the wave function collapses into a par-ticle. In his *Paradigms Lost*, John Casti defines the wave function not as a substance but as an abstraction—pure information.[65] It's usually thought that this information wave collapses when it hits a measure-ment device in the macroworld (our world as we normally experience it). But Casti wonders how an abstraction could possibly be affected by a physical object.[66] So, the question becomes urgent: What *is* a measure-ment? In other words, what does it take to get probability to become certainty, the Infinite to become finite, the indistinct to become dis-tinct, the enfolded to become unfolded, the quantum world to manifest the macroworld? In a certain sense, wave collapse by measurement, *whatever* that is, is *the act of creation* of the cosmos!

Three observations before we get into the bizarre realm of the several interpretations of wave function collapse—that is, *creation*: (1) Wave col-lapse, if it occurs, is an immediately observable instance of what seems to be instantaneity—no time elapse between the assumed existence of some kind of wavicle and its sudden actualized appearance as a particle. This strongly suggests that, below the surface of our observations, there is nonlocality—no time, no space. Therefore, wave collapse is a rabbit hole. (2) It's amazing, as the astrophysicist Adam Becker observes, that most quantum physicists have missed this point entirely. (3) Jim Baggott claims in *Quantum Space* (2018)[67] that wave function collapse is "entirely hypothetical." In one of his hypotheses about this issue, the quantum physicist Richard Feynman (1918–1988) suggested that there are no waves per se, that the particle is literally everywhere in the universe—again, nonlocal. When we measure it, or when it is measured, it has taken every path—an infinite number of paths—to our detector, or to whatever has disrupted the wave function. This hypothesis is called the *sum over histories mechanism*.[68]

Now, at the risk of enormous oversimplification, what follows is a summary of the nine major interpretations of the measurement problem or, otherwise put, *the creation of the world*.

The Copenhagen Interpretation

The Copenhagen interpretation was first put forward by Niels Bohr.[69] There are several versions of it, but Bohr's remains the most central and is the one still most common among quantum physicists. In effect, the Copenhagen interpretation claims there is no quantum world, at least not for practical purposes or, put another way, one that can be understood or even accessed by us. Whatever it is or isn't becomes reality for us with the act of measurement. In other words, and with a little more interpretation on my part, the quantum world is spaceless and timeless until, by measurement, a boundary is created between Infinity-Eternity and our finite space-time experience of reality.

The Local Hidden Variables Interpretation

The local hidden variables interpretation was Einstein's.[70] In his view, apparent wave collapse upon measurement is caused by local "hidden variables" that are always there—local factors (at the site of the measurement) that are indiscernibly present along with the particle's wave function. Einstein disliked the probability side of Schrodinger's wave equation, but he endorsed its deterministic character. It's important here to note that in Einstein's proposal for hidden variables, these were envisioned as entirely *local*—this, in vehement distinction from Bohr's idea that the quantum world is *nonlocal*. It is everywhere, all at once.

The Conscious Act of Measurement Interpretation

In slightly different ways, quantum physicists John von Neumann (1903–1957), Eugene Wigner (1902–1995), and Erwin Schrodinger endorsed the conscious act of measurement interpretation.[71] They did so because they couldn't find, or find convincing, any sort of physical boundary between quantum events and objects (like wavicles) and macroevents and objects (like measuring devices). In a way, trying to determine a physical boundary between micro- and macrorealms is a replay of the ancient Greek problem of the so-called sorites, to which there seems to be no solution other than by fiat or arbitrary proclamation. The Greek sorites problem involves things like, as you remove material, at what point can a mountain be called a hill, at what point does a hill become a pile, at what point does a pile become a heap, and so on? Or at what point does a burning log become a heap of ash? Or, one of my favorite modern versions: How many molecules of H_2O does it take to make water?

The basic idea common to these three theorists is that consciousness as focused observation causes the wave function to collapse into a particle.[72] Especially for Wigner, while things in the outer world in general, not just subatomic things, are probably "there," it is the subjectivity of the conscious observer that determines how they will look, behave, and so forth—at least to the observer, which is all that really matters. You can see a mixture of Immanuel Kant (1724–1804), J. G. Fichte, and German idealism in general behind this perspective.

The Quasi-Solipsistic Interpretation

The quantum physicist John Wheeler (1911–2008) is the architect of the quasi-solipsistic interpretation,[73] which has certain points in common with the consciousness interpretation—most importantly, the idea that human consciousness is central for any valid interpretation of the measurement problem. But in Wheeler's view, the outer macroworld is not just *influenced* by the observer; the observer *creates it en toto*. This is very close to solipsism: the realization that everything is experienced only within the psyche—but not only experienced, everything exists, is created, only there. The "I" is not reducible to anything else (actually, there *isn't* anything else), and so the psyche, or Psyche, is inescapable.

Maybe the most shocking part of Wheeler's interpretation is that, in making a measurement, we can create not only the immediately present wave collapse (and so, create the future) but also dictate the past. And if we can create the past, we are also creating the present and future too. Needless to say, there are serious philosophical not to say real-life problems with this whole scenario. But there are also some work-arounds. One is the idea that everything has already been determined—made— including our present-and-future-causing act of making the past in the present. This and other work-arounds require something called the *block universe*, in which everything always *is* in a spaceless and timeless Now. The apparent unfolding of that Eternal Now as space and time, and the events and objects in It and that make It up, is, if not an illusion, a kind of alternative way of experiencing It. Wheeler's interpretation, along with maybe more than flirting with solipsism, also seems headed toward another rabbit hole. Well, solipsism itself is a rather gigantic rabbit hole!

The Potential-to-Actual Interpretation

In some ways, the potential-to-actual interpretation is a variant of the Copenhagen interpretation.[74] In particular, it agrees with Copenhagen that little can be said about the quantum world before a measurement is taken. But the potential-to-actual interpretation affirms that the quantum realm embodies some kind of reality, even when unmeasured. That unmeasured reality it calls *potential*, while it terms *actual* the aspect of reality that's been measured. The potential becomes actual when a measurement is made. But this raises the questions: Is potential in some way actual in its own realm? And, whether it is or not, how does that realm transition into ours, which we claim is actual? As we'll see in a moment, this is very close to David Bohm's hypothesis of an implicate and an explicate order.

The Backward Causation Interpretation

Building on the work in electrodynamics of John Wheeler and Richard Feynman, which used both forward-moving and backward-moving electromagnetic waves, John Cramer proposed a type of backward causation for understanding the wave collapse, or, more probably, the failure of waves to collapse.[75] In Cramer's hypothesis, a wavicle sends out ahead of it a wave function, while whatever is going to receive it sends backward in time a wave indicating what state of the subsequent particle it will accept. As Maudlin suggests, though, the idea of backward causation leads to a host of worldview problems that can't be readily solved, or solved at all.[76] It seems to me, though, that some comparisons could be made between the backward causation and the quasi-solipsistic models in quantum physics and at least some precognitive events. Both seem to envision dynamics within a block universe.[77] However, strictly in terms of quantum physics, as Maudlin points out,[78] the backward causation interpretation does not actually result in wave function collapse. And that's a problem for the actualization of matter.

The Many Worlds Interpretation

The same is true for the many worlds interpretation (different from the multiverse) of Hugh Everett III (1930–1982).[79] In Everett's view, whenever a wave function collides with a measuring device (undefined, could be anything), the new compound system splits into innumerable, perhaps infinite, versions of itself.[80] A fraction of a second later, these decohered wave functions interact with the different wave functions of their alternative universes, and yet more worlds are born. No wavicle collapses, just infinite splittings occur. This is yet another vision of nonlocality. These, at least functionally, infinite number of universes all exist *right here, right now*. They are, as the physicists say, *superposed*. Nothing but wave functions crashing into each other, splitting a new space and time universe off from ours, or from theirs to ours, and stacking up in Eternity. As Adam Becker sees it, there is no wave function collapse—only an ever-multiplying and complexifying "universal wave function."[81]

No particles. "And yet," as Inspector Poirot says in *Evil under the Sun*, "we have a body!" We still have a material universe, which we couldn't have without some kind of local somethings-or-other, whether we call them particles or something else.

There *is* one virtue the many worlds interpretation may be said to have. It avoids the difficult questions about wave collapse into particles *by denying that it occurs*. Yet, in addition to leaving questions about particles aside, this "solution" violates Occam's razor in a stupendous fashion. Not that William of Occam (1287–1347) is always, or even very often, right.

The Emergence Interpretation
Back to Earth?

Robert Laughlin's take on all the inventiveness of these and other even more radical interpretations of the quantum world and its relationship to our macroworld (for instance, the Ghirardi-Rimini-Weber theory of spontaneous collapse)[82] is that it's all pretty much a waste of energy and very good minds. The main problem for Laughlin (along with what he calls the "deceitful turkey effect")[83] is that they fail to take the phenomenon of *emergence* into account.[84] Laughlin claims that the detectors and measuring devices that are seeking to record quantum objects and events record those submicroscopic goings-on through the filter of large objects. The large objects are *not* influenced by quantum objects and events because they are (comparatively) huge aggregates of quantum objects and events that, by the law of large numbers, cancel out the ambiguities and bizarre behaviors of the quantum world.[85] A consequence of this cancelation is the emergence, seemingly out of nowhere, of whole new sets of rules and laws—those that govern large objects and events. In something resembling an emergentist variation on the Copenhagen interpretation, Laughlin suggests that particles may only arise when they are detected at the interface between large objects like detectors, the latter of which behave in a this-or-that, yes-or-no unambiguous manner. This emergent definitiveness misinterprets the objects and events appearing from the quantum realm, like seeing the distortion of a stick standing in water.

I like Laughlin. He's fun. But it looks to me as though he still has the measurement problem because he hasn't defined at exactly what point in the aggregation of quantum objects and events his hypothesized "phase transition" between micro and macro takes place. He also doesn't seem to make clear his view of quantum objects and events *in themselves*—that is, whether he thinks that the large-object detectors are completely mistaken in their readings of quantum world behavior, or whether he thinks quantum behavior as observed is accurate to some degree but irrelevant. It *does* seem to me, from my attempted close reading of his *A Different Universe* (2005), that he in fact does regard quantum behavior, whatever it might be, as largely or even wholly irrelevant to objects and events in our macroworld.

The Implicate Order to Explicate Order Interpretation

I'm going to give David Bohm's quantum potential interpretation the last word in this brief run-through of interpretations of the measurement problem within the context of our Weirdness of Nature discussion (I'm referencing his book *Wholeness and the Implicate Order*).[86] A full discussion of Bohm's proposals is far beyond what we can do in this book, so I'm going to focus on the aspects that *I* think really get to the point. This is my summary, laced with my interpretations, of those aspects.

Undivided wholeness or the implicate order—in which all things and events *are* at one and the same spaceless and timeless "location"—unfolds as if it were a staggering multiplicity of objects and events.[87] These make up the explicate order. This multiplicity displays varying degrees of what we take to be disorder, chaos, randomness, ambiguity (indeterminacy, in Heisenberg's view), but which are fragments of a higher order Organization that lies above all subsystems. The quantum world's messy behavior *appears* messy at the basement level of the *explicate* order but actually obeys higher orders of organization within the *implicate* order, which are not fully disclosed in the explicate order.[88] While appearing out of the blue from our limited perspective, emergent ordered systems manifest out of the implicate order in which they are *potential* rather than *actual* . . . from *our* perspective.[89] All order, as well as apparent chaos or indefiniteness, which are characteristic *for us* of quantum behaviors, is present always . . . Infinitely and Eternally . . . in a completed and rational (or suprarational) way within the implicate order, which, again, unfolds systems (and subsystems) from the apparent chaos or indefiniteness of the quantum realm to the more comprehensive systems (and subsystems) of the large-scale realm—this, by means of any number of temporal scenarios.[90] In acts of measurement, the implicate order of wholeness unfolds further: it is more *un*folded in the measuring device than in the quantum level wavicles' nature and behavior . . . again, *from our explicate perspective*. But when interacting, the relatively *un*folded measuring device forces the relatively *en*folded state of the wavicle to unfold more fully . . . *as a particle* . . . into the explicate order.[91] In agreement with Schrodinger, Bohm believes that the characteristics of these particles—locations, trajectories, momentums, spins, and so on—unfold through time in a completely deterministic way.

Furthermore, because, as Bohm believes, the implicate order is present in every bit of the explicate order (although not fully unfolded in its wholeness), he uses the analogy of the hologram for thinking about the explicated universe (or multiverse, as the case may be).[92] He suggests that we abandon reductionism as a full explanation of systems (of whatever size and complexity)[93] and look to the ultimately undivided whole in order to understand how the explicated parts, such as quantum and supraquantum, micro and macro, work and interrelate.[94] For Bohm, there is no collapse of the wave function and there is no measurement problem because these are appearances, or misinterpretations, of the expressions of the implicate order into the explicate.[95] Finally, if the implicate order is present in every bit of the explicate order, and since the implicate order contains All-space/No-space and All-time/No-time, Reality for Bohm is fundamentally nonlocal . . . *a rabbit hole* . . . at that level, while making the appearance of locality in the explicate order. In his *The Holographic Universe* (1991), Michael Talbot (1953–1992) takes Bohm's more general holographic principles and shows how they appear all over the place and really do seem to govern beings and events in every corner and at every level of the explicate order.

As a variety of commentators say about the number and incompatibilities of these nine major interpretations of the extreme strangeness of changes in the states of quantum objects, when there are this many competing hypotheses, we've hit a wall, and our thinking about Nature at this level has, in effect, splattered and scattered. We are certainly missing *something*. And that something is probably *very important*.

One more instance of quantum Weirdness: the double slit experiment.[96] You may already know how it goes. Here's the basic experiment; the results are bizarre and have serious implications for the nature of Nature at the quantum level but also at our level, and perhaps beyond. Okay. There is a panel set vertically. It has two vertical slits, spaced apart. In front of the panel is a photon (or other sub-atomic particle) gun, which, in this example, will shoot photons through the slits toward a photographic plate, also set vertically. Now things get strange. When you have both slits open, the photons create a wave interference pattern on the photographic plate, like two sets of circular ripples overlapping on the surface of a pond. When you close one slit or, oddly, put detectors on the slits to register the photons' passing, the photon stream creates not wave patterns, but one or two solid bright bands (depending on whether you have one slit open or one or two detectors). So far, no fully plausible physical explanation for this change in the photons' behavior at the photographic plate has been offered. But things get even more odd. If you have both slits open and you slow down the stream of photons from the gun so that they aren't continuous, and you, instead, shoot one photon every min-ute or so, they somehow "know" ahead of time—in the future?—to make the wave interference pattern. This is very strange. It strongly suggests that a photon's (in this case) wave function *is* continuous, while the particles that will collapse out of it don't have to be. Rather, the wave function seems oriented toward the future completed wave interference pattern. It apparently anticipates that pattern, completely oblivious to the timing of the photons' release.

My interpretation of this quantum Strangeness goes something like this. *Something* continues to guide individual photons (and so forth) to their predetermined collapse locations, but something that "imagines" *instantaneously where* the photons *will* appear in space and time, *in the future*. In other words, the wave function just *is*, above time and space . . . in something resembling Infinity-Eternity . . . while the particles are moving *in* space and time. I think it's possible that in the double slit experiment we may be getting an indication of the presence of Bohm's implicate order of undivided wholeness expressed *as if,* and *as,* his spatial and temporal explicate order. I'm reminded of Plato's suggestion that "time is the moving image of eternity."[97] If my musings here are on the right track, then we have just found *another* rabbit hole.

Space-Infinity and Time-Eternity

Nonlocality

The discovery of the fact that, beneath the level of space and time as we know them, there is a quantum reality in which space and time seem not to exist has been and continues to be deeply disturbing—not just to physics but, when we think about it, for all of our daily life, common-sensical assumptions about physical, psychological, and even spiritual Reality. That means *us*!

As we've seen, the Copenhagen interpretation of wave collapse, electrons jumping their orbitals, and so on—all appear to be instantaneous. According to Einstein's theories of relativity, the speed of light in a vacuum represents the upper limit at which objects can travel and communicate with one another. But the instantaneity shown by Copenhagen seems to defy this limit and show what physicists call supraluminous (faster than light) events. Einstein saw this as a flaw in the Copenhagen interpretation. As I mentioned, he believed there must be what he called hidden variables that accounted for the strange instantaneous coordination between, say, two protons that had once been together but were now separated and yet still coordinated. Niels Bohr basically shrugged off this oddity. But Einstein, who rejected, as he put it, "spooky action at a distance," was determined to prove the existence of his hidden variables. Important note: as we've seen, Einstein required that these variables be *local*—that is, that when particles that had once been together and entangled showed coordinated behaviors when they were separated, they were simply showing their original entangled state at a distance from each other. There was *no communication* between them. That would be impossible because such communication would have to be faster than light (again, since it appeared to take no time at all) . . . and *that* was forbidden by the special relativity theory.

So, he teamed up with his colleagues Boris Podolsky and Nathan Rosen, and together they published what has since become known as the EPR (Einstein-Podolsky-Rosen) paper in 1935.[98] In the paper, Einstein and company tried to prove that the Copenhagen interpretation was wrong. But the EPR paper actually suggested the opposite of what it attempted to prove. Instead of demonstrating that the hidden variables were local, it strongly suggested their *non*locality.

In 1964, the physicist John Stewart Bell (1928–1990) created a thought experiment in which he attempted to prove that Einstein and his colleagues were right and Niels Bohr was wrong.[99] But instead of upholding Einstein's continued resistance to nonlocal hidden variables, the results of Bell's experiment showed conclusively that these variables were *not* the result of local factors but were in fact *non*local—not only faster than light but indeed instantaneous, *as if there were no space or time!* A few years later, John Clauser,[100] Alain Aspect,[101] and subsequent investigators performed actual physical experiments that put the nail in the coffin of local hidden variables.

This was a shocking development, not lost on reflective quantum physicists and cosmological theorists. It has powerful and bizarre implications for our fundamental notions about physical . . . and perhaps psychical or spiritual . . . Reality. Indeed, nonlocality signals another, and very large, *rabbit hole.* In completely unforeseen ways, nonlocality goes far beyond Einstein's relativities and seems to restore a greatly altered yet still recognizable kind of Newtonianism. When carried out to its logical conclusions, nonlocality appears to at least *bump up* against something Absolute.

Maudlin comments that the correlations seen between the entangled then separated particles are not due to a *force.* He says they might be due to a structural dynamic that may underlie the *appearance* of relativity, just as relativity underlies the *appearance* of Newtonian (static, absolute) space and time structures.[102] At the same time, if the nonlocality experiments are pointing to an underlying Absolute, *that Absolute is not isolated or cut off from our apparently relativistic dimension.* Rather, as these and other experiments show, this Absolute, or at least quasi-absolute—*whatever it is*—responds to our prodding and poking at it with our experiments. This is true of other quantum experiments, like the double slit (which we just looked at) but others too (like the delayed choice experiment).

I can compare the discovery of nonlocality to Bohm's idea (yes, he's my favorite quantum physicist) of an explicated surface, where things seem—and are—local, localized, localizable, and locatable. They are also relativistic—individual things and events being and behaving relative to one another. In part, this is because they are constrained by time—one-thing-after-another—and also because they appear to be only semi-autonomous and thus constrained by one another. Toward the interior, both physical and psychological-spiritual, things show a more ambiguous nature—some expressing, I think, a not fully definable shading off into a flowing and flexible semi-individuality and semi-unity mode. Deeper still, at some point, even less definable or even thinkable, everything is fully within Bohm's undivided wholeness. All of these levels are equally real, equally valid. Wholeness is not fully expressed at the surface—the explicate order—but, rather, fragmentarily (as individuals). At the same time, each fragment does somehow show, even though in a half or even wholly obscured way, the underlying Oneness—the implicate order—that it is an embodiment of. Speculation—interpretation—of course. But not without signs in that alien realm of the quantum level of Reality. And not without evidence from *our own* altered states of consciousness, climaxing in mystical experience, the summit (or abyss in a good way) of the world's spiritual and religious and also philosophical and even secular traditions.

In our discussion of quantum Weirdness and the Weirdness of Nature in general, we've already been mulling the mystery of the juxtaposition of time and Eternity. So, before we leave this discussion of Nature's

Weirdness, I want to bring in my favorite near-contemporary Platonic philosopher, Stanley Rosen (1929–2014), explicitly on this theme. From all the reading I've done on this subject over the years, his work stands out (to me) as the most insightful. In his *Metaphysics in Ordinary Language* (1999), he tries to think through this slippery problem in four places. I'm not going to go through the details of his thinking here but, rather, cite his use of the Present as the key to thinking about time and Eternity. His insight into what the Present *is* is startling to say the least.[103] To enormously streamline his thinking, he says that it's easy, but not accurate, to imagine that we've entered the Present from the past or the future. Why not? Because the past and future do not exist except in the Present—at least for us. (Note: he is excluding—at least for present purposes—the idea that the past and the future, like the present, are already "There.") The only "temporal place" we *ever* are is the Present. He says, just as we can't *enter* the Present from what does not exist—as *we* don't in the past or future—we also can't *leave* the Present, because, outside of the Present, we do not exist.

Rosen's second discussion moves us toward what is going to be, as I say, his shocking conclusion.[104] Here, he goes a step further and suggests that we—whatever "we" are—*generate the Present from desire*. Desire for what? He says for Immortality, Self-validation, and Completeness. Furthermore, it is this desire that *makes* time—past, present, and future. (Let me just say, I think there are shades at this point of Plotinus in particular and, more generally, Platonism as a whole as well as the Romantic movement.) Then Rosen says that the experience of the Present must be generated by "something other than time."

Rosen concludes his third discussion of time and Eternity with the shocker.[105] He claims—and I agree—that that "something other than time" that is experiencing, or even *making*, time is *Presence* (Greek *parousia*), Self-consciousness. And that *That* is atemporal—always *is*, which is to say, always is *outside time*. Unquestionably, from my perspective, this is the Eternal Now, Which takes no time at all and is (and isn't) the *dimensionless points* that are synthesized into clock time, or temporality as we normally think of it. The *Presence* Rosen is talking about, although he doesn't say this directly, is the Presence of a, or *the, Person*, because *only persons are self-conscious and so irreducibly present.* Other things may be present, but they are all present *to persons* (at whatever level of awareness). Therefore, at least in what I would call their Essence, persons are Eternal-Immortal, *however* we think about Eternity and Immortality (a question we will come back to). In other words, it is *we*, or *We*, in our Essence who are Eternal—outside time; the universe in its explicated presentation to us is temporal! Something *outside time* is generating the space-time universe, and that universe includes the layers of *us* that are *not* atemporal, the parts of us that are partly or fully *inside time.*

Rabbit Holes

I want now to sum up what we've been looking at in terms of the Weirdness—for me, this also means the Terror—of Nature in the form of a brief discussion of rabbit holes. So . . . beneath the surface of the things we're most familiar with, including ourselves at various levels and as a multitude, is an unthought . . . un-think-able . . . Infinite and Eternal Background. Reality, as we limited creatures know It, is shot through with sheer drops into No-thingness/All-thingness. We have to be careful of our footing—both mental and emotional—or we'll find ourselves falling toward that Unknown and Unknowable. We cannot *know* It because It swallows everything we *can* know . . . everything we seem ourselves to be. And that fall lasts forever!

Most of us, understandably, try to avoid—even deny that rabbit holes exist.

Science knows they're there, however.

So does psyche/Psyche.

Here are a few of them:

Singularities. These include the hypothetical singularity at the beginning of our universe, as well as the singularities at the centers of black holes. By definition, singularities are infinitesimal—infinity imagined as spaceless and timeless on an infinitely small scale. They also seem to demand infinite gravity, as do the point particles of quantum physics.

Absolute Unity, Symmetry, and Isometry. Related to the mathematical concept of singularities is the hypothesized state of *absolute unity* in which many cosmologists believe the universe began—that is, before rising entropy (diffusion and cooling) occasioned the spontaneous breaking of the initial symmetry and unity into asymmetrical states and the instantiations of energy fields and then the matter that emerged from them. Physicists strive to imagine the hypothesized unity-symmetry-isometry of the original state of the universe through what are called GUTs (Grand Unified Theories)[106] and TOEs (Theories of Everything).[107] I might add, with only partial success.

Field Theories. Energy fields are thought to be infinite in extent—if not perhaps actually, then at least functionally. In field theory, as well as quantum theory per se, particles are imagined to be infinitesimal points (of wildly varying masses), not unlike singularities (of infinite mass). The fields surrounding such infinitesimal points spontaneously generate, or are the products of, infinities—at least numerical (as in virtual particles and gravity).[108] The equations that result from trying to calculate these quantum entities can only be worked if these infinities are cancelled by being subtracted out of the equations (infinity minus infinity), which then leaves workable finite numbers. This is done "by hand," as physicists say, by a process called *renormalization*. Many physicists regard this process as a form of cheating in terms of the Reality that is actually presenting Itself, but concede that it is necessary in order to do the math.[109] It seems to me this should alert us to the possibility that we're seeing only what works *for us*—in other words, that we're (however understandably) reducing Reality to fit the size of our imaginations.

In addition, field theories seem to demand—at least within the framework of Einstein's general theory of relativity—a *continuous* (rather than quantized, or broken up into discrete bits) medium for fields and the waves that ripple through them. Continuous mediums are believed to be infinitely divisible: you can divide them forever, more than a little like Zeno's arrow that can never reach its target because we can keep dividing the tip of the arrow's distance to the target in half. That's at least a *functional* infinity. Leibnitz (one of the inventors of calculus) concluded that we can't reach infinity by dividing infinitely. We will get closer, but never arrive.[110]

Quantum Physics Equations. Not unrelated to this problem of the manifestation of infinities in field equations, quantum physics equations: (a) assume an absolute space-time background (Euclidean-Cartesian, Minkowski-Lorentz) on which these equations are dependent; and (b) show symmetry in both space and time. That's to say that they can be worked forward or backward in space (at least what's called *configural space*)[111] and time. Taken together, these two characteristics of quantum equations can be said to require an absolute space-time. This is contrary to Einstein's theories in which space-time seems to be flexible and multiple (in the relativity of its "nows," among other things), and therefore, as I've mentioned, background independent. Philosophically, what is Absolute is Infinite and Eternal. It's also in some sense Static, Immutable, Unchangeable, Invariant.

Cantor's Infinity of Infinities. Georg Cantor (1845–1918) discovered that every spatial and temporal measure can be visualized in every direction, from zero to one and from zero to minus one, as divisible into infinities—an infinity of infinities. He also believed that some infinities are "larger" than others.[112] These realizations literally drove him crazy. That is, he had an endless fall into a *rabbit hole*.

The Mathematical Object. If, as many mathematicians believe (currently the most outspoken, Max Tegmark), the universe is either an expression of or is itself per se a mathematical object.[113] This mathematical object is, as mathematicians say, outside space and time. That means it's outside finitude and therefore, in effect, Infinite and Eternal. Tegmark believes that only an "infinitely intelligent" mathematician could understand it.[114] A related idea is that if the universe and/or its mathematical background is Infinite and Eternal . . . or at the very least Eternal (in some way) . . . it is, as it is termed (and we've seen), a block universe.[115] In this universe, although objects and the events that accompany them are experienced as moving, in the end, from what is called a *geodesic* or *global perspective*, we can see that nothing moves at all! Things traverse neither space nor time because space and time are both All-at-Once.

Special Relativity. In special relativity theory, there are an at least functional infinity of frames of reference. Furthermore, these are absolutely symmetrical—that is, of absolutely equal validity. While the simultaneity of the "nows" in each frame of reference is denied, they are all equally experienced as *now*. This gives them *an Absoluteness that transcends their relativity in terms of each other.*

General Relativity. In general relativity theory, there is an objective condition of asymmetry of space and time—once more along the lines of an at least functional infinity of frames of reference.

A Preferred Manifestation of Space-Time. A number of quantum cosmologists and physicists (especially the philosophically inclined) believe that, in the midst of the relativistic space-time frames of reference within the universe, there might be a preferred manifestation of space-time, one that, among other things, might be responsible for the correlation (not identity) between rising entropy and the direction of time. Such a preferred manifestation of space-time might or might not arise from *an underlying Absolute*. If we set such a hypothesized (and perhaps actually indicated) manifestation side by side with ideas of the mathematical object or block universe, an Absolute, Geodesic, or Global Frame of Reference might, once again, be thought of as outside space and time and, consequently, Infinite-Eternal.

The Speed of Light. If there is such an ultimately Absolute Manifestation of space-time—with a possibly Infinite-Eternal-Absolute Background—we might be getting clues for Its existence from the (usually) constant speed of light in a vacuum. Remember that the speed of light is constant in all relativistic frames of reference?

Instantaneity. Quantum physics clearly shows the reality of instantaneity in the change of locations and/or states of subatomic particles or, as I've called them before, materialized wavicles. Instantaneity does not mean faster than the speed of light because no movement from place to place or from state to state seems to occur in those experiments that have demonstrated instantaneity. This suggests that these changes of location and/or state occur without in any way traversing space or time. From my perspective, this implies that particles manifest from a "placeless place" and a "timeless time." And that is the very definition of Infinity and Eternity. As we've seen, instantaneity has been demonstrated in such events as the collapse of the wave function, electron orbital jumping, and, maybe most spectacularly, in experiments confirming nonlocality.

Implicate and Explicate Orders. David Bohm's idea that a probably multilayered implicate order, at least at its Core, is identical to Infinity-Eternity. This implicate order causes the objects and events of the explicate order by some form of projection. Maybe the closest analogy to this projection and its results, as Bohm proposes and as we have seen, is the hologram.

The Present as Presence. We just looked at Stanley Rosen's proposal that the *Present*, Which is momentless and is not in space and time, may define time itself (as past, present, and future) or even, in some way, create it. He also proposes that the Present is known and constituted by *Presence*, Which, at its Essence, is Eternal-Immortal (and perhaps Infinite). From where I sit, that constitutes yet another rabbit hole, and maybe the *rabbit hole of rabbit holes*, at which all of these (and other) rabbit holes converge and from which they emerge. I've also said that I believe this Presence *is* the Infinite Psyche or Person.

Our Psychological-Spiritual Capacities. Finally, assumed in all of the above, is our psychological capacity to engage in abstract thought at what *might* be an or *the* Ultimate Level. At this Level, not only do we take the stance (usually unconsciously) of the omniscient observer in a rational, or discursive, way, but we also intuit (feel-think) the appearance of the Infinite-Eternal-Absolute timeless if not spaceless Background of our relativistic, finite, time-bound observations and assume This into many of our calculations. For example, we can think of ourselves outside space and time. From that position we can look back at the universe as a whole to imagine its form, its evolution in time, its place in relationship to possible additional universes, and so on.

Also, some of us do claim to have had direct experiences of the Infinite-Eternal Now—Absolute Oneness. If we are willing to accept such experiences to be as equally truthful as our experiences in usual states of consciousness—which I am—then we might consider the idea that human beings, in fact, have both intuitive and discursive knowledge of the Absolute. So far as I'm concerned, these both cognitive and feeling-toned experiences are direct evidence of, as I've already suggested, a major *rabbit hole* built into the very Center of our own psyches!

The Character of Nature's Evolutionary Unfolding

Another one of those magical Rock Island summer nights. I was, as so often, standing in the backyard under the stars. A humid breeze was gently swaying the tops of the elm and maple trees. I watched for a while, then raised my eyes to the sky with its host of unimaginably distant sentinels. I "heard" a Voice—a male Voice. It seemed to come from inside my head, and at the same time from everywhere. My inside was somehow outside, loose in the cosmos. The cosmos was inside— speaking through the neural architecture of my brain (I assume). The Voice said, "Did I do well?" It had a deeply poignant tone. There was an almost plaintive quality to the Voice, a deep touch of what felt perhaps like Self-doubt. I don't remember what I answered, if anything. But I do remember feeling haltingly ambivalent. "Good, yes . . . beautiful, fantastic! And yet . . . "

Some Evolutionary Drivers

Given the mathematical values of the three elemental forces plus the specific geometric parameters of exploding space-time—in addition, the presence of the processes of particle and Higgs field(s) formation and sustenance, as well as the phase transitions all of these seem to have required, which kicked in as the newborn universe rapidly cooled in the midst of dramatic expansion, cosmic evolution in the direction of greater and greater complexity seems to have been inevitable.

In certain "bubbles" of low entropy and high energy, where chemical complexity was able to go from a slow creep to a startling hypersonic dash for the acquisition of energy and information, life appeared . . . at least on our planet. By fits, starts, stupendous catastrophes, and ferocious recoveries, it took charge of Earth's chemistry and climate and, as far as possible, made the planet in its own image, to serve its own purposes.

I want to take a moment to give my take on what Nature as life on

Earth has been doing, and/or done to. First, I want to talk about what I'm calling Nature's drivers, then Its Intelligence (however one defines that), even Personhood, and Its Goal(s), if any. To do these things, there are terms that must be defined, most important of which, I think, are words like *random, determined, meaningless, accidental, intentional, directional*, and so on. These are terms for evolutionary drivers that are often used carelessly, inconsistently, and, therefore, incoherently by both scientists and laypeople. Consequently, trying to see what's going on in evolution, especially biological evolution, is seriously impaired and, I suspect, sometimes even maliciously obscured by professionals and laypeople with ideological axes to grind. I do admit that Nature's processes and motives (again, if any) are subtle, hard to discern, and show every sign of being genuinely ambiguous.

Random, Determined, Purposeful?

Take the loaded word *random*. In *Merriam-Webster's Collegiate Dictionary* (eleventh edition, 2004), random is defined as "lacking a definite plan, purpose, or pattern." The crucial qualifier here is the word *definite*. Definite in what sense and according to whom? Would we say, then, that it has no cause, or at least that its cause, whatever it might be, has no plan, purpose, or pattern? But how do we know that? The pattern part is in the eye of the beholder. Indeed, it has been suggested that the so-called statistical residue[116] or the empirical residue[117]—what's left over after the observer has identified the patterns (as in pattern recognition) that impress him or her, what his or her mind has been able to pick out— is just that, a residue of no import. That seems a little arbitrary to me, as it does to the philosopher Bernard Lonergan (1904–1984). Indeed, sometimes that bit of information that the statistician has excluded, in the eyes of a perhaps genius-level observer, turns out to be a gateway to a whole new level of knowledge—an undiscovered continent that just needed someone with a little more expansive imagination, like Copernicus over Ptolemy, or the discovery in genetics that the so-called junk genes, at first assumed to be redundant or useless, turn out to regulate the on-off switches for other genes and may hold at least part of the key to unlock the mysterious presence of "ghost populations" in our own genomes.

In other words, I'm inclined to think that much, most, or *all* of those elements—in whatever field of study or even just life, *our* lives—are *not* planless, patternless, or without intention. They may very well be the mountaintops of those submerged continents, evidence of higher orders of organization, very much planned and intended—hence, meaningful. I also suspect that they are necessary for *really* understanding that small bit of Reality that we seem to know something about. They are for us the unthought, or not-thought-well-enough, context for what little segment of Reality we have deciphered. We are fish who've never become aware of water (or appropriately aware) because we've never dreamed that our part of Reality is (please excuse the pun) a drop in the bucket.

Then there's the evidence that the future, like the past, is already "there." If that's the case, what place could there possibly be for randomness? Okay, we could certainly say that, compared to the order we *do* experience, it *feels like* some other events are random. From my perspective, "feels like" is a valid level of experience. At the same time, I would propose that the randomness we are feeling about certain elements of our existence, in the face of evidence for, say, the block universe—determinism on steroids—opens up the probability, maybe even the certainty, that this feeling of randomness is part of our experience of that Eternal Reality that both does and doesn't move.

So, does randomness mean meaninglessness? As you've gathered by now, I don't think so. Rather, I think there is no such thing as meaninglessness.

Nonetheless, evolutionary biologists use the word *random* to mean purposeless, meaningless, pointless, and also without direction or goal.[118] Don't tell that to any organism—that it has no direction or goal! *All* of these live their lives with a sense of purpose (however vague, however sharply sentient), every aspect of their lives, from minutiae to feeding, fighting, mating, raising offspring (as the case may be), surviving and flourishing in a partly supportive and partly annihilating environment. They all have direction and goals, inherent to their sense of purpose and meaning, and vice versa. That includes the quest for the Theory of Everything and, in a somewhat different vein, devotion to trying to become one with God.

Evolutionary biologists are fond of saying that genetic mutations are random, or that the great upheavals that have led to mass extinctions are accidental. My position is that, the more you can't see the forest for the trees—the overall patterns—the more you're inclined to think that individual events, like a genetic mutation or continental drift (which, over time, substantially reconfigures land and ocean surfaces, dramatically alters climates, and so on), are random. But they all have causes, indisputably. And while they may look random at the minute level—especially in the case of genetic mutations—they do seem to result overall in life's ability to garner increasing amounts of energy and information and so to make it more resilient and smarter. Better adapted to its ever-changing environment, and better able to remake that environment to suit its own purposes. That's the forest. I might also mention the evidence presented by heretic biologist Rupert Sheldrake (*Morphic Resonance: The Nature of Formative Causation*, 1981) and Simon Conway Morris (*The Runes of Evolution: How the Universe Became Self-Aware*, 2015) for recurring patterns over vast stretches of time. Both point out the startling convergence toward, for example, Mind across families, genera, species, and even phyla. These insights too are signs of a forest. In other words, of meaningful patterns and patterns that look at least *as if* they have long-range intentions or goals.

And "as if" is good enough.

So, here's another evolutionary question: If we admit that there is *direction* in all of this, which I think is undeniable, is direction the same thing as *goal oriented*? Can something have a direction but no intention or goal? Maybe.

It's clear, for instance, that evolution (both cosmic and biological) is directional—greater and greater complexity. At least up until now. It looks to cosmologists like the time will come when this direction will gradually shift to less and less complex and a long, eons-long, final dissipation as the universe expands and evaporates.[119]

But does it—does life, do *we*—have meaning if all energy and the things it was the agency for manifesting fall off into what from our present perspective looks like No-thingness? I believe the end of the cosmos, like the end of our individual lives, does not have anything to do with the cosmic, terrestrial, biological, and psychic meaningfulness and goal orientation of who and what we are and do (feel, think, and so on) right here, right now—the experiences of the *persons* we are in this Supracosmic moment. This Supracosmic moment, this *Present*, is the occasion for our *Presence*. When the universe can no longer support persons, they have already been . . . and then they have gone Elsewhere and Elsewhen. So, it doesn't matter how the universe will end, or *that* it will do so. What matters is that, at a certain stage, it provided the conditions that enabled persons to become within its context . . . persons who *were* it and who transcended it, which, I believe, was its own major goal orientation, its primary (but probably not its only) reason for being. Sound like some version of the anthropic principles? With certain qualifications, that's where I'm at.

It seems clear to me that goal orientation, intention, striving, purpose, meaning—most fully manifested by persons—must hitch a ride on directionality; the purpose that persons display is an added dimension of directionality, emergent from it as its intended goal. Maybe, once the goal has been reached, or at least a major effort has been made toward it, the directionality that supported it ceases to be important, or in that sense meaningful. Perhaps it never was meaningful in its own right but was always nothing more than a necessary dynamic for the emergence of persons.

The Emergence of the Potential into the Actual

One fun thing I like to do in my classes is write on the whiteboard the symbol H_2O and ask my students what it stands for. They inevitably say, "Water!" At which point the fun begins. I say, "No, this actually isn't water. It's not wet, it has no surface tension, it doesn't flow, it doesn't form crystals when it freezes, it doesn't taste like anything, and it won't quench your thirst." Of course, they know they've been tricked into realizing that it takes x-number of these molecules for the emergence of a whole new thing with characteristics and laws that were not prefigured—but nonetheless potential—in that single molecule. It's certainly true that H_2O does have unique properties that enable it to bond with others of its kind in a powerful *and* slippery way, which, when conditions are right (many conditions), forms water.[120] How many of these molecules does it take—five, a hundred, forty thousand . . . more? I don't know. I do know that we are now back at the ancient Greek sorites problem. The point is that for anything to become what it is, there was a very real *potential* that preceded it.

Here's a more complicated example. When I was a little kid, I wanted to be an astronomer, but a little further on I discovered I couldn't do the math. Then I wanted to be a fighter jet pilot . . . but I had to wear glasses (which in those days were a disqualifier). So then, an archaeologist. But by high school, an internship in archaeology had convinced me of the tediousness of most of the work. Then, as high school was ending, I wanted to be an Egyptologist (theoretical, not field). But a conversation with an Egyptology professor at the Oriental Institute of the University of Chicago indicated that there were no jobs. Throughout those years—from earliest childhood to college—I read voraciously in the fields of cosmology, comparative religions, philosophy, and theology. A number of years later, I became fascinated with depth psychology. Upon reflection as a young adult, I realized that there was a common theme through all these adventures of the psyche—*Expansiveness of Consciousness*. Expansive Consciousness was what I was after—going beyond the everyday, going beyond every-*thing* to . . . . Awe, Wonder, Exhilaration . . . in my experience, the Divine. There is nothing more expansive than that! And the *potential* for the person I would become and the adult interests I would express were all present in my baby being, maybe even before. Along the way, they were moderated and modulated by the interactions that potential encountered outside of my forming identity as I gradually became as actual as this earthly environment in general and my specific life course would permit.

In the course of the evolution of life on Earth, we find the same potential-to-actual dynamics as those we experience in our personal lives, albeit on a grander scale and in some ways more mysterious, partly because of the scale and the enormous variety of organisms, past and present. Among the several evolutionary developments that Simon Conway Morris tracks in great detail in his *The Runes of Evolution*, one of them is what's called *inherency* (otherwise known as *preadaptation*).[121] Preadaptation is the presence in animals (and to some extent in some plants and fungi, not to mention protists and other groups) of mechanisms, whether molecular pathways or even larger structures, that seem to serve no purpose (or another purpose) until they are pressed into service to be used for a creative advance in adaptability or furtherance of an organism's active mental or physical capacities, which we could view as superadaptability. I can't rehearse Morris's examples; there are way too many of them. I'll just defer to his book in the bibliography. Once again, Rupert Sheldrake's morphic resonance may be at work here too (*Morphic Resonance*).

Here's a question about potentiality and actuality that philosophers periodically chew on: Is the entire oak tree that will be contained *en potencia* in an acorn? And if so, what about the potential oak forest that might be generated by that first oak tree? Is all of that, plus all the behaviors of all the animals and plants that will flourish in and interact with that actualized oak forest, also present potentially in that acorn? My answer is yes.

But what happens when potentials are thwarted—when lives are cut short or become distorted in some way, when species go extinct and so their preadaptations never get appropriated, or the budding oak forest is stricken with disease, drought, fire, and so on? What, if anything, does that say about the substantiality (in some way) of potentials? Clearly, potentials can be thwarted, cut off at the pass, before they can be fully actualized. But, in my view, this doesn't mean that they never really existed in the realm, or space, of potentials . . . wherever that may be! It seems to me that that could be in David Bohm's implicate order or in other (not necessarily oppositional) envisagements of Eternity in the experiences and speculations of philosophers and theologians.

The Beauty

It probably goes without saying that much of Nature at essentially *all* levels, from cosmic to microscopic, shows Itself as profoundly Beautiful in Its organization, Its intricacy, Its forms and colors, the individual creatures, both animate and inanimate, It expresses, Its light and darkness (literal, in this case, not metaphorical), and, of course, in its crowning manifestation . . . *persons*. Since "it probably goes without saying" (as I just indicated), I'm not going to say it!

What I do want to say is that when people, including me, feel romantic about Nature, or one with It, they're caught up in and overwhelmed . . . specifically, by Its Beauty. This works best when there are few, if any, other humans around. It also works well, I suspect, when panoramas are involved rather than nitty-gritties. Or when certain individual elements are so radiantly colorful and well-crafted that they catch the breath, and we are struck with wonder.

The romance about Nature's Beauty and, by extension, its Goodness (in a non-moral-ethical sense) don't work so well, for *me* at least, when I witness the little horrors that take place just under the surface of that Beauty and that to some significant extent seem to be essential to that Beauty and Goodness's illumination, appearance, being-at-all. My guess is the romance doesn't work well either for ourselves or our loved ones' diminishment, or for our or their sharp and lingering suffering, whether emotional, cognitive, physical, or all of the above. It's difficult to feel one with unmitigated suffering. Nature is, of course, rife with this. And to the extent that creatures are *persons*, that suffering, in my view, is *un*acceptable and finally unforgivable.

But, as I've often said, "'They' give us just enough Beauty and Goodness (pleasure, satisfaction, fulfillment) to make (most of) us want to keep going." And right there is the almost inescapable dilemma of *persons* who can imagine something better . . . including themselves . . . being pressured to accept the medium in which they dwell as it irremediably *is*. That, as James Luchte says, is "tragic."[122] And, I would add, it *is* so . . . nontrivially.

If Nature Were a Person

What if Nature were a Person, or at least Person*ish*? Comparing It to human persons, what could we say about It? Okay, I know that's maybe a bit of a stretch. I'll no doubt be accused of anthropomorphizing. On the other hand, perhaps anthropomorphizing is what Nature Itself has done. Perhaps we and any other relatively sophisticated self-and-other conscious beings are Nature's way of becoming aware of Itself. Not necessarily the only way, but the way most available in terms of Its Self-expression in the misty medium of matter. As I've noted before, we *are* Nature . . . whatever else we might be. Also, even if I'm using Nature as a Person in a completely metaphorical way, it still seems valid, and at least potentially insightful, to play with the idea. Anyway, *I'm* going to play, and I invite you to play with me.

Let's imagine that Nature was once Something Else, Something Whole—say, the Pythagorean All, or David Bohm's implicate order, or the Divine beyond or within Them. And that for reasons I'll speculate about later on, It fell out of that Wholeness, completely lost Consciousness, went to zero, and became dormant, comatose, we might say. When It eventually began to come to, It was really out of it, dazed and barely functioning . . . I mean Its Mind, Its Psyche. It found Itself in some kind of a medium completely alien to It. It didn't recognize *Itself* in these surroundings, and at this very minimal level of Consciousness, It was what we would call Dissociated, Schizoid, and consequently Indifferent (at least to morality and ethics, as we view these things). Either while It was in the coma or at Its most rudimentary, Mind began to function; It had a series of nightmares— terrifying, disorienting, crazy making. Neither this nor that . . . *both* this *and* that . . . forward and simultaneously backward in time . . . not *in* time . . . at the same time, time itself, teeny-tiny things. And the idea of space . . . get some room, spatial and temporal, stretch it out. Quantum world, quantum Mind.

Quantum theorists believe that below the Planck measurement of space—very, very subquantum—space-time is violently thrashing.[123] Anthropomorphizing, could we say that Nature is expressing extreme Anxiety and Anger, perhaps as It begins to come out of its coma?

Next up, Cruelty. By the best human standards, which include, of course, kindness, compassion, empathy, fairness, the desire to alleviate suffering, and so on, Nature is Cruel. Cruelty can be unintentional or intentional. From a human perspective, unintentional cruelty may be due to indifference (lack of empathy), while intentional cruelty may have many sources. These include, but are not limited to: cruelty in the service of a perceived higher Good (whether protecting or advancing one's cultural or individual norms and identity—even, let's say, creating art of one kind or another); cruelty incited by extreme anxiety and anger (which can include overwrought competitiveness, on a collective or individual level); cruelty evoked by existential dread (again, on a collective or individual level); and cruelty as an expression of pleasure (sheer meanness) (ditto). The Neoplatonic philosopher Plotinus believed that Nature's Cruelty, including our own, is an expression of Its Lostness in the realm of matter and Its Anxiety to return to Its originally Whole State of Oneness with the One.[124] As I've often said to my classes, "Whoever made all this—the universe as it's given—has a fantastic eye for beauty and is morally and ethically bankrupt!"

Another of Nature's anthropomorphized qualities is Its enormous Inventiveness and Creativity. This is, of course, startling and wonderful. Expressed through space and time, Nature rushes (in the long view) from one invention or creative expression to another. Indeed, to me, It seems to be so intent on creating . . . Beauty among other things . . . that It has essentially no other value. As we've already seen, and actually all know, It indifferently dispenses with individuals, including persons, and whole panoplies of species, not to mention genera, families, classes, orders, and even phyla. Cruelty here is on shocking and disheartening display. But there's more downside to Nature's Creativity: it seems to be doing this in an opportunistic, jerry-rigged, and slipshod way—grabbing at whatever is the next adjacent possible to make new creatures. The results, as Richard Dawkins rightly points out in his *The Greatest Show on Earth: The Evidence for Evolution* (2009), are malformed individuals and species, not to mention genetic mutations that have *positive* effects on groups and species (like protection against malaria . . . for most), but that ruthlessly destroy individuals. In addition, the hurried and somewhat inept creation of bipedal apes, which advanced their survival as groups in their increasingly savanna (rather than woodland) environment, resulted in a misrouted *vas deferens* (looped over the ureter that leads from the kidney to the bladder), which can cause partial blockage and considerable discomfort in adult males.[125] And anyone who's experienced back pain can testify to the post hoc way that bipedalism was gained. As Woody Allen is supposed to have said, "I don't think it's so much that God is evil, as that he's . . . well . . . an underachiever."

If Nature were a Person, or at least Person*ish*, what might all this add up to? Maybe, Someone Who once knew Wholeness, stricken by a devastating coma, and feverishly trying to regain Its full Consciousness and functioning, using every means available (no matter the cost to others) and so, we might say, trying to get Home before the material scaffolding on which It is forced to actualize Its project collapses or, as in one hypothesis about the future of the universe, melts away and dissipates into No-thingness. Someone Who, as a Whole and as individual entities and living creatures, is and expresses a Beautiful Terror!

Okay, I know. This is a myth. But as I discuss further in chapter 8, "My Likely Story," it squares really well with my own experiences . . . at least *some* of them . . . of altered states of consciousness, especially those that seem to involve direct dialogue with the Divine as Creator. It also makes some kind of sense to me in terms of my experiences of daily life, Nature, and my own body and *person*.

Still, Nature is fabulously Beautiful! And, I would say, wishes to be even more so.

4

Persons:
Presence Fully Visited*

The fiery globe of Sol, yellow as an
incandescent bulb,
ascended through a swoon of mist-strewn
phosphorescent gauze
across the fields, gilding these with otherworldly
ambers, greens.
Untangling from
the limbs of trees, he floated up into that day-lit
vault of self-wrought
dreams,
declared with fanfare of the stirring birds his
freedom and his majesty.
I was present there. I saw, and knew that I was all
of these.

DOUGLAS M. GILLETTE,
AT THE THRESHOLDS OF ELYSIUM

---

*This phrase—"presence fully visited"—originates from my poem "Dora's Self-disclosing" in *Thresholds of Elysium*, page 201.

Persons, whether the Divine Person or the multitude of persons that Person has Imagined and Made, are the highest expressions of Reality there is or ever will be, in this world or any other. From my perspective, they are the reason for the existence of Reality, including Nature.

Clues to the Infinite Worth of Persons

Our backyard is magnificent, really. It's the size of a small park and looks the part. There's the globe-shaped redbud tree a little south of the center, the fantastic ash (a little west and north) that in the autumn flashes brilliant yellow against the blue sky. On the east side are maples and swamp oaks, and all around the edges, stately buckthorns, which we trim to make a fourteen-foot-high green wall. Under and out from these is a wonderland my wife has created of vetch, sedge, violets, and wild-flowers. In the southeast corner is an area where the trees' roots have surfaced, making it a miniature version of Harry Potter's Forbidden Forest. And covering the open area of our "park" is a nearly weedless lawn, nourished by our lawn service and our own tender care. There's a birdbath on the eastern side, up under the overhanging limbs of the maples. Over the brick patio, up against the house on the east side, years ago I built a huge grape arbor. The vines are still flourishing, and every fall, the Concord grapes hang in heavy clusters, emitting the most intoxicating aroma, sweet and musky. When our daughter was little and home, our backyard was transformed from time to time into Hobbiton, the various trees and the Etruscan-style garden shed serving as the homes of the most famous Hobbits. There was bubble blowing, bucket toss, catch, badminton, water fun "fights." The whole thing was, still is, glorious. Oh, I forgot to mention my statues! The only one still missing is the one inspired by all the life we lived there—"The Laughing God of the Summer Backyard." It's too late now for that one. I don't have the heart.

The point is, now when I walk out there, or just look at it through what in effect is the glass wall that is the east side of our dining and garden rooms, it's still beautiful, especially on fresh spring mornings and high summer afternoons. But now that our daughter's grown up and gone, and my wife and I have more work (not less) in our professional capacities, it's empty, hollow, without laughter or games . . . a museum piece.

I remember who we were then, there—the games we played, the hammock in which we swayed and laughed and dreamed together, the inflatable pool. There are echoes and whispers of our lives as they were, still, but they're fading further and further into an unrecoverable past. They're less than vapor now . . . a gradually dispersing mist. The absence of us as we were has made our yard—except for those echoes and whispers—a beautiful but meaningless void. It was everything to me when we were there together. Of course, *It* wasn't everything . . . *we* were. That's one way I know that persons—in this case *us*—are of Infinite Worth. When we're gone, there is what feels like a No-thingness that goes down and down forever. Our absence, *as we were*, is *Absolute*—another clue that Eternity is always Immediately Present, at every slice through time, utterly unrecoverable. The emptiest rabbit hole of all. *Infinitely* Empty.

Another way I know that persons are of Infinite Worth is what happens to them when they're cast aside and abandoned, as if they were trash. What happens to them is that they are wounded with a wound that also goes down and down Forever. It goes down and down Forever because, if they had been held and loved, they would have gone up and up Forever. *Forever* is another word for Eternity.

Of course, in relationships, abandoning is sometimes the only healthy, self-affirmative thing to do. Sometimes we have to give each other back to the One Who Created us. Yes, that can be devastating to some or all of those involved. Hopefully, they have the emotional and cognitive resources to deal with that or can get help developing them if they don't.

But I'm talking about the truly help*less*—babies, children, the irre-vocably poor, the sick, the elderly. That's why we took my senile mother in to live with us her last years. That's why we provide day care in our home for, as I write, our four-month-old granddaughter. The thought of the indescribable horror of her total inability to understand that her mother *had* to go back to work—and so, the existential terror at feeling abandoned she would have had to live with if we hadn't . . . were too awful for my wife and me to contemplate.

While we're talking about abandonment, I'm thinking again about my lost-in-space dream I had as a little kid. Whatever else it was about, I *do* think it was an abandonment dream. Abandonment feels existen-tial, Absolute, Infinite, Eternal—a condemning to death, physical and/or psychological (they often go together).

I was never threatened with physical death in the family I grew up in. But I was very definitely sporadically-to-chronically threatened with what amounted to psychological death. For me, that was somehow a deeper kind of death than the physical version. Utter and total aban-donment in an infinite space, with no way to return to my finite home . . . where I am *me*. *Infinitely* Abandoned. That's part of our Infinite Worth . . . but reversed into the negative . . . to Infinite Worthlessness. Asteroids may be equally adrift as I was in my dream. But they are not abandoned. Only *persons* are.

Then there's the most fulfilling, completing, validating, lifting, and exalting feeling at the very peak of all life experiences a person can have—Love. Giving and receiving. It's hard to say which is greater, but my vote is for giving. Ultimately, at its highest peak, Love feels like the *Infinite* Valuing of another.

As I mentioned earlier, when I first met the woman who would be the love of my life, she was married. I assumed she was *happily* married, which turned out to be very wrong. Over the months that I picked her up and dropped her off after a day of cooking and cleaning in my apartment in Chicago, she slowly and shyly unfolded the story of her marital *un*happiness. I learned that she lived with her husband, an at-times violent alcoholic, and his two brothers (one of them wanted for murder in Mexico) in a tiny, rat-infested basement apartment. I saw in her a wonderful person—intelligent, strong, warmhearted, a woman who would be a fantastic mother, a woman who was open to new experiences, someone who shared my basic values, a really quality *person* in awful circumstances who *deserved* a life of Love, emotional security, and personal fulfillment.

After about nine months of getting to know each other, we began to make a plan for her escape. For the plan to work, the brothers had to be out of the apartment late into the wee hours, which they usually were. She'd call me when the coast was clear, and I'd go pick her up and drive her to the Indianapolis airport. We decided on that airport because if the brothers came home early and found her gone, they'd likely head for Midway Airport in Chicago to look for her, figuring she would fly to Houston, where most of her family lived. Running into them would have been a really bad scene. Who knows how that would have turned out? Also, I had a video shoot with the T.V. program 20/20 in Indianapolis the next day. I'd put her on a plane for Houston there.

We executed the plan, and then began talking on the phone regularly. Soon I started flying to Houston every weekend. Finally, my mother in tow, I rented a house there, and we began our wonderful life together—twenty-eight years and counting.

The thing is, all through the days of getting to know each other, I felt the purest, most selfless Love I've ever felt for anyone other than God. Even if we were never going to be together, I wanted to empower her to live the life that would fulfill her. The Love for her I felt was startling to me and wonderful. It opened up in me a vista, a panorama, a whole new incredibly Expansive Dimension of Love, what It is in its most pristine form and, to my surprise, delight, amazement, and an overwhelming sense of gratitude, my own capacities to give that kind of Love to another person.

That whole time of getting to know her—discovering that, while from radically different cultures, educational backgrounds, races, and languages, we shared values—I never made any advances toward her or touched her, although she was, and is, the essence of Mexican beauty for me. That was wonderful too! While magnetically attracted to her physically, what I really felt was that I was in love with her magical magnificence as a *person*—embodied to be sure but indescribably more than that . . . and yet, there *is* nothing more, from my perspective and experience, than embodied persons. I knew that *she was of Infinite Worth*. I didn't *think* that or opinionate about it. I *felt* it—directly, compellingly, as a matter of fact, not as a product of fantasy or wishing.

That selfless Love that I felt for my wife—still feel twenty-eight years later—is the same Love I've felt for God, the *Person*, all my life. It's a kind of In-Love-ness—Rapturous, Joyful, deeply Peaceful, inexpressibly Grateful, powerfully infused with Wonder and Awe! It has informed almost everything I've done—my life in the theater (directing, acting, designing, set construction), my alternative service for the government during the Vietnam War, community organizing, life guiding, pastoring, teaching, writing, my art, my love of music, (most of) my personal interactions—nearly everything!

Remember the Italian song, hugely popular in the 1950s, "Volare"? When I first heard it, and still today, I *soared* with it. Into the blue sky! Into the sun! I felt, and feel, it as one of my love songs to God. In fact, I've come to experience many love songs as God singing to me, to us—and me or us singing to God. When I hear Juan Gabriel's "Amor Eterno," written for his dead mother, it is, for me, also about loving and missing God—grieving the Separation from Him/Her/It that is and is not forced upon us by being here . . . "below" those blue skies, with all the incredible mixture of yearning to fly when we can't . . . yet somehow *can* . . . and the Exultation of rising into Bliss!

I've realized in recent years that all of my paintings and sculptures were never meant to be sold. They were meant as love songs, gifts of gratitude to God for the Magic of my life. I'm thinking of one sculpture in particular right now—the eight-foot-tall piece I've named *Father El*, for the High God of the Canaanite pantheon. But really, in my mind, it's a living testament to the whole tradition of Western monotheism.

There are Egyptian elements, Jewish, Islamic, and Christian, with a hint of the pagan oracular. I won't describe the whole thing, but I want you to see the twirling, shimmering narrow tree trunk that rises from the primeval waters of the ancient Egyptian God Nun, the Infinite, the blue branches, the green leaves, and the yellow- and orange-colored fruit, the leafing staff held in front with mysterious markings carved into it, and the head with its long beard and its twisted goat horns. The Face! A look I can't easily describe—Tranquility, Benevolence, Joy, Sadness, Gentle Authority, Radiance, Love. Which, of course, is how I predominantly experience the Person Who Is God . . . to *me*. I've seen that look in people's faces now and then.

I remember one evening, after my wife, daughter, and I had gone to a mosque with my friend Ibrahim. After prayers were over, Ibrahim stayed for a long time praying, meditating, reciting. We finally went outside to wait for him. When he did come out, his face was radiant with Tranquility and Joy. I believe he had touched, and been embraced by, the God of Love . . . in love himself with the Divine Person!

That's a rush words are not able to communicate. The most wonderful feeling in the world!

Love—the royal road to *the actual fulfillment of personhood*. What that's *for*. And when you feel the Real Thing—the Thing in its Fullness, you know It has no boundaries. You know It is Infinite, of Infinite Worth. As are the persons who feel It.

But even at less full expressions of Love, at levels of simple warmth and affirmation, where all that's needed is respectful recognition and validation, the wonder of person making and upholding takes place. I'm thinking right now of two incidents in which I was being threatened by persons who, as it turned out, just needed my recognition of them. The first happened when I was in junior high school and being bullied by two guys who roamed the halls together. Not knowing any better, I tried ignoring them (as we passed classes) and, from time to time, anger and confrontation. Neither worked. So, I thought of a totally different strategy. I asked one of the teachers, I think it was the wrestling coach, what their names were. The next time I saw them heading for me, I called out, "Hi Jim . . . Hi Jack!" (not their real names.) They looked confused but a little pleased. They never bothered me again.

The other incident took place when I was a graduate student in the Divinity School of the University of Chicago. I was walking from the campus to my apartment when two black guys showed up and positioned themselves around me, one in front and the other behind. I knew what was coming next. Without any trace of fear, felt or expressed, I said cheerfully, "Hi guys!" I pulled out my wallet and showed them there was nothing in it. I was dressed in my somewhat raggedy student clothes. They were dressed in literally shiny slacks and jackets. I compared my clothes to theirs. They laughed, and we started having a conversation that ranged from their and my anticipated futures, through racism, social issues, and politics. They soon saw that not only was I not afraid of them, but also that my social and political views were similar to theirs. I treated them as human beings, as equals, and with respect. We parted with high fives and best wishes.

I'm certainly not suggesting that all potential muggings, far less assaults, could end this way. Far from it. What I *am* saying, though, is that, escalated emotions and situations excluded, people *do* usually respond positively when they can feel that we intend them no disrespect or harm but rather an adequate degree of what amounts to Love. Most people know when they're in Love's Presence. And it feels good.

I want to tell one more story here about my experiences of the Infinite Worth of persons. The subject of death comes up in a number of my classes. I sometimes have an opening to communicate in a way that really does hit home for my students and feels real to them by asking something like: "Have you ever felt the absolute absurdity of the death of *persons*?" When I do it right, and at the right moment, there's almost always an immediate and enthusiastic chorus of *yes!* I'm not asking them to *think* about or to construct a philosophical or theological argument for why the death of persons might, or should, be experienced as absurd. I'm asking them to *feel*. And they do! The total and final end of something or someone of extreme—and I'm proposing Infinite—Worth, *is*, plain and simple, absurd.

There's yet another clue about the Infinite Worth of persons. All persons, at whatever level of complexity, experience needs and strive to fulfill them. As I've already mentioned, living things seldom if ever know when to stop. Needs, and the striving to fulfill them, seem to be limited only by environmental constraints. But for highly sophisticated persons, like humans, some needs (and the drives to fulfill them) really do appear to be ultimately unconstrained. For instance, the need for Infinite and Eternal Validation and more—the desire for Infinite Being, Knowledge, and Bliss. The sense that this is our Ultimate Goal suggests to me that Infinity—and the realization of our Ultimate Worth as persons—is built into our being as such.

Some Definitions of Incarnate Persons

Following the lead of Lyall Watson in his *Beyond Supernature* and Simon Conway Morris in his *The Runes of Evolution*, I'm going to suggest that personhood has very deep roots among organisms, be they Protistans (of one kind or another), fungi, plants, or animals, possibly even complex molecules such as DNA and RNA. More radically, according to the panpsychism school of philosophy of mind, any event—any change of any kind—may trigger an experience, which suggests some kind of personhood, because only persons *can* experience. For example, as the philosopher David Chalmers notes, a thermostat has three phenomenal states, cooling, heating, and no action, which suggests to him that it has experiences and therefore is a "person." Chalmers asks: "What is the character of these phenomenal states? What is it *like* to be a thermostat?"[1] If there is something *it is like*, the thermostat is *experiencing* in some way alternating states of information—hence, being—at whatever level of psyche it has.

At its most rudimentary level, an incarnate life-form is an entity with sentience of some kind, at least a vague sensitivity and a simple awareness (probably unconscious by our standards) of itself as an individual other than other individuals and things. It acts on its own behalf, securing nutrients (energy) for itself by ingesting chemicals and/or other organisms, gaining information as it can, and seeking the "practical immortality" of reproduction. Psyche is present in, I assume, a very simple way—the maximum possible in this kind of material structure. Even simple single-celled organisms such as prokaryotes show a complexity of internal organization and speed of chemical reactions completely and starkly incomparable to their inanimate environments. Once Protistan eukaryotes emerge with complex internal structures, including organelles (miniature organs per se), a wall around the nucleus, and mitochondria or photosynthetic inclusions, psyche/Psyche has enormously more to work with. Remarkably, some eukaryote Protistans seem to coordinate in, as Morris says, "cooperative hunting."[2]

In more complex expressions, an incarnate person is an organism made up of a number of individual cells (individuals) that have banded together in such a way that cooperation and specialization of cell types has given rise to a sense (probably still unconscious) of "we're all in this together." This stage of psychic expression goes far beyond the simple colonies of bacteria, like early stromatolites, and involves an organizing principle of some kind that causes the cells to differentiate in order to work together. Lyall Watson cites the German biologist Ernst Haeckel's (1834–1919) research on, among other tiny complex organisms, *Volvox*,[3] a miniature plant about the size of a pinhead, which has a somewhat pronounced head and tail. The head, which is more photosynthetic than the tail, is kept upward (by the cooperative work of the other cells) so that it receives the most sunlight and undergoes a complicated series of inter-cellular reorganization to make sure all cells, especially the inner ones, are fed and that reproduction is assured. Haeckel called *Volvox* a *person*.[4] It's interesting to speculate that this and other primitive multi-celled organisms are being organized by Psyche, however, rudimentary in Its expression—again, expressing Itself up to the maximum that the materials at hand will allow.

In still more sophisticated persons, as we saw in chapter 2, a whole panoply of actors crowd in to contribute to the making of a psyche-in-matter creature. The "I" implicit in less complicated expressions of Psyche-as-psyche reaches, in at least *some* humans, the high perch of *self-reflective consciousness*. The degree of *consciousness of being conscious* var-ies enormously from individual to individual and species to species, but we can clearly see it happening in other animals (perhaps even in some plants). I'm thinking here of both wild and domesticated animals, espe-cially those in the primate family, but others as well—for example, our household pets. In humans at least, not only does reflective conscious-ness vary among individuals, but it also varies in all of us from hour to hour or even moment to moment.

Obviously, the above assumes evolutionary trajectories for an ever-fuller Presence of Psyche-as-finite personhood, at least in this particular world of space and time. The details of this evolution I leave up to Morris.

I feel compelled here in this context to say something more about the Evil that plagues personhood. We've already looked at the probable origins of moral-ethical Evil at the foundations of biological being. I just want to reiterate and suggest further that, as Psyche-as-psyche expressed through material organisms becomes more complicated, it also becomes more fragile and more vulnerable to the moral-ethical Evil of exaggerated narcissism. The very structures and dynamics that make them sophisticated and precious—their layer upon layer of consciousnesses, fragmentary consciousnesses, and other factors that we looked at in chapter 2—make the cohesiveness and integrity of persons more and more difficult to maintain. This, along with the needs for which they strive, which, because of environmental constraints, cannot be satisfied—at least not in this material realm—cause them to become anxious and frustrated. As we've seen, this anxiety and frustration very often lead to anger and cruelty. A sad fact of psychic evolution indeed.

Solipsism and the Irreducible "I"

Solipsism is usually defined as the school of philosophy that says that the self is the only thing that exists, or (fallback position) the only thing that can be *known* to exist. In my view, solipsism cannot be defeated by any philosophical argument. The commonsense argument that we behave as if there are other things than the self doesn't do it. Neither does the "consensual consciousness" proposal. The consensual consciousness hypothesis is the belief that if some, or many, (presupposed) selves agree on what something experienced as outside of themselves is, that validates that there is, in fact, an objective reality other than the single self. But, no matter how you finagle this, in my view, these presupposed other selves, and the things "outside of" them, are still *within* the self that is experiencing them—both the selves and the things. But before we go there, however briefly, we have a problem with the definition of the self. A number of schools of psychology pretty much equate the self with the ego. But, as we saw in chapter 2, the various schools of depth psychology believe they have discovered that each of us is made up of multiple selves. Some of these are true alternative persons (as emphasized in John O. Beahrs's system); some are more or less fragmentary consciousnesses and complexes (as in Jung's map of the psyche); and others, somewhat less defined in these terms, are subliminal and supernormal entities (as in F. W. H. Myers's panoramic view). As we've seen, depth psychological theorists define the self (lower case *s*) as the ego, and the Self (upper case *S*) as the transcendent Core of every sophisticated psyche, as do I. So, the question for solipsism is: Which self is meant?

From my perspective, all of the above can be thought of as the self for the purposes of the solipsistic definition. How? First, the ego. In a kind of comprehensive sense, the "I" I normally think of as me is the only consciousness that exists for me, and anything that comes into ego-consciousness is real only in so far as it, in fact, shows up in my ego-consciousness. When it does, it is known to exist in me. If it doesn't, it isn't. Still, this "coming into" suggests that there *is* something, probably a lot, that is outside my usual ego-consciousness that I need to, or in any case *will*, sooner or later (in this life or some other), end up incorporating into my ego-consciousness. Second, what about the rest of the psyche/Psyche that, according to depth psychology, is outside my ego, but still inside my psyche/Psyche? Depth psychology speaks of these consciousnesses, partial consciousnesses, and other entities as things other than the ego—outside it—and so unknown to it, until, through various life events and, of course, analysis, they become known. It seems to me that for Jung, the self of solipsistic self-awareness is ultimately *the* Self, the all-encompassing and organizing Center of the psyche. This Self can be thought of as the Cosmic or perhaps even the Supracosmic Psyche—Atman-Brahman-God—outside of Which there is nothing, literally, because It is Infinite. So, at least at that Level of Selfhood, the Self *is* the only thing there is or can be known.

Until we get to this Ultimate Level of Selfhood, though, it's clear that the "I" at all other levels does propose or experience itself as self and other—both as inner and outer. This isn't something we think about, at least not at first, but something that feels given. From a

solipsistic point of view, this is a strange but compelling self-division . . .
ultimately between *subjective* and *objective* aspects of itself. The self can
even objectify its self, as when we think about ourselves or make claims
like "I was not myself today." What self are we talking about? Or when,
as often happens, a child first learning to talk speaks of herself in the
third person: "Julie wants some milk." Who—what "I"—is speaking for
Julie to her caregivers? Clearly, there is an "I" other than Julie (who,
perhaps, has not become conscious of her own "I" yet).

The most developed version of solipsism in the West (Eastern psychospiritual traditions have their own way of elaborating solipsism)
is German idealism, especially as developed by J. G. Fichte, Friedrich
Hegel, and others. Here, I'm going to use Fichte as my springboard for
this further discussion because his thinking seems more basic to me
than, for example, Hegel's . . . without the latter's history-manifest-
ing complications or, depending on how one feels about it, "claptrap."
Fichte's main concern seems to be trying to understand how we get
from a singular Self to a Not-Self[5] . . . then to all the multitude of
selves. In a nutshell, the only way to become aware of Me is I have to
be thinking (and feeling) of Me as if I were a Not-Me. Only then can I
reflect on Me. I stay the Subject, and I make the Not-Me an Object. So,
now I can experience Objects, but it's I Who is doing this—thinking
about Myself . . . always . . . as if I were these other things.

So, Fichte is trying to understand how we get from a singular, Infinite
Self to a multiple, finite me as Me and Not-Me. (The capitalizations here
mean that, on my reading, Fichte does not clearly distinguish between
the Supracosmic Self and our individual selves; almost certainly he means
both at the same time.) I can only *reflect* on Me in the context of a
Not-Me that *I* have thought of *as if* It were Not-Me. As I just mentioned,
the Me divides Itself into a Subject and an Object—in Its primordial condition, Me the Subject thinking of Me as if I were Me as an Object. But
then, I'm *already* and *necessarily* Me and Not-Me (because the only way
to experience Myself as Me is if there is simultaneously a Not-Me). I can

never get behind this duality, not even in Mystical, or Unitive, Experience. I am *given* to Myself as Me/Not-Me. So, *both* Me and Not-Me are *as if.* Descartes's *cogito, ergo sum* ("I think, therefore I am")[6] goes immediately into the Multiplicity. The "as if" Me/Not-Me, implicit in Descartes's thinking, shatters like a broken hologram, and then, through cosmic and terrestrial evolution, as if waking up from a coma, glues Itself back together in the unitary thinking and feeling of Mystical Union. Evolution, of course, is nowhere and nowhen except within the Psyche, or even the "I." Which gets us to the irreducible "I" part.

The "I" is irremediably and without recourse irreducible, even if we're largely unconscious of It, because nothing can be sensed, felt, known, or thought about without It. *Nothing.*

Some Western thinkers talk like Buddhists when they suggest that the "I" is really an illusion. There's only a bundle of random thoughts and feelings going on that creates the appearance of an "I," but this is delusional. *Someone* is picturing the "I" as a bundle of random thoughts and feelings. That someone, of course, is the "I." There's a phenomenon related to this sort of skepticism, which we all experience—forgetfulness of our own "I's," as when we're intensely engaged intellectually, emotionally, or creatively in some project or experience. Or playing tennis, or riding a bike. Or in moments of passionate Love. Or, again, in Mystical, or Unitive, Experience.

We take this forgetting of the "I" for granted. However, some philosophers and scientists (others as well) make this everyday fact of temporary forgetfulness into a doctrine. They not only pretend that the "I" is delusional; they also *forget* that *they've* forgotten! What I mean is, they lose awareness of the fact that their work is not even possible without its foundation in the subjectivity of the "I." They seem to think that there is only objective truth. What they don't seem to realize is that it is inescapably some *subjectivity*—an "I"—that is searching for and perceiving that objective truth. Anyway, what could determine what is true except an "I"?

I sometimes ask my classes such questions as "Where's the brain?"

Answer: "In my head."

Question: "Where's the head?"

Answer: "Part of my body."

Question: "Where's the body?"

Answer: "In the universe."

Question: "Where's the universe?"

Answer: "In my mind."

Not unlike Stanley Rosen's realization of the Present as Presence, it's clear that there's nowhere for the universe or anything else to be except in my awareness. I'll add the caveat "for me" . . . that is, the "me" of my immediate ego awareness. But, if I'm thinking of me/Me as the Supracosmic "I," my caveat disappears!

Take the question: If a tree falls in a forest, but there's no one to hear it, does it make a sound? At least on the non-Supracosmic level, the answer is unequivocally no. But still, you might say, as my students regularly do: "But it still makes sound waves." I then say, "Okay, now you've played a trick on us (and yourself) because you're still there! You're still 'there' imagining the tree and forest, pretending that you're not there to hear the tree fall. But what if there were no one at all, could there be a forest, silent or not? The answer again is no. But notice that you're *still* there, imagining that there is 'no one' to imagine the forest not existing."

So, there is no object without a subject, as far as anyone can tell— and that includes you (or me). That's if we're speaking from any level of the Me that is less than the Supracosmic Me. At the Supracosmic Level of Consciousness, I at least have no real idea what's going on, though I suspect that *Someone* is *always* there to hear the tree fall in the forest, or to imagine no tree and no forest.

That's why the "I" is irreducible. And that's why I say that solipsism cannot be defeated. We can never get outside the psyche/Psyche because, ultimately or immediately (although in the latter case hidden by the "as if"), the "I" as Me/Not-Me is all there is.

Only *persons* are "I's." That's why they are "presences fully visited."[7]

5
Divine Self-Disclosures: Unsettling and Ecstatic Intimacies

When to ecstasy I have been hurled,
and known that one benevolent Immensity,
that stupendous Presence over-flowing I'm
impelled to denominate and indicate as
"God," I have been made as grave as iron,
entered into a state of wonderness, still
a man, yet so large and strangely deep
I cannot respirate or think. I cannot tell
you what I've heard or where I've been.
"Everything" and "Nowhere," is all that
I may venture.

DOUGLAS M. GILLETTE,
AT THE THRESHOLDS OF ELYSIUM

God seeks communion with persons "other than" God at whatever level of their development and then lures them toward fuller expression of God's Goodness and Beauty. This is the point of the Infinite Person's Self-expressions that we know of.

157

Some Divine Self-Disclosures I Have Loved and Felt Loved By

As always, I'm telling my personal stories to show as honestly as I can the actual experiences that have led to the reflections and interpretations that will follow shortly and also in the hope that you may find some similarities with your own experiences and maybe some inspiration. I'm presenting these stories of some of my personal encounters with what I take to be God's Self-disclosures to me in something like a chronological order, at least the chronological order of their beginnings.

The Divine Self-disclosures I believe I've experienced range all the way from what feels like being grazed or touched lightly by the Infinite to a very much human-sized God adjusting Himself/Herself/Itself for communication and companionship with humans. The accounts I'm presenting in this section are all about some of the more or less human-sized experiences I've had of the Divine, although there is the sense within most of them, I think, of the shading off toward Infinity. I guess I'm presenting the human-sized because, in a sense, they're the most important to me—more easily graspable as *Person to person*. For me, that's where the rubber hits the road in my relationship with God, so long as I keep the continual sense of openness to the Vastness and Ultimate Unknowability of the Divine. For my personality type, that's the easiest thing in the world.

I think God Self-discloses to us wherever we're at, as we're able to take these Disclosures in, whether that's at different stages of our lives, at different moods and intellectual capacities and interests, or according to our cultural framings, levels of education, basic personalities and temperaments, and so on. My experience is that in each Self-disclosure there's all of that—necessarily—but also frequently (but perhaps not always) both a comforting and a disquieting element—in each case an ecstatic element, the one calming, the other a little, or a lot, discomfiting. The discomfiting or disquieting part, for me, is about being drawn out, lured to venture further into the More that's always present within the experience, however obscure and mysterious at the time, beyond whatever resting point we've reached.

As I'm saying, there's a kind of chronology in the way these Disclosures came to me and so in my account of them. But as I've actually experienced these Self-disclosures, many of them closely overlap in time, at their beginnings, and especially as they unfold further, and then flow together like tributaries of a river. In their origins and development, they often have to do with the various things in my environment that I was exposed to at any given time. I think of them as enriching, complexifying, mutually reinforcing, and eventually merging into a mostly coherent God-image or ongoing God-experience.

In addition to those Angels I talked about in chapter 2, I want to mention these strange entities again a little bit later on—this time, in the present context of God-images, or Divine Self-disclosures, which I believe they are, but at a lower level.

I know I've already told the following story (not about Angels), but I want to represent it again here in the account of the unfolding of a lifetime of what I believe are Divine Self-disclosures to me. After my birth night "memory," the first spiritual experiences I remember were seeing the moon from the windows of our upstairs apartment—serene mystery, soft sheening, the feeling of expansiveness, the eerie, the uncanny, the slightly threatening, the calming, the exalting. Behind all this was the vague sense of a Wondrous Presence. These were experiences I sought out every night. After the first, whenever that was, I wanted to feel it again and again. These moon moments were my first series of experiences of what I later came to see as the Divine's Self-disclosures to me—my first personal experiences of both the *fact* of Its Presence in my otherwise very small two-year-old world and It's Care and Concern, Its Love, for me, Its simultaneously Unsettling and Ecstatic Intimacy with me.

It's possible that I was already going to church by two years old. I remember a handkerchief with a lamb and ivy on it that was for church and that I had at a very young age. I was certainly going to church before five. As I was growing up, I went to two Presbyterian churches until I bailed out of confirmation class at eleven or twelve. As far back as I can recall, I had trouble with Jesus as God, even more with the Trinity. The three-in-one system seemed contrived to me, and I had the feeling (in the exclusivistic one-way-to-God-through-Jesus doctrine) that Jesus stood *between* God and me. That was off-putting, as I felt that I already had a direct, even intimate relationship with God, and Jesus was in the way . . . a step *above* me, and God's *especially beloved* Son. I also found Jesus and his Father a strange mixture of Severe—Severe enough to send people to Hell forever—and Loving in a kind of pure way that I couldn't match. Anyway, how do you get these two Elements of their Personalities together, I wondered. The Loving Part was fantastic, if out of reach for me, certainly in terms of loving other people. As applied to human relationships, mine, for example, "Turn the other cheek," "Love your enemy," and so on were impossible. And at the Divine level inconsistent, to say the least, with Eternal Damnation.

The God I had sensed *in* Nature, and/or as *coming through* Nature (and toning or coloring It in the process) in my early moon experiences expanded to include the forests, fields, meadows, streams, and rivers, the animals and plants, and the sky—day and night—just outside my door. Eventually, the enthralling Presence of Nature included the oceans, deserts, and jungles, all the creatures therein, even the ruins of the temples and cities of ancient peoples who still lived intimately with Nature and that I frequently visited around the world, especially in Mexico. The Maya became—and still are—an especially sacred aspect of my own soul, my own self-knowing and my creative self-expression. Driving down a strip of road in the Yucatan, the rainforest rising thick and green, towering above the road—a combination of Wonder, Joy, and the vaguely

Threatening Presence of a God far more ancient than *Australopithecus* and apparently not even remotely interested in human beings, their cultures or beliefs—is a thrill that goes through me, reaches unconscious depths of my psyche, and reverberates there. Or seeing the crumbling roof combs of Maya temples rising above the forest at night in thunder and lightning storms. Mysterious! Exhilarating!

That God is not tame, knowable in Its Essence, or in anybody's back pocket. The God Who Self-disclosed to me *as* or through Nature *way* outside church was … is … Wild with Mystery, Ecstatic, free of all human attempts to box Him/Her/It in with doctrines and orthodoxies and *loves me as a part of Nature*, somehow *as* and *beyond*, or *transiting*, Nature's Indifference while *not other than* Nature, in some not fully thinkable or communicable way. What It is I don't know—the so-called Divine Economy of It. But, seemingly, there is no Son of God required!

At the same time, the more human-centered and Humane Love of the Christian God-image and Its revelation in the teachings and life of Jesus calls upon human beings to go definitively *beyond* Nature, including their own; that form of Love eventually lodged within the deepest deep of my psyche. It became my ideal, for myself and others, and the standard by which I have come to judge all other Divine Self-disclosures and all other ideologies and worldviews. Along with this, and with more life experience, I began to feel the basic pattern of the Christian *mythos*—Love is offered; Love is rejected; Love is triumphant—as the truest and most central insight into Reality ever experienced.

Years later, in seminary at Meadeville-Lombard Theological School, I read J. R. R. Tolkien's essay "On Fairy-Stories," in which he claims that the Christian "Fairy-Story" is what every human deeply yearns for to be true,[1] and I realized with a bit of a shock that that's what I also believed. At least in the archetypal form in which Tolkien presents it. I *knew* it to be true for me. It had been at the core of all of my personal experiences of Divine Self-disclosures throughout my life—*to* me and *as* my life. It made conscious for me the feeling that the Wild Mystery that had been disclosed to me in, or through, Nature *was* that Love and that, while It was *in* Nature, It was not *from* Nature per se but came from outside It. Of course, this contrast between the Dark or Indifferent side of Nature and the God of Love revealed and lived by Jesus (and others) raises emotional and conceptual problems that are not as prominent for belief systems in which Love is not (at least supposedly) the highest value. So, it's back to the persistent issue of Evil.

So far as Jesus is concerned, with Tolkien and others' archetypal framing of the Christian story internalized as another Divine Self-disclosure to me, I became free to love Jesus as just about what a God Who is a Loving Person would be like in human guise. And I could really begin to see human beings as those manifestations of the Divine uniquely (though not entirely exclusively) gifted for at least the emotional glimpsing of Divine Love—and, consequently, of Infinite Worth.

But to go back to an earlier stage of my Divine Self-disclosures. When I was four or five, I knew a strange and gifted man and his large family who lived on the other side of our magical alley (which was at the back of our back yard, and ran the length of the block) in a big house on higher ground, beyond a mysterious white retaining wall. His name was Don Wooten, and he and friends would make wonderful things in his garage. They turned out to be costumes, props, and masks for a series of ancient Greek plays. The name of their theater group was Genesius Guild.

The plays were performed in a beautiful, oak-tree-shaded park called Lincoln Park, which was on a series of hills overlooking the Mississippi River. At the center of the park was an old Greco-Roman-style bathhouse with a wading pool and, on the opposite side, just before the precipitous slide to the river valley below, a semicircle of Doric-style columns with a grassy area in front of them, originally for sunbathers to lounge and flirt.

One summer afternoon Don asked me and my parents if I would play the part of the boy who guided the blind seer Tiresias to his confrontation with Creon in Sophocles' play *Antigone*. It was the first play of the Guild in what was to become an established community theater in the Midwest, performing Greek drama, Shakespeare plays, and opera right up to the present.

I fumbled my part a bit, but I remember the powerful sense of the Holy I felt that night, of Zeus, which in ancient Greek was not primarily a name for *a* God but meant simply and directly "God." I felt His Presence as the Terrifying Force of Divinely Mandated Justice in the service of Humaneness—the heroic ethical stand of Antigone, vindicated by Zeus even in her unjust death, the judgment from Olympus on the cruel and autocratic Creon . . . Zeus's deep, perhaps Infinite Caring about human beings and their actions toward one another. I felt the Presence of that in the twilit park, the smell of the pitch-burning torches, the ancient Greek architecture of the bathhouse and colonnade, the dark tops of the huge oak trees (Zeus's vegetal hierophanies) against a summer night sky. Terrible Beauty; Beautiful Terror! All in the service of holding human beings accountable for their sins against one another and, ultimately, their sins against the God of Love.

How could I not accept this Supranatural Reality, enacted in the play, as an authentic Divine Self-disclosure? That magical and terrible night of the first Genesius Guild performance of *Antigone*, Zeus became an indelible part of my God-image, and with this, the realization that the Divine has *always* been Self-disclosing to *all* peoples, not just Jews and Christians and, by extension, Muslims—this, as cultural and personal conditions have allowed.

In the years that followed, I frequently attended Genesius Guild plays and became a theater major and an avid student of ancient Greek mythology, philosophy, culture, and history, eventually earning a master of religious studies (with an emphasis on religion and literature) and a master of divinity (emphasis on religion and depth psychology). Many of my interests, passions, and studies flowed to some great extent from that wonderful and terror-inducing first Greek play performed in Lincoln Park.

With *Antigone* (and other Greek dramas) came more Divine Self-disclosures in the forms of ancient Greek Gods and Goddesses—all ultimately understandable to me as Expressions of God. First, Dionysus, the God of Theater itself and of Ecstasy. That Ecstasy is originally Dark, as in "divine madness," but madness as the agent of insight into the depths of Psyche . . . uprushes of genius, of F. W. H. Myers's sub- and supernormal consciousnesses, the evoking of psi phenomena. As we've seen in the mysteries of Eleusis, Dionysus is also Hades, the Abductor of Persephone. That makes Him the God of savage but also of a profound Sexuality that, as we've seen, leads to Eternal Life.

A second Divine Self-disclosure from the Greek spiritual tradition that has been important to me is Hermes, the Wayfinder. In Greek mythology, He's certainly the Wayfinder as Conductor of the soul from earthly life, through death, to Eternal life. For the Hermeticists of the Ptolemaic and early Roman periods in Egypt, He was the Conductor of the soul Who led it to ever-greater spiritual growth and through that to a Blissful Eternal Life in Elysium. For me, invoking Hermes is a finite-sized, yet still mysterious (shading off into the Infinite) channel for accessing the Divine in an "at my side" form. I have felt Divine Guidance throughout my life, from small to major decisions and undertakings, or just flow. For me, prayers, both of gratitude and of requests, have been important in my trying to mesh with Divine Purposes for the course of my life. When I'm asking for Guidance specifically, I speak to God or to God-as-manifested-as-Hermes.

And then there's Athena. She is the most intimate to me—most trusted to always be there for me, most beloved to me of the named ancient Greek Divine Self-disclosures. I say *named* because God Himself/Herself/Itself is neither a name nor nameable. God, as I'm trying to show, is for me Someone Who is a composite of many and various Divine Self-disclosures as I've been able to take them in. Athena, the gray-eyed Warrior of civilization, wisdom, the arts, humanities, sciences, and the adventure of seeking ever more knowledge—near and far, inside and outside—and so, the Defender and Advancer, ultimately, of the Humane, is, in my experience of Her, my closest Divine Ally, Patroness, and Friend—again, of the named Aspects, or Expressions, of God.

Suited in ancient Greek armor—cuirass, helmet, and greaves, shield on one arm, spear in the other, Gorgon head on Her chest, and the Attic owl beside Her as her bird hierophany—She is still intensely Feminine, with doe's eyes and flowing hair. She is forever Virgin, so belongs to no one and thus freely protects all who strive in the causes She advances and defends. In the Greek myths, She was born directly from the Mind of God and so is intimately present in psyche/Psyche of whatever form and level of sophistication. In the *Odyssey*, She is always at Odysseus's side on his long journey home to Ithaca. In later interpretations of Homer, Ithaca is Heaven, our true Home.

There's another tributary to the river of what I believe to be Divine Self-disclosures to me—again, as I was, and am, able to internalize them. It must have started when I was in grade school. It was Sunday school at the First Presbyterian Church in Rock Island. Our teacher was the minister's wife. She focused on the so-called Old Testament, and fascinating to me, she created models of the legendary battlefields of Joshua's purported conquest of the Canaanites. She also dwelt on the story of Moses and how evil the Egyptian pharaoh had been—to a somewhat lesser extent, perhaps, the "idol-worshiping" Egyptian priests and people. At the time, I was actually more interested in these non-Christian stories about the ancient Hebrews, their sup-posed monotheism, and the (in my eyes) young Warrior God Jehovah, Whom I later learned should be called Yahweh, or something like that.

Although He was portrayed as an exceedingly Ferocious Deity, much like Zeus with His stern Justice and Athena's absolute devotion to the project of civilization, He was, I believed, fighting for the freedom of his people to worship Him and live lives devoted to Him. I admired Him for that. In addition, He was free of Trinitarian complexity, and there was no Jesus standing between me and Him. I later learned that He was the Champion of the poor and oppressed. He went straight to my heart with His ringing condemnations of corrupt authorities[2] and His subversive declarations about His expectations of human beings.[3]

As a middle-aged man, I studied His altered but still recognizable form as Allah in the Qur'an and the Hadith literature in Islam. Then I studied the schools of jurisprudence in Sunni Islam, the theological schools—the Mutazilites, Asherites, and others—and the philosophers. And then I became deeply engaged in the study of Islamic mystical theology, Sufism . . . and especially the theology of Ibn 'Arabi.

I remember my introduction to Ibn 'Arabi through William Chittick's *The Self-Disclosure of God: Principles of Ibn al-'Arabi's Cosmology* (1998). I was with my wife and (at that time) young daughter in the fantastically and wonderfully claustrophobic bowels of the Co-op Bookstore in the basement of Chicago Theological Seminary. The store no longer exists in the form that it did then. The claustrophobia was thrilling and intensely cozy at the same time—very narrow aisles lined from floor to ceiling with what felt like miles of largely academic books. Really, a paradise for me then. I had just rounded a tight corner, and there on the top shelf of a narrow bookcase unit in the Islam section was Chittick's book. The spine glowed white, and I had the immediate feeling of the Presence of what it announced—the Self-disclosure of God!

I grabbed it and began a years-long adventure, mostly into Ibn 'Arabi's voluminous writings (and the equally voluminous commentaries—medieval and modern—on them), but also into the works of other Islamic Sufis, including what the history of religions scholar Toshihiko

Izutsu (1914–1993) in his *Creation and the Timeless Order of Things: Essays in Islamic Mystical Philosophy* (1994) calls "Iranian existentialism." All of it, for me, an extraordinary series of, as Chittick's book promised, Divine Self-disclosures. Allah came alive for me, not only as the threatening Warrior and strict Upholder of Justice, but also as the Great Mystery That surrounds us while inside us at our Cores and That beckons us deeper and deeper and further and further out ... so far as anybody can tell, Forever.

Another strand of Divine Self-disclosures became visible to me by sixth or seventh grade. It first came into my consciousness as a love of ancient Egyptian art and architecture. Soon, though, after several years of my Sunday school's bad press on Egypt, I became curious to see if there was another side to the story. So, I went to the Rock Island Public Library. James Henry Breasted's (1865–1935) *A History of Egypt* (1905) hit me like a thunderbolt. Not only did the Egyptians actually have a history, known in significant detail, but they also had a sophisticated mythology and theology and a monotheism, complete with absolutely beautiful hymns to the Deity that depicted Him (or occasionally Her) as Mysterious beyond human comprehension and, at the same time, Lovingly Concerned for the poor, disadvantaged, and all those in distress. Accompanying the hymns were extraordinarily high moral-ethical standards displayed in proverbs, stories, and the so-called negative confessions in the Book of the Dead.

I'll never forget the first time I read the Nineteenth Dynasty hymns to Amun, the *Great Hymn to Aten*, the *Instruction of Amenemope*, the Egyptian Book of the Dead. It was a revelation to me: these biblically vilified pagans were actually a major source for essentially all of Western civilization, including most centrally the teachings of Judaism, Christianity, and Islam—of ethical monotheism, the Judgment of the dead, their assignment to Heaven or Hell depending upon the Humaneness (or not) of the earthly lives they'd lived, and much more.

I've continued to study ancient Egyptian culture, history, literature, and religion my whole life.

The Divine Self-disclosure called Amun and His pairing with Re, as in Amun-Re, have become an integral part of my experience of God—merged with all the others. Theologically, I appreciate the at least latent mysticism in the Amun-Re conjunction—Amun, the Hidden One, that Aspect of the Divine that can never be directly known; and Re, the Light, the Visible One, He Who gives Light and Life to all things, Who is so obvious He is taken for granted but if looked for can certainly be found and known.

Put all of the God-images I've been sharing here together, along with some other Divine Self-disclosures of lesser definition and intensity for me, with the God of Love at the Center, absorbing and integrating them all, and that's pretty close to my lifelong experience of living within the Presence of God.

Okay, there *is* one more I want to mention (I've already referred to Him)—"The Laughing God of Our Summer Backyard." He's All of the God-images I've sketched above, Self-finitized by my awareness of the Presence of the Divine in and, in a way *as*, our daily lives as a family as they were on summer afternoons that I dreamed would go on forever. I've already described our backyard and the play, laughter, and Joy we've had in it. It has been there, too, that I crafted many of my large-scale sculptures. I can still picture the Laughing God overseeing, entering into, epitomizing, emerging from, and being Present *in the form of* our lives there, as well as indwelling all the creatures—both animate and inanimate—that have lived, passed through, been born and died there, only to be lifted up on wings of Light to an even more Joyful Place—a Place that I believe replicates our yard but in a way that completes and fulfills it. There laughter—*our* laughter together as a family—is Forever.

As I mentioned earlier, I also want to represent what I call Angels or Minor Deities—spirit guides, helpers, consolers, all of whom I have experienced as protectors. They show up more or less regularly in my dreams, and sometimes I feel them as Presences when I'm awake. They come in a fascinating variety of forms. I'd like to show just two more of them to you here, and do that as they appear in two of the lyric illuminations in my *At the Thresholds of Elysium* (2016).[4] The first is called "Hallowed, Hushed Yearning." It goes like this:

> *Who is that young summer woman with the sky-blue*
> *   eyes,*
> *puffs and concentric creases around them, as if she*
> *were aged,*
> *yet with the face of a girl, cream-colored skin,*
> *blonde as sun*
> *on bleached corn tassel?*
> *Who is that girl at our screen door, wanting to take*
> *my hand—*
> *not smiling exactly, yet certainly not unpleasant,*
> *who wishes to walk with me across the fields to the*
> *"University,"*
> *so that I can further my "education"?*
> *And who is that in the shadowed back bedroom,*
> *representing*
> *herself as my dead grandmother, lying on her side,*
> *greyish,*
> *like a half-overturned*
> *baleen whale, offering me her money, blessing me*
> *on my way?*
> *I would say both are angels,*
> *or God Herself, appearing to me as these in this*
> *dream. What*
> *I feel is such joy and gratitude, a great weight*
> *lifted, and a hallowed, hushed yearning.*

The second, "Angelic Messenger":

Should some angelic messenger, claws of bronze,
black-bristled,
with iron arms like Assyrian warriors carved in
relief,
bash the hinges from my bedroom door, seize me
at some moment
of extremity, collapsed in tears and grief,
or drag me from beneath those buckthorn
hedgerows Jesus preached,
and haul me to his Master's wedding feast,
I would kick and scream, shake whatever fist I'd
left at his feathered
face and beak, challenge him with my perplexity,
charge him as a thief. He would no doubt laugh, or
roar, stripe me
with his tongue of fire, shot out between his teeth.
Noting my condition then, he might sit,
physicianish,
at my bedside, bury claws into the mattress
springs, glossolalic, begin to sing
some Word deeper than my bewilderment and
seething,
loosening those losses which have embittered me.
Then he'd raise great rainbow wings.
I would shout, "I've turned my back on God and
all His crowd of griffins,
snakes, and sphinxes! I don't believe in anything!
Nor will I yield to you or go with you to your
euphemistic 'wedding feast'!"
His beard would quake, azure as the sea. He would

uproot me
then, from bed or hedgerow, and pronounce my
doom. He'd thunder,
"All are hoped, even those that never do!" And
he'd reveal
sliding films of skin across the eyes—saurian, I
would guess, nictitating
membranes, like those of serpents or of basilisks.
And I would go with him.

And I'll leave it at that.

Reflections on Some Puzzles in Divine Self-Disclosures

Oneness and Multiplicity—Again!

To speak temporally, I can accept that before and at the moment of the Big Bang everything that's in our continually expanding universe (again, temporally) was present *as*, in some incomprehensible way, the supposed infinitesimal point that exploded. As we've seen, cosmologists and physicists continue to search for a way to make everything one thing before the explosion. Grand Unified theorists try to make the four foundational forces one force, and the Theory of Everything enthusiasts are even more ambitious, seeking to find the four foundational forces *plus* everything else as a singular something-or-other (or nothing-or-other).

A couple of definitions. When I say "thing" or "something-or-other" or "nothing-or-other" in this context, I mean *all* fields—force fields but also the Higgs field, proton fields, electron fields, and whatever else requires a field. Perhaps Max Tegmark is right and behind it all is a massive "mathematical object" that only an Infinitely Gifted Mathematician could understand . . . or create. But in that case, the mathematical object would itself be infinite, or Infinite, although the Big Bang people are talking about an *infinitesimal* "object"—the point. Of course, infinite and infinitesimal are the same thing—*in*-finite, at which point there is nothing either big or small. So, Tegmark's mathematical object is in-finite . . . neither big nor small, nor even an object, because all objects have size. Or do they?

The other definition I want to put forward here is of "thing" more generally. When I say thing in a wider context I mean, as well as fields and forces, particles, planets, moons, stars, galaxies, time, space, every grain of sand, every fungus, plant, animal, bacterium, virus, every manufactured item, every thought, feeling, event, action, motivation, every molecule, every word, spoken or written, every note of music, every atom, every person, incarnate or not—and on and on.

If all these things (and much much more) were once one thingless Thing, then at least three major problems arise: (1) How did all of that unfathomable multiplicity develop from single, simple oneness? (2) Wasn't it all present *in/as* the oneness in some way? (3) If it was all present, even only *en potencia*, wasn't it nonetheless "there" (which, from our standpoint, was actually nowhere)? That is, if something is *potential*, doesn't it already exist in some way? Isn't it already really *actual*, but not yet (or maybe ever) here and now? We've looked at these questions before, but it's worth repeating the exercise from a little different perspective.

From my perspective, nontheistic philosophical and scientific systems of thought might be able to contrive some mathematical-physics way to get a number of later things out of earlier things—temperature gradients for one thing (closely related to the interactions of energy and entropy), colliding fields, and so on. And they *do* do this with some success. Iteration and iteration with mutation or novelty. But they don't seem to be able to account for the most basic things like: How do you get something *at all* and in the first place from nothing? And how, philosophically, do you actually get the one to become two, much less the multiplicity?

Fichte and Hegel (who was *not* an atheist) could hypothetically—really by fiat—finagle two out of one, in Hegel's case, three.[5] But the *multiplicity*—furthermore, *these specific exemplars* of the multiplicity? How *this* particular ant, *this* amoeba, *this* species, *this* asteroid? Not a peep on specifics, just hypothetical generalities.

Looked at from a theistic point of view, the One becomes the Many by fiat all right, but not that of philosophers. Rather, everything that is—in potential *and* in what we call actuality—is what it is, even through the agency of evolutionary processes (like thermal gradients), by *Divine* Fiat. After some very long meditations on the problem of getting the Multiplicity from the One in many of his writings, Ibn 'Arabi simply concluded that the One and the Many are the Same Thing and, furthermore, that there's nothing further to say about the matter.[6]

I, somewhat reluctantly, agree. No matter how we turn the problem around and look at it from different angles, we cannot reach a solution. As we've seen, this is because, in Nicholas of Cusa's terms,[7] we run into the unscalable Wall of Paradise that permanently separates finite creatures from the Infinite Person—except when that Infinite Person, through His/Her/Its infinite Power, Self-finitizes for us. In the case of the mystics, they may be able to see better than the rest of us *that* Multiplicity happens from absolute Oneness. But even they can't see *how* it happens.

So, I'm going to leave this problem at the foot of Cusa's Wall and with the final words of Ibn 'Arabi on this topic.

Personal or Impersonal Self-disclosures of Ultimate Reality

In the context of thinking about a God Who is a Person and Personal with us, I occasionally ask my classes, "What has Infinity done for me lately?" Of course, I'm joking. But not completely because I mean Infinity as the *im*personal notion of a thingless Thing—like an Infinite Mathematical Object. If Benoit Mandelbrot is correct, I may be *made of* Infinity.[8] But Infinity per se did not make me. Some-*one*, not some-*thing*, did.

Emerging from this Impersonal notion of Ultimate Reality as Infinity is the issue of so-called pure consciousness,[9] purged of personhood, or Personhood, but still, from my perspective, implying a Person*ish* State of Being and Consciousness. I want to think about this first, and then come back to the question of the Absolutely Impersonal versus an Absolutely Personal Foundation for Reality because the "pure consciousness" thing can be dispensed with rather easily—in part because, in my view, it's really a disguise for the Impersonal and can readily be revealed as such and because I want to tackle the *truly* Impersonal (which is more honest) afterward and offer a reasonable way for how to think about It *within* a theistic context.

A reminder: as always, my interpretations of Reality flow from my personal (and, of course, subjective) experiences of It.

Pure consciousness is much talked about, mostly in Eastern spiritual traditions. For me, all that talk is a signal that it isn't what it's purported to be. Up front, I'm not sure there is such a thing, at least not as an End-State of Ultimate Reality. I do believe some people believe there is, that it is such an End-State and that they've experienced It. But for all the business of emptying the mind—an enormous amount of work here, especially in terms of what Western psychology would call *repression* or, more actively and intentionally, *suppression* (specifically of the ego and company)—the effort is, I think, in vain. If not ingenuous, it is, in my view, delusional. Here's why.

If *pure consciousness* means, as it seems to, both thinking about nothing and no one doing it, what kind of sense, even mystical, does that make? You're still there, or some higher form or version of you— call it Buddha Consciousness, Atman, the Self, or whatever you want— *is* you or *some*body. And *whoever* it is is imagining not thinking and not being there. Furthermore, if you *weren't* there in *some* form, you couldn't talk about it later. So, again, some form of you was there, and you were thinking about not being there and . . . well, perhaps thinking about not being there, thinking about nothing. If you don't like the

word "thinking," then substitute "experiencing." But if you were thinking "nothing," you were, as philosophers call it, reifying it—making it a
something, however contentless. Sometimes it is argued that those who
talk about No-thingness are actually talking about All-thingness, as
in "No-thingness and All-thingness are the same thing." I agree. But,
I think, not only has no one ever thought No-thing, no one has ever
thought Every-thing-all-at-once. I believe we can touch or intuit That,
but that we're always stopped from the full experience-less experience at
the foot of Cusa's Wall.

The same goes, I think, for Islamic *fana*—the occultation of the
ego in the Presence of the One.[10] As I've mentioned, losing track of the
ego whenever we're engaged in a concentrated activity doesn't mean
the ego has gone away or ceased to exist. It's still watching on the side-
lines. If it weren't, there could be no *baqa*—no recovery—and certainly
not a recovery in which we could talk about our consciousness of having been occulted.[11] In most cases of our losing track of the ego, we're
actually *thinking* about *something else*—like sculpting, composing,
making love, doing work of some kind, and so on. We aren't thinking
about nothing. But, of course, there is the case of dreamless sleep. In
dreamless sleep, however, it really seems as though there isn't anyone
thinking nothing. As far as anybody can tell, there is no thinking at
all because there's nobody doing it. Except that we can talk about that
state, which, again, suggests that *somebody* is experiencing not experiencing. In ancient Egyptian thought, dreamless sleep was a return to
Nun—the precreational nonstate of utter blankness. Nun was a source
of renewal, a rest in No-thingness. Somehow the psyche was born from
That, as was the whole of the individualized and animated world. (But,
notice again, we're still thinking of "no thinking," "no-one," "Nun," and
"No-thingness, "precreation nonstate," and so forth . . . which means
that someone is still present, thinking about them, as *we* are right now.)

But, to speak conventionally, since precreation cannot be experienced (supposedly) and since we return to that stateless condition every

night and perhaps at death, it mystifies me why anyone would make the rather prodigious effort to go there during the day and before death. Along with that, why would you *want* to go to the *lowest* state (again, wording our discussion conventionally), and why would you regard that as the *highest*? And, for me, there's the question of trying to undo *personhood*, which is what all of this represents. Isn't there an implied *devaluation of individual persons* here? I understand life weariness, and I understand physical and psychological pain so great that we might actually *want* to go to No-thingness (or nothingness). I've been there (not No-thingness but wanting to be erased). But such a state of consciousness seems to me really to be suicidal. I say this without judgment. But I think we should be honest about the suicidal desire in the whole "no-mind" spiritual traditions.[12] And there are more questions for me in all of this. For example, in my understanding, there are certain forms of Buddhism in which this world and the persons in it are thought of as errors. I've sometimes asked Buddhists such questions as: "Whose errors?" "How could error (whoever made it) arise from error-less-ness (whatever that is)?" "Does that mean there really is Someone (or Something) behind the supposedly Person-less pure thought that could have engineered this . . . and been in error while doing it?" I have yet to get anything like a straight answer.

Still, many people undoubtedly do experience Unitive States of Consciousness, even if these are not "pure thought." What are they encountering?

Generally, these Unitive States come in two major flavors— Impersonal, or Transpersonal, and Personal. We can't go into all the variations of such described experiences and their even more varied interpretations. I'll just say that, from my point of view (born of my own Unitive Experiences), the so-called Transpersonal[13] view of Ultimate Reality (as I just mentioned) is a euphemism for the more honest notion that Ultimate Reality is, in fact, not personal (trans or otherwise) at all, but, instead, *Im*personal. Period. As I've already said, it seems extremely odd to me that, in this view, persons are of *less* value, or even validity, than that which, by being nonpersonal (like minerals, atoms, interstellar dust and gas), is clearly *sub*personal.

Again, what must one think of one's self and other persons to value interstellar dust or abstractions—such as the laws of nature, infinite mathematical objects, whatever—above personhood, especially human personhood (but really any)? I find it incredible frankly to be awed by distant galaxies and certain types of rocks on the moon and not by a baby's smile or the mature Love of couples who've been together a lifetime or any other of the many manifestations of personhood at its best. I mean, the image of samadhi or nirvana as the full moon over still water is certainly a beautiful picture (where, by the way, there aren't supposed to *be* any . . . pictures). But how does it even *begin* to compare with the experience of old and deep friendships?

I suppose it's obvious at this point (if it hasn't been clear earlier) that I favor the Experience of Ultimate Reality as a Person, no matter Its Infinite and Eternal dimensions . . . or maybe *because* of them.

So, what is the Infinite and Eternal Impersonal that some mystics do encounter . . . that I perhaps encountered in my upstairs bathroom mirror in my own eyes and in my dream of being lost in space? I think one of the Things It is (we'll see another possibility shortly) is that It is first Background—the *necessary* Background—of creation by the Infinite and Eternal Person, a clearing of the way for the manifestation of the at least ostensibly finite multitude of beings.

I got that idea from the sixteenth-century Kabbalist Isaac of Luria, whose life and thoughts are presented by Gershom Scholem in *Major Trends in Jewish Mysticism* (1946).[14] It's Isaac's doctrine of *tsimtsum* that opened my eyes. Let me elaborate. Like many philosophers and theologians before him, Luria asked the question: If God is Infinite, how can there be room for anything else? A related question: If God is Infinite, how can He create anything (and everything) from nothing, since there is no nothing; there is only God? In Isaac of Luria's tsimtsum, God "withdraws"—Self-finitizes (without losing any of His Infiniteness).[15] He evacuates a Part of Himself in order to make room for His return to it in Self-manifestation—that is, He creates a finite world that will be considered by God "as if" it were *other* than Him. Of course, this is mythological language that Isaac is using, much as Plato did when he intuited a truth that he couldn't adequately put into discursive language, and then concluded with, "Well, it's *something* like that!" Or, a likely story.

I think *this* is one candidate for the Void that mystics bent on self-extinguishment and the no one and nothingness thing encounter. In my theistic view, God, the Infinite Person, dwells on the other side of this first (speaking temporally) of His creations. As God withdrew, He split into the Unknowable Aspect, Which is behind Nicholas of Cusa's Wall, and His Knowable Self as the form of Self-disclosure as the world, and all the things of the world, all dimensions of time and space, at the Big Bang, but still outside all that. He "holds Himself back"[16]—like the cubic centimeter idea in physics and how it slides out of the way of forces, fields, and matter. If God did not do this, nothing would or could exist. Behind the veil that protects us from the incalculable mass-energy on the other side, described by David Bohm, as we've seen, there is the Unknowable God, perhaps dwelling at the Center of Bohm's implicate order. Across and into the Void, God Projects what He is thinking and feeling—the things of the world. And through evolutionary processes, He is continually—every picosecond—Withdrawing and then Surging across and into the space He has Vacated. This is the Self-finitizing that God does to Create a world so that He can be interrelated with Himself-as-us, yet with a gap between Himself and us. The gap is the necessary one that separates the last number from Infinity and makes finite creatures, as well as interrelationship, possible. At the same time, being Infinite, God recognizes *no* gap and is immediately and intimately *beside* us and *within* us.

Luria apparently taught that, because they *are* God (at least at their Cores), all things have an indissoluble oneness (as God is One) that, once God has manifested them, protects them from vaporizing into the No-thingness/All-thingness represented by the universe (and any others), including any other dimensions beyond.[17] With God's tsimtsum, *negation* becomes expressed within God and, on the level of sentient creatures, becomes *the negation of God*, on the one hand, and, on the other (eventually), *the negation of others*. These negations are, in my view, a central source of Evil[18] . . . the negation of the Divine Person and the (necessary) limit-setting that actually allows the appearance of discrete finite things. The finite things then unconsciously, semiconsciously, or consciously identify themselves with the Infinite and Eternal Person of God, an identification that, if not handled in a clued-in or spiritual way, produces malignant narcissism (as I've already talked about).

And that's one way I reconcile the two major versions of the Experience of Ultimate Reality. Except that, from my perspective, the Impersonal Experience is *penultimate* (next to ultimate), not Ultimate. The *Person* is the true, the One-and-only Ultimate.

Divine Self-Disclosure and the Fact of Evil

It goes without saying that there are very many Facets to Divine Self-disclosures and so many intellectual puzzles. Here, I want to focus on the fact of the existence of significant Evil as a part of the Beautiful Terror of the manifest world as we know it, and how several spiritual traditions have attempted to explain it (or explain it away) in the context of an essentially Good God. Note: traditions in which there is no God, or in which the Divine as encountered appears to be both Good and Evil, the problem of Evil is sidestepped (sometimes completely) in the former case or turned into a "just so" story in the second.

We've already looked at the problem of Evil a couple of times. I want to do that again—this time as it relates to the hypothetical Structures and Dynamics of a (for the most part) Good God, and whether that God is assumed (more or less unconsciously) as a Background Something-or-Other or explicitly experienced as a Person. I'm just going to sketch a few of these systems as they've tried to solve the issue of what historians of religions and theologians call theodicy, the study of how Evil can possibly be squared with an Absolutely Good Divine Source. This all may seem a little like trying to count the number of angels dancing on a pinhead. But our God-images, and how we imagine Their dealing with Evil, have profound and far-reaching consequences for how we actually live our lives—with what values—and so how we treat one another. I've chosen these particular spiritual systems because they are representative of strongly influential currents in human thought about Evil and a Good God.

Plotinus

We briefly looked at Plotinus's system earlier. But I want to take a deeper dive at this point as it relates to the problem of getting Evil from Absolute Goodness. Plotinus's system for mapping Divine Self-disclosures and trying to account for Evil uses the sun and its radiation as its main model (*Enn.* V.1.6, V.3.13*).[19] Importantly, the One, or the Good, is supposedly *Absolutely* One, although whether and how It is Infinite or not is a matter of debate (*Enn.* V.2.1, V.3.15),[20] and as such, It, presumably like the sun, is completely Unconscious. It generates Being, Aliveness, and Awareness as an unintentional consequence of Its overflowing Fullness (*Enn.* V.3.12, V.4.2).[21] This continuous outflow surges into an unspecified space that is apparently outside It. There are three stages of Its radiated effulgence—four, if you count Matter.[22] Actually, five, if you unorthodoxly count supposed No-thingness, as I do, as a Thing in certain spiritual systems other than Plotinus's . . . Which It is and isn't.

---

*This parenthetical citation and others that follow refer to the specific volume, book, section, and lines in Plotinus's *Enneads*. In the endnotes are page numbers to the modern translation referred to (full publication details provided in the bibliography).

The first is what Plotinus calls the "Intelligible Realm"[23] (equivalent perhaps to the sun's corona). This stage abruptly becomes Conscious by looking back at the One (*Enn.* V.2.1),[24] Which It Itself no longer is. As It becomes Conscious, It suddenly and all at once (*Enn.* V.3.7)[25] generates the Mental archetypes of all things, and yet, since It is fresh from the One, It is still a kind of One but also the Multiplicity that It has (somehow) thought of at the momentless Moment It realized It was other than the Absolute One.[26] In It, all things are archetypally themselves (little onenesses)—proton fields, butterflies, atoms, molecules, and so forth . . . and yet still One. At the same time that the Intelligible is looking at the One, It is also anticipating the next stage, the simultaneous Unity (not Oneness) of the soon-to-be multiplicity of material things within the Soul, or Psyche, of Nature, which we might equate with the sun's atmosphere (*Enn.* V.37, V.3.10–12).[27] This second stage—Nature—looks back at the Intelligible and so produces the unity and order that we will soon see in Nature. It looks out or down at Matter and, using That, creates a world of concretized things. These are what we usually think of as Nature. Concretized or individualized Nature is a mixture of what we would call the spiritual and material.[28]

Scholars of Plotinus are divided about whether to think of Matter as the final stage of the One's radiation or as the alien space into which the One radiates (*Enn.* II.4.1.2).[29] In any case, Plotinus views Matter (somewhat ambiguously) as the Source of Evil (*Enn.* I.8.3)[30]—that is, the Absolute Goodness and Being of the One's Life is finally spent, dispersed, and lost,[31] just as the farther we get from the sun, the dimmer its light and the less its warmth. Beginning with the Soul of Nature—although anticipated by the downward-looking Aspect of the Intelligible—Eternal Being ceases, and time, or Becoming, begins (*Enn.* III.7).[32] For Plotinus, time is the medium that the Soul of Nature (or the World Soul) uses in this process—to *Become*, rather than *Be*, or to evolve (as we would now say it) from one material form to another.

In Plotinus's system, Nature's Becoming is a hurried, misguided, and desperate attempt to recapture the Oneness of the One, Which Nature dimly remembers, by manifesting as fast as It can and, carelessly, as many things as possible—discursively or one-thing-after-another (*Enn.* II.4.3, V.1.1).[33] This is the only way Nature, Which is bound by time, can try to regain that Fullness from Which It fell, or had the misfortune to be radiated from, and return to the "sun." All the horrors of what I've called the feeding machine that is Nature are due to this frantic effort to reproduce the One within Nature's own environment—space and time. The malignant narcissism I've talked about as associated with Evil is the product of this Uncaring and Relentless but doomed effort. Why doomed? Because the generation of things can never *be* the absolutely thing-less One, in Which is not only No-thing but also no space and no time.

There are many problems with Plotinus's system, but we can see that it's trying to explain how we get from Pure Goodness (however Unconscious) to Evil (in terms of at least moral-ethical Evil, Which is at least Semiconscious) by means of a kind of "step-down transformer model."

Does this model work as a whole? My take: Pretty well for accounting for the layering of Reality. That's why I'm a Neoplatonist, although of the theistic variety, as I've mentioned. But, as a system for how exactly Evil is produced by Absolute Goodness, it does not.

Kabbalism

Next, the system of the Kabbalist Sephirot as the Self-disclosure of God . . . and the issue of Evil. This medieval Jewish mystical system is found primarily in a book called *Zohar*, written in the late thirteenth century CE. It describes the gradual unfolding of God into the space that would become the created world.[34] "Before" Its unfolding into a Self-finitized Form, God-as-God-is—the *Ein-Sof*—was Unknowable.[35] Mystical Judaism refers to the Ein-Sof—the Infinite and Eternal Aspect of God, or God in His Fullness or Essence—as "It." This

It-ness is still present when the unfolding gets underway. But by the end of it—when all ten of the Sephirot have become manifest, we might say, on this side of Nicholas of Cusa's Wall—God has become an "I," a Person.[36] The fullest account of this process that I've encountered is in Gershom Scholem's *Major Trends in Jewish Mysticism*, to which I've already referred. Once God has become a Person in the process of Self- and other-creation, the Ein-Sof Aspect is, in concert with Plotinus's One and the Ultimate Reality of Eastern religions, an Impersonal Whatever.

As the Sephirot (or Aspects of the Knowable God) unfold, three of them seem to go haywire. *Hokhmah*—the Divine Wisdom—does not completely deploy as It goes about the business of creating the world. The result is a flawed creation and a faulty representation of God's Wisdom.[37] According to Scholem, this partial deployment of Hokhmah is not explained.[38] Its companion Sephirah in the manifestation of the world is *Binah*—the Divine Intellect—Which is responsible specifically for the fashioning of all defined things.[39] Here, too, we find a failure to make these things "perfect."[40] (Here, I'm pushing Scholem a bit to be more explicit.) However, a third Sephirah—*Din*—the Severity of God—somehow tears Itself away from the rest of the Sephirot and, independent of the integration and modifying influences of the others, goes over into what modern psychology calls . . . again . . . malignant narcissism. Staying within the area of moral-ethical Evil, this rebellion of Din creates the conditions for human beings to become Its agents, and express malignant narcissism at their own level.[41] Some readers of the *Zohar* found this explanation for the Presence of Evil unacceptable and put forward the hypothesis that God intentionally broke Din off from the rest of His Self-disclosures, so that human beings could make free moral-ethical choices between Good and Evil.[42]

Whatever. Scholem concludes his discussion of the unfolding of the Sephirot and the expression of Evil by saying that somehow or other, Evil derives from God.[43]

So, does the Jewish version of a basically Neoplatonic system for accounting for the existence of Evil finally work? My take? Again, No.

Gnosticism

So, let's try Gnosticism. According to historians of religion, it's difficult to know exactly where or when Gnosticism as a movement began. From the surviving literature (as in the Nag Hammadi Library), it looks as though Gnostic thought was well established in Egypt, the Near East, and throughout much of the Mediterranean area by the late first century CE. It shows signs of a very complex mixture of some late Egyptian thought, a dark version of Platonic philosophy, disillusioned Judaism, a world-abhorring Christian strain, and Zoroastrian dualism (so-called).[44] There were a number of more or less independent sects. But all agreed that the world is a place pretty well dominated by Evil—natural and moral-ethical—and ruled over by a Dark Lord and/or Lords. It is an abortive creation, mis-made through ignorance and incompetence or outright malevolence.[45] At the same time, the Ultimate Deity—Who is not wholly an abstract One (as in Plotinus) but, at least in some Gnostic systems, a Person—is completely Light and Goodness.[46] How did this disjunction between the High God and Evil, both spiritual and physical, happen, and what, if anything, can be done about it?

The Gnostics (knowers) tried what Plotinus did and the Kabbalists would—the step-down transformer model—but in an excruciatingly complicated way, with all kinds of twists and turns by all kinds of Angels, Demons, Lesser Deities, and all their intricate plotlines.[47] In my view, to no avail. No matter how complicated you make the stages of "radiation" and the series of "transformers," and no matter how many mythic figures you interpose between Good Origins and Bad Results, you *never* solve the problem. You can never get Evil out of Goodness in this way. However, theology and mythology aside, there *is* hope for individuals, and that consists in their nearly total withdrawal from the world and gaining states of consciousness that get them within shooting distance of the Good God.[48] The psychospiritual work this involves, though, is prodigious, and there is still dependency on the world of Nature in the form of others who are still enmeshed in the natural world—making a living and, from those proceeds, *paying you* to escape! That is to say, you don't really escape fully from the world because others foot the bill to keep you alive; they make your living for you.

Zoroastrianism

As previewed in chapter 1, if you exclude Mithraism, Zoroastrianism seems to be the final product of native Iranian spiritual traditions, as documented by William Malandra in his *An Introduction to Ancient Iranian Religion* (1983). Depending upon how you account for Zarathustra's use of an antique form of an Iranian dialect in his surviving *Gathas*, or hymns, he can be dated to either around 1200 or 600 BCE.[49] As we've seen, Zoroastrianism appears to be a mixture of Old Iranian Religion and Zarathustra's teachings.[50] His teachings about God (as a Person), at least as they go through the filter of a resurgent Old Iranian Religion, are usually (mis)interpreted as dualistic—that is, as bi-theistic. As we saw in chapter 1, in this view of Zoroastrianism, there are two major though second-order Gods—Spenta Mainyu, the Good God, and Angra Mainyu, the Evil God. The mythology of how these two Gods came into conflict in the creation of the world as we know it varies, but that They are struggling with Each Other until the Final Battle at the end of the world, in which Good will triumph over Evil, is not in doubt. Indeed, it seems both intuitively and commonsensically obvious that at both the natural and the human level, Good and Evil are in a life-or-death war. That's the power of the Zoroastrian message. That message passed into Christianity as the struggle between Christ and Satan.

But there are problems with this simplistic approach. As I've mentioned previously, the main one is that the two Gods are Brothers, both Sons of the High God, Ahura Mazda, Who is all Light and

Goodness[51]—again, both natural and moral-ethical. We can maybe see how Spenta Mainyu could be a Self-finitized Version of His Father. But if that Father also Expresses Himself as the Evil Angra Mainyu, which He *must*, since Ahura Mazda was originally the *only* God, then we have the problem (again) in this system of how Evil could have arisen from Pure Goodness. As I just said, it seems clear to me that a similar issue presents itself in Christianity. It doesn't come up in the same way in Islam (although it does come up) because Islam includes what we judge to be Evil within the "Character" of Allah, but It's glossed over by assigning Evil to any number of the "Ninety-Nine Most Beautiful Names of God.[52] The gloss, of course, is the adjective *Beautiful*, which is used, in this case, for courtesy's sake.

It is often missed that Zoroastrianism is, in fact, a *monotheism*. I'm afraid that, from where I sit, the buck stops with God, however you try to evade or spin it. Zoroastrianism presents the origin of Evil as a "just so" story. Evil as well as Goodness already, inexplicably, exist. Choose Goodness. End of report.

Christianity

There are many ways to come at the problem of theodicy in Christianity. Here, I'm going to briefly discuss the particular focus of Carl Jung, who strongly suggested that what was for him the glaring moral-ethical failure of Christian Trinitarianism must be resolved by re-envisioning what theologians call the Economy of Salvation or the Divine Economy— the Structures and Dynamics intuited to be present within God. Jung noticed that the three Persons of the Trinity were all Good. Where was Evil? He was concerned that psychological-cum-spiritual health is not possible without inclusion and integration of the Shadow, in this case, God's. He maintained that this is obviously the case with human individuals, and he insisted that the God-image, in order to be made healthy, we might say, for human consumption, must include the Divine Shadow—*integrated* with the Divine Light (not split off as in

Zoroastrianism . . . or Christianity . . . or to some extent Judaism . . . or, in its own way, Islam).[53]

I think that's an okay idea . . . maybe. But exactly how this is to be done so as to make God a fit Subject of worship, not to say emulation, is something of a mystery to me. In Jung's book *Answer to Job* (1952), for example, I get the part that, in the Book of Job in the Bible, God overwhelms Job with what Jung rightly calls out as God's bullying Shadow. But with that moral-ethical failure of Yahweh-Elohim, Jung puts Job's innocence and ethical maturity *above* God's lack of integration.[54] Okay . . .

I don't see, for all of Jung's depth-psychological eloquence, that he provides an explanation for the *origin* of Evil in God's Goodness, Which is what we're mostly concerned with right now, nor a path for God to take to integrate the two. Besides that, it really does look to me as though Jung is actually envisioning the Divine as a supersized analysand-client—his, perhaps? Furthermore, even if God *could* complete a successful course of analysis, would the result be Someone I could worship, look to for aid and comfort, consolation, inspiration, and salvation from Nature, including my own?

Actually, not.

Eastern Religions

When it comes to the Eastern religions, which, I know, should really not be lumped together—for example, the many forms of Hinduism, the several of Buddhism, Taoism, and so on—it should nonetheless be said that, with the possible exception of Hinduism, none of them has a serious cosmogony or any explanation for the origin of Evil. Along with this, these spiritual systems lack an Ultimate Deity that is in any important way Personal, or a Person. It's true, of course, that Hinduism and (Mahayana) Buddhism are packed with Gods and Goddesses. But these are really concessions to popular demand, on the one hand, and, on the other, finally ephemeral and transient, as are we . . . and everything else. Brahman, the High God of Hinduism, is an image of the proposed *Im*personal nature of Ultimate Reality, and the Buddha, who was once a human being, is finally now an *Im*personal Consciousness.

Furthermore, as a number of scholars of Eastern religious systems have noted, the morality and ethics of these systems are not directed at concern for others but are self-interested—as in, like Western Gnosticism, "Get me out of here!" In Hinduism, the major God-images of Brahman, Brahma, Siva, and Vishnu are, as A. L. Basham (1914–1986) in his tome *The Wonder That Was India* (1954) says, morally and ethically neutral.[55] Continuing, he claims that what we experience as Evil in the world is pretty much completely sidestepped.[56] The morally and ethically neutral part, I think, "solves" Jung's problem with the Christian Trinity; the Shadow is definitely incorporated into Hindu notions of Ultimate Reality. But, I would ask, at what cost?

There is, of course, the law of karma, which seems to be, at least when humans are involved, a moral-ethical code that is absolutely binding. Karma, in turn, is an aspect of dharma, the universal law of the cosmos, which has to do with "the way things should be." Both karma and dharma appear to have no particular origin, and they are both, I would say, mechanical, devoid of the passionate Will of a God (or any feeling at all . . . or any Deity behind them), rather like the laws of physics or the rules of mathematics. They just are. And neither they nor Whatever (unspecified) set them up has any concern for human persons or their fates. We must simply try to conform to them, or else. The "or else" is about the possibility of being reincarnated in a less pleasant form or, worse, *never* being released from the endless round of reincarnations per se, which all involve suffering and the fear of death.

This world is experienced as exceedingly Dark, and those few pleasures that creatures can enjoy are distracting them from the work of Salvation, and so, they are deluded and themselves Evil. Salvation is about escaping all this and reuniting with the great *Im*personality called Brahman. Indeed, the *whole* of this world is ultimately delusional,

merely the dream of Brahman, Who spends most of His time sleeping or, we could say, Unconscious. At best, it is the "play" of Brahman.
But, for me at least, this idea of impersonal playing as an adequate
description of what persons go through in their incarnated existences
fails utterly. As we've seen a number of times, Hinduism says that the
only thing human beings really want, although they seldom realize it, is
Brahman's sat, chit, and ananda—Infinite Being, Knowledge, and Bliss.
That may be, at a deep level. But then, there are all these other levels,
informed in my view by the ultimate desire, but chock-full, not only of
physical pleasures but, more positively, with inter*personal joys.*

I do agree that egoism—or malignant narcissism—is a danger . . .
not only to salvation in the spiritual sense but, more immediately . . .
and probably more importantly, for the horrors, large and small, that
human beings inflict on one another and on other species. In this
respect, the Hindu virtues of self-control, selfless giving, and mercy
are noble attempts at mitigating moral-ethical Evil. But, again, they
aren't practiced for their own sake, or for the sake of other persons,
but in order to achieve one's own annihilation in Brahman.

So-called Bhakti Hinduism seems at first like a kind of theism, and
its basic virtues—benevolence, tolerance, compassion, and action without attachment (to its effects or outcomes)—are laudable. Yes, and yes.
And yet, while various Gods and Goddesses are passionately loved by
Their devotees, the ultimate Hindu truth-claim that these figures are
the transient products of the Impersonal remain in place.[57]

Okay, but doesn't Buddhism offer something more refreshing and
genuinely elevating? For me, yes and no. As I've mentioned (several
times, I guess), Buddhism has no explanation for Evil's origins except
to say that Something committed the error of believing this world of
suffering, old age, and death to be real, whereas the only thing that is
actually real is . . . well, nothing or No-thing. Leaving aside the question
of how a Some*thing* could make an error, when we turn to Buddhism's
morality and ethics, there is the sense of a genuine warmth and concern

for other human beings, not to mention all other living things. The great cardinal virtue of Love is, indeed, elevating. It approximates the central position of Divine Love in Christianity. Still, though, Love in Buddhism generally means something like conviviality, goodwill, and compassionate kindness—all really good feelings, yet not quite the passionately Self-sacrificial Love of God in/as Jesus.[58]

And again, the purpose of practicing these virtues is not for their own sake, or even for others, really. Instead, once again, it's for saving one's self from the world of things, events, and so on . . . and *persons*, including *one's own person*. When I look at the Noble Eightfold Path, I immediately see the impossibility of following it. *There is no way to stay in the world*, much less the world of inter*personal* interactions, without violating it.[59] Perhaps the impossibility is the point. Again, "Get out of here . . . correct the primordial error of being here . . . as quickly and as efficiently as possible."

I'll conclude my perhaps irreverent survey of the major world religions, some past, some present, with Taoism. There's no question in my mind that Taoist scriptures are often beautiful and that they sometimes convey profound truths—for example, that in the heart of what we think of as Evil is Goodness and in the center of what we normally experience as Goodness is Evil, and that, consequently, we would be wise to look more carefully at people, things, and events before making judgments.[60] Yet, in my view, the Taoist teachings actually make no more progress in solving the puzzles I'm raising in this section than any of the other systems we've looked at. I hate to say it, but it is and isn't surprising to me that much of Taoism has degenerated into the rather dark regions of the occult.

A note: In suggesting with Basham and other scholars of Eastern religions that the sometimes very high moral and ethical standards are *quite* high but ultimately self-centered—this is true even of the Bodhisattvas, in my opinion—I'm *not* saying that followers of these systems are less genuinely loving than followers of the Western spiritual traditions or that the Eastern systems do not effectively foster humane values. Beneath the shaping of our psyches that our cultures and ideologies accomplish, human beings are human beings, and we all show pretty much the same range of feelings (and indifferences) to one another. We do have the marked capacity to act "as if" we felt kindness, fairness, even Love for one another. And, as I was taught in my undergraduate theater classes about creating characters in a play, if we act "as if" often enough, we actually do become (or at least show) what we're acting.

Divine Self-Disclosure in the Form of Humane God-Images

Although my experiences with what I believe are Divine Self-disclosures do include encounters with some dark characters, I interpret these as split off, and lesser versions, ultimately of God, but more immediately as angry, even vicious, entities (of some kind) that have pretty much lost contact with their Source. We've just looked at attempts to derive such entities, as well as maliciously dysfunctional human beings (probably animals as well)—their complexes, psychoses, and so on—from the Pure Goodness and, I would say, Humaneness of the Supracosmic God. As I mentioned, I, at least, have found no completely believable solution to this problem. From my perspective, if there is one, it lies beyond Nicholas of Cusa's Wall and Ibn 'Arabi's conclusion that the One *is* the Multiplicity, and *vice versa*.[61] So, I give up on trying to figure it out.

My experiences of the "best" of the Divine convince me that any God worth worshiping embodies in an Infinite Way the most humane values that human beings have discovered in themselves— kindness, celebration of differences (where this is possible), respect, fairness, mercy, forgiveness, going the extra mile, compassion, and, above all, Love. The giving of Love to others and, yes, receiving it from them too is unarguably the most pleasurable, most joyful, most satisfying and *completing* of all of our desires . . . actually, of our *personhood*. It is, in fact, Love that makes us fully and authentically human. Being fully and authentically human means being *humane*. Loving is the acting out of the truth we deeply feel that *persons are of Unlimited, even Infinite Worth*. I think this realization is what makes Humaneness the Highest State of Consciousness we can experience, and it obviously can be experienced only between *persons*. That includes *between finite persons and the Divine Person*. It is the best of us . . . and we all know that (at some level). The firmest proof that an Infinitely Loving God exists is precisely this feeling, which, because of Its Power to absolutely fulfill our natures, so that, finally, we desire nothing else, is this very fact of Its overwhelmingly felt *Presence . . . Its Presence as a Person.*

As we've seen, Nature per se has other things in mind, of which Love is only one of a suite of feelings—all of them vital to our flourishing within Its Sphere. While I don't share the Gnostic or, in general, the Eastern view of Nature that It is overwhelmingly Dark, mostly or completely Evil, or an illusion or error, I *have* experienced transcending It, rising above It into a Realm of Pure Light and Goodness, where the Darkness of Nature—Its Beautiful Terror—are either left behind completely or transformed by Divine Love into something absolutely wonderful! I presented a few of these experiences in previous chapters. They are (mostly) what I base my world view on, and here, why I'll make the claim that Humane Divine Self-disclosures are the only, or at least the most valid, fulsome, and true Self-representations of God.

I'll also claim that nonhumane God-images serve no moral, ethical, or psychospiritual purpose (which is always about growth in *personhood as humaneness*) and so have no justification as Images of the Divine. For me, they're actually just the worship of Nature, and you can see how far that's gotten those who are in awe of them. Only God-images that *transcend Nature without denying the reality and purposes of Nature* (intuited, perhaps, but not known)—most importantly in terms of a higher, compelling, and finally Absolute set of moral-ethical values—are worthy of human devotion.

But what about Divine Justice . . . Divine Judgment on our lives? I do believe that God is Infinitely Just as well as Infinitely Loving. How these apparently Absolute, and absolutely opposite values, which seem *necessary*—and I mean the Justice/Judgment part too—for a God-image of Infinite Love are reconcilable, I have no idea. But if Love and Humaneness are Absolute, then our continual crimes against them must be judged in a way that somehow can be accepted by their victims. Love requires validation, and Its Truth enforced in some way. Here, again, I'm going to punt and accept that I can't see over Nicholas of Cusa's Wall into the Essence of God, Where I believe all contradictions are resolved and all questions answered. I suspect it's even presumptuous to try and, with that trying, to play God ourselves through the absolutizing of *our own* finitely limited judgments.

A Few Final Words about Divine Self-Disclosures and the God-Images They Produce

I strongly suspect that God has many Purposes, not all of Which (by any means) are disclosed to finite creatures. And couldn't be anyway. I think those are not my business. What *is* important to me is when I feel the Divine loving me, holding me, challenging me. In fact, I think I exist at all because God is gazing with His/Her/Its Infinite Gaze fixed upon me. Also, and equally, on everyone and everything else. The probability that since God's Gaze, by definition, is Infinite, as everything about God *is*, all things other than me are receiving that same Infinite Significance. Does that diminish or relativize His/Her/Its Love for me? Not at all! Anyway, the only thing that's important *to me* is that *I* am gifted with that.

Last note . . . and a reminder. Of course, all of the experiences

I've related in this chapter (as in all others) and the interpretations I've asked you to ruminate on with me (ditto) reflect the structures and dynamics of *my particular psyche* and the experiences and life it has undergone and lived. I also think, not just mine, probably, but the Universal Psyche (short of God's) in the bargain. True. But, like the mathematicians who believe they've *discovered* mathematical structure in the universe rather than *imposed* it, through pattern recognition and so on, I believe my finite psyche, as well as the Psyche of Nature, have *not* imposed their structures and dynamics on Reality but, rather, have *received* those, in however incomplete form, *from* the Ultimate Reality, the God of Love.

6
The Immortality
of Persons

That sweet-and-tart and disinhibited vanishing
drops back and back forever,
and I, running or dancing, push off from my own
earth,
and loft into this far-flung exultation
until I thin to nothingness, extinguished in a
boundary-less crescendoing—
then, astounded, reconvene with all my joys about
me ringing— .
those and that which I have loved and those and
what I did not—all alighted with me
in a flood of sun and thunder.

DOUGLAS M. GILLETTE,
AT THE THRESHOLDS OF ELYSIUM

God wishes to commune Forever with the persons God has created within the medium of matter (and any other such media).

Logic for the Immortality of Persons

If there must be Infinity for there to be finitude, there must also be Eternity for there to be time.

> Eternity is the time-related form of Infinity. (Verified)
> Persons are beings of Infinite Worth. (Presupposition)
> Beings of Infinite Worth must also be Eternal. (Specifiable)
> Therefore, you and I—and all you's and I's—must be Eternal, or Immortal. (Conclusion)

This is *my* logic. I don't claim it *proves* anything. But then I don't think *any* logic does. About the deep things of life, I think there is only intuition. A switch clicks. There's light. And then there's seeing. Logic can be a succinct way of verbalizing what has already been intuited (correctly or incorrectly).

Here's an elaboration:

All things and events are Eternal-Immortal because, in their Becoming, they *are* (above time) even as they *become* (in time). And everything that is *is* because its Creator-Envisioner-Manifestor, being Infinite and Eternal, Gazes upon it with an Infinite and Eternal Gaze. Persons (of any and all degrees of awareness), being that which is "Presence fully Visited," are the height of what God Gazes into Being. And because they are *conscious* of themselves and their Creator (albeit to a necessarily limited extent), they are the only things that are *aware* (to a necessarily limited extent) of their Immortality and so, in *that* sense, the only things that have it.

A second logic: All things strive—some more than others, especially living things.

There is striving only if there is a goal that already exists to strive for.

Living things strive for Immortality.

Therefore, the Goal of Immortality exists.

Evidence for the Immortality of Persons from Personal Experiences

Physical Effects as Incipient Apparitions[1]

We've already looked at some of these in the context of their upwellings or intrusions into our individual psyches from the Collective Psyche, or the Psychic Medium from Which we ourselves have come, and within which we ever are and become (chapter 2). But here I want to look at incipient apparitions to see if they might give us evidence of Continued Life after biological death—at least some of them.

Here are some we've reviewed in chapter 2: my wife seeing the wet footprints on the upstairs hallway carpet in a client's house; raps on the floor and footsteps coming down the tiled hall that I experienced in two different houses; following my mother's death, the condolence and Valentine's Day cards on the wall; and what I'm calling the Oak Park Demon. Here are three more:

A night or two before my mother died, when she was in bed in her bedroom, and my wife's sister was in the bed next to her, my mother repeatedly called for her long-deceased parents, "Mother, Daddy." My wife's sister witnessed an attempted turning of the doorknob from outside the room. The knob never turned far enough to release the catch, probably indicating that whomever it was (presumably my grandparents) did not have the force to open the door and enter the room. While, according to the literature on such things, disincarnate souls don't need to open doors to appear in a room, a lot of psi phenomena is counterintuitive, odd, even tricksterish. This story is suggestive of longevity of life after death, as my grandparents had died *years* before.

My students sometimes tell me about strange physical effects they believe, and I'm inclined to agree, are generated by dead loved ones, sometimes years after their deaths. Ruth, one of my students, felt her dead son's breath on her face while she was driving. All of the car windows were closed, so no breeze could have entered the car from outside, and the air conditioner was off. The puff of air was strong enough to ruffle her hair. Her son had been murdered exactly a year earlier, and that day was the anniversary of his death. She was driving to her synagogue to observe the yahrzeit (the Jewish ritual of the anniversary of a loved one's death). This is an example of what I'm calling a midterm post mortem incipient apparition.

This next story is more involved. It also involves a midterm post mortem incipient apparition. Kara was one of my parishioners at Oakton Community Church in Evanston, Illinois. I'd been doing pastoral counseling with her for probably close to a year around the issues of her sense of self-worth and, related to that, not being able to find a man (ultimately, to marry) who was taller than she was. She finally did, though—Robert, a strapping firefighter from Chicago. I married them and, within a couple of years, baptized their two children. In the process of all that, I got to know their family pretty well. I remember Robert's mother as a wonderful combination of serious, firm, and very warm. It was probably a year or so later that she was killed instantly in a car crash. I remember doing the funeral and the terrible sadness that was such a jarring contrast to what had been the happy life of their extended family.

Several months later, Kara called me and told me that Robert was experiencing his mother frequently entering the house suddenly. He could feel her presence as a rushing in of her personality any time of day or night, a focused consciousness that was definitely his mother.

And he was very upset about it. He wasn't at all frightened of it, but his life was feeling less and less predictable and increasingly interrupted by mixed feelings of grief and a kind of nostalgia that would unexpectedly overtake him. He was losing his focus both at work and at home. Kara asked me if I could come over and talk to him.

He and I met in an upstairs sitting room. We talked for a while, and then his back arched and his chest swelled as if he'd had a sudden in-rush of air. Breathily he said, "She's here!" I asked him what he was feeling right then, when he felt her suddenly enter the room, and I helped him calm down somewhat. Even though his mother was still in the room, as he said, he asked me if I wanted something to drink. I said yes, and he went downstairs to get iced tea. As soon as he left the room, the floorboards just to the right of the chair I was sitting in began to creak—rhythmically. *Eek-eek, eek-eek, eek-eek.* I've lived with floorboards most of my life. They occasionally creak and pop. But I'd never heard them creak rhythmically, as if someone were shifting their weight from one foot to the other.

I took this as a sign that his mother was standing right beside me and was very agitated. I decided to talk to her—almost in a therapeutic way. I told her that she'd been killed instantly in that car crash and that she might not fully realize that she had passed out of this dimension. I told her I had no idea, of course, what medium she was in, but that she was not going to be able to come back into this one. I tried to reassure her that Robert would be fine and that I was sure she would see him again. And I suggested that, if she could see a Light, she should move toward it. The creaking of the floorboards stopped, Robert came into the room with the iced tea, and immediately said, with amazement and relief, "She's gone!" I told him about the floorboards and what I'd said to her.

A month or so later, Kara called me to thank me for what I'd done for Robert and to tell me that his mother had never come back.

In my years of pastoring, I've heard many stories from parishioners whose judgments I trust about feeling the presence of dead loved ones—some shortly after their deaths but some many years after the fact. They don't seem to experience their loved ones as a general or defuse presence, or as memories, or as the result of (at least their conscious) yearnings. Rather, they tend to experience their presences as focused—that is, with a definite location in a room, usually in a house or apartment they shared for years, but sometimes beside them on the street when out for a walk, or really any setting. And they experience them unexpectedly, spontaneously—not when they're wishing for them or necessarily thinking of them. That was true for me in Elise's mother's living room at three in the morning. That was also true for Robert's experiences of his mother . . . and my own experience of her creaking the floorboards next to me.

Voices as Incipient Apparitions

As I've mentioned in chapter 2, I "heard" my mother's voice in our bedroom in Miami a day or two after she'd died. The voice, which was indeed my mother's, nonetheless had a kind of tone and use of words that was not characteristic of her in life. It seemed to come from a corner of the ceiling to my left as I lay in bed on that beautiful sunlit morning. Stranger, perhaps, was "hearing" my father-in-law's voice a couple of months after he'd died alone in the family home in Mexico. He spoke only Spanish. But when I heard his voice in our house in Palatine, Illinois—I remember, just as I was crossing from our garden room to the living room—he spoke perfect English! And it was exactly the kind of thing he really would say but that I'd never heard from him. Meanwhile, my wife had been pleading with him *not* to appear to her, as it would terrify her. Still, she wondered why he would communicate with me, and not her, until, about a year after his death, he *did* appear—but in a dream. According to the research in this area, dream experiences of dead loved ones are pretty common, although I've never had such a dream, at least not in which a dead loved one has appeared, I guess I would say, undisguised. In my wife's dream, her father was separated from her by something like a glass partition, from the other side of which he waved and smiled at her. She says he looked about forty years old, as he was in his prime. The main message of the dream seemed to be to reassure her that he was fine—in fact, in a *really* good place—and that he was waiting for her and for all his family.

Probably the most shocking and unexpected "voice from the dead" experience I've had was that of Sandy, a former student, exactly two days after her death, as I was just beginning to wake up in the morning. I heard her voice saying, "Doug?" incredulously. Her voice sounded very distant, but it was clearly her distinctive timbre and tone, but a tone filled with wonder and amazement. Here's why the incredulity and amazement.

Sandy had taken many of my Emeritus classes over the eighteen years (and counting) that I've taught them. No matter what the subject, she was always the resident—and outspoken—atheist. Which was fine with me because I've always taught in a welcoming and inclusive way and really enjoyed our discussions. About two years ago, Sandy and I became close friends. This happened because we both developed severe intestinal distress at about the same time. Eventually, mine was diagnosed as a hyperallergic gut reaction to the second Covid shot, which has gradually gotten better with massive daily doses of cimetidine. Sandy's condition was eventually diagnosed as metastatic abdominal cancer.

She was dying. Our conversations were at first mostly about medical stuff but became extensions of what we were discussing in class, and more. As she grew worse, she kept taking my classes. She hung in there for the very last session of "The Decay and Collapse of the Roman Republic." And, on the last day, she said good-bye to her fellow classmates, and they said good-bye to her. There were lots of tears. Something she said about being ready to "go into No-thingness" prompted me to do what I had never had done in class before, which was to suggest that a student might be fundamentally wrong in his or her worldview. I said cheerfully, "Sandy, you might be surprised." Those were my last words to her . . . while she was still in her body.

So, two mornings after her death, she woke me up with incredulity . . . "Doug?" I started out of sleep and sat up in bed and said to her, "Yes, I'm here!" She said something more, but it got muffled and lost as I became fully awake.

Fully Manifested Apparitions

I and people close to me have occasionally experienced visible and, at times, interactive apparitions. Here are a few instances.

We've already looked at a couple of these—my friend Frank's seeing the apparition of the murdered boy in the guest bedroom, our toddler daughter's seeing my mother in her bedroom within a day or two of her death, and Elise's dead father appearing to her in her mother's bedroom. For me, he was an incipient apparition, but for Elise, he was a full apparition.

This story was reported to me by my first wife's father. He was sleeping in a completely dark bedroom, when his sister, who was dying in a hospital a few miles away, suddenly appeared in a softly glowing beam of light in the corner of his room. He was awakened by the glow or by her presence . . . he wasn't sure which. He sat up in astonishment and said, "Sis!" She smiled and vanished. He later confirmed with the hospital that she had died at about the time he saw her apparition.

There is a rather large body of case studies of apparitions—both incipient and fully manifested. I've listed some of the books in this field in the bibliography. Three books I would strongly recommend are Edward Kelly, et al., *Irreducible Mind: Toward a Psychology for the 21st Century* (2007), especially chapter 6; F. W. H. Myers's *Human*

Personality and Its Survival of Bodily Death (2005, originally 1903), especially chapter 7, "Phantasms of the Dead"; and David Kessler's *Visions, Trips, and Crowded Rooms* (2010), especially chapter 8.

This next apparition story suggests very long-term survival after death. And it's my only full apparition experience—unless something further happens before this book goes to print. Which it might (not the print part, but the something further). It's complicated, shocking, and perhaps worrisome. Because it's complicated, I'll have to give you a fair amount of detailed background information as well as recounting the event itself. I hope you'll hang in there with me.

Let me begin by saying that, although in the early parts of my life I was (largely) devoted to rationalism and the Enlightenment, no more so than in matters of religion and miracles (like the parting of the Red Sea and Jesus's resurrection), as well as so-called supernatural phenomena, I can no longer hide behind modernity to protect myself from the emotional and cognitive consequences of accepting the supposedly nonrational. I don't think, actually, that psi phenomena (including at least some miracles) are exactly nonrational. But accepting their reality does make me convincedly open to dimensions of Reality that I guess I would have preferred to have been able to continue to deny. Having said that, though, I've had, by now, so many experiences of what we conventionally call the supernatural that they seem to me pretty much like just a part of the natural world—an odd, sometimes tricksterish, certainly uncontrollable part. And also, at times, genuinely alarming but no more alarming, really, than quantum physics, mass extinctions, or the coyotes that come through our yard eating rabbits alive and leaving little tufts of hair or intact bunny tails on the lawn.

Okay, first installment of the backstory. My great-great-great-grandmother was a Dakota Sioux "princess" who married an English American horse trader whose last name was Metcalf (my middle name). They were rejected by both sides of the family, and so as family legend has it, they became early settlers of a new town in Iowa, Sioux City, established by mixed-race couples. Supposedly, my ancient Native American ancestress was still alive when my mother was born and came to the hospital to see her. That would make my great-great-great grandmother quite old at the time. She must have been in her late 70s—maybe more. My Metcalf grandfather had Native American facial features, white and brown splotches on his forearms (sometimes a characteristic of interracial mating), and sinodonty (the extra tooth roots inherited from northeast Asian ancestors). My mother occasionally referred to herself as "a dangerous Indian."

Next bit. As I've mentioned, my wife is Mexican Native American, a Huasteca. Our daughter is, of course, half Mexican. Her husband, with whom she produced our granddaughter, is also half Mexican. Our granddaughter would then also be half Mexican. Except, so far, she doesn't look half Mexican. She looks like something else.

This last summer, when they came to visit, and we were lounging in the backyard—our granddaughter was about a month and a half old—and we were talking about her, our son-in-law said, "She looks oriental—the eyes and the downturned mouth." I said, "Not oriental—Plains Indian." I said, "Look on your phones for late-nineteenth-century and early-twentieth-century photos of Plains Indians." Which they did. And their jaws dropped. "That's it!" our daughter exclaimed. So, I told the story of my great-great-great-grandmother and of how those genes had been carried down the generations in my family. I should probably also say that when my wife and I carried our granddaughter around the backyard, she got a trancelike look on her face and became very still. She was focused intensely on the tops of the trees and the sky—just fixedly taking them in. My impression of what she was experiencing was that, as I told my wife, "I have the feeling she's seen this before, and she's remembering. I think she's an old soul."

Okay, next bit. The nurses at the hospital in the neonatal ICU where she fought for her life after her birth all told us that our granddaughter, even with her harrowing birth, was "extremely aware, extremely alert." And our daughter and son-in-law told us that when they saw her through the viewing window for the first time, when a nurse held her up for them to see, they both had an uncanny feeling that she was looking straight into their souls and saying, "I've got this! I'm stronger than both of you!" Many people who've seen her—among them, my students and some friends—have said things like, "That's not a baby! There's a *person* in there, looking right out at you!" An old soul? Maybe . . .

Another piece of the backstory. For two and a half years I've been teaching my Emeritus classes from my home office via Zoom. In fall 2022, I began teaching a class called "In Whom We Live and Move and Have Our Being: Supra-Cosmic Consciousness." The class's first book was Elizabeth Krohn and Jeffrey Kripal's *Changed in a Flash* (2018), in which Krohn writes about a near death experience and the sudden precognitive and other psi abilities that followed, and Kripal analyzes them, mostly from a comparative religion standpoint. We were at the point in the book where he speculates, from what I think is a careful and well-informed standpoint, about the likely connection between the electromagnetism spectrum and psi events, including apparitions.

On that day (November 3, 2022), our granddaughter was in our house. I had volunteered to be her full-time nanny, and she'd just started coming to the house a few days before that class. My wife stayed home that morning to be with our granddaughter in the basement office on the sofa while I was teaching—about two hours. My students, of course, wanted to see her, so my wife brought her over to sit on my lap for a few minutes in front of the Zoom screen. That was just after we'd been talking about apparitions and the electromagnetic spectrum. With our granddaughter there, I gave a little background about her ancestry, including my great-great-great-grandmother, and how our granddaughter looked more Plains Indian than Mexican. Then I handed her back to my wife, and they went back to the sofa.

All of a sudden, among the little boxes on my computer screen displaying my students, a very old Native American woman appeared. Her hair hung in long braids, and she was wearing several bead necklaces, some kind of headdress, and what might have been a buckskin shirt. She didn't face the camera—or whatever she was using—directly but mostly showed her heavily creased left cheek. Her eyes were hooded and very black, and these she *did* have turned toward the screen. The name that appeared in the box with her picture was Sinoda. She didn't look like the kind of person I should cheerfully greet with "Hi Sinoda! Welcome to the class!" So, I just said, rather carefully, "Sinoda." She immediately smiled. I would say, a sly, concealing, and perhaps a little mischievous smile (but not hostile or evil) and nodded her head slightly in acknowledgment.

As I do with most possible psi phenomena, I passed it by and, in this case, kept teaching. The next time I looked for her—probably five minutes later—she was gone. Later in the class session, one of my students asked, "Did anyone else see that Native American woman?" Five students raised their hands. Most either didn't have the full screen on their devices, and others might not have noticed her. There's also the possibility that Sinoda *chose* who to appear to and who not.

Meanwhile, on the sofa in the office that faces the plate glass window and two side windows, which give a view of the front yard, my wife and our granddaughter were sitting looking out. That was right after I'd shown her to the class. Now something strange and totally unexpected happened, something we'd never seen our granddaughter do before: she got a look of stark terror on her face—wide eyes, curled-back lip—and she started to tremble and cry. My wife stood up, turned her to her shoulder, and left the room with her, reassuring her that everything was okay. She had almost certainly seen something directly in front of her that my wife did not see.

A few days later, as I was telling one of my student friends about the Sinoda event and our granddaughter's reaction—a student who

hadn't seen Sinoda, but who'd been in class that day. I was saying—
stupidly—something like, "She must have been outside, bending over to
look in the window and see our granddaughter on the sofa." My student
replied, "Doug, Sinoda is a spirit. She doesn't have to bend down to look
through the window. She was in the room!" Of course.

In the afternoon of that same "Sinoda day," the student who'd
asked if anyone else had seen the Native American woman emailed me
and asked, "Did we just see an apparition?" I emailed him back, and
told him I was checking out natural explanations, and I'd keep him
posted. I was indeed checking out natural explanations for the Zoom
appearance. I contacted the Oakton administration and IT to see if: (1)
anybody named Sinoda had registered late for my class; and (2) to see
if anyone could crash the class. The answer to both questions was no.
There *was* the possibility that one of my students had shared the link
and class code with one of their friends. I asked my class about that during the next session. The answer again was no.

I called my boss in the administration back then, and we worked
through the odds of a naturalistic explanation. For instance, "Have you
ever seen an old Native American woman in full nineteenth-century
regalia ever walking around the campus or in the office registering for a
class?" "No, of course not." "What are the chances that such a person—
urban or from a reservation—could be a hacker herself or would hire a
hacker to crash my class and exactly and only at the moment we were
talking about apparitions using electromagnetism (as in computers) and
our granddaughter's Plains Indian ancestry?" "Extremely remote." "Of
all the Zoom classes floating around the Internet . . . *this* one, at *this*
moment? And how would she even know about it?"

To my great surprise, my boss, the admin person, who I'd thought
would really resist the possibility of an apparition using one of Oakton's
computers to enter my class, actually agreed with me that, in all probability, just such an event had occurred. We asked each other: Which
was more plausible—a contemporary, very old Native American woman

in traditional tribal dress hacking my class or an apparition? Well . . . ?
My boss said, "I'm on board!"

But who *was* she? Given the circumstances, I thought it could be
my great-great-great-grandmother looking in again, as she had at my
mother's birth, on one of her female descendants. And I wondered if
she'd been a medicine woman, a shaman, when she'd been alive (from
an Earth perspective). Our daughter certainly has some psychic ability, and our granddaughter showed, and shows, some of the same—the
trees and sky look, the trancelike state that she continues to fall into
when out in Nature, the possibility that she saw Sinoda in my basement
office.

I got on the Internet and tried to find the name Sinoda among
the names Native Americans give their children. I'm still trying to
research that. Somewhat alarmingly, one match that *has* come up
identifies the name Sinoda with "a molesting spirit from space." I'm
trying to find out how that name originated for such a spirit. Did it
come from a Native American source? Could that have been my great-
great-great-grandmother's actual name? Was that *her* on the screen,
or was it this spirit masquerading as her? If *not* my ancestress (and
our granddaughter's), why would the spirit Sinoda be interested in our
granddaughter or in showing up in my class? If not my great-great-
great-grandmother, could Sinoda be sensitive to the kinds of discussions we were having that day and want to show us that what we were
talking about is *real*?

I don't have the answers to these questions yet. But one thing
seems clear: whether Sinoda is my, and our granddaughter's, ancestress or a non-incarnate spirit that likes to make trouble, survival
after—or at least outside of—death is *some* kind of *fact*. Either way, I
and at least six of my students experienced an apparition and, furthermore, not an *eidolon*—an automaton or psychic residue—but a *person*
(of some kind) who *interacted*, at least with our granddaughter and
with me.

Dreams

According to depth psychological theory and my own experience of dream analysis, many—perhaps not all—dreams have several or even multiple layers of meaning (like most of the rest of life). I've sometimes felt as though some of my dreams might be symbolic portrayals or prefigurations of aspects of my own afterlife. I've already mentioned my dream of the boutique run by three feminine figures and the coming to meet me of a mysterious male figure, dressed in white, who seemed to be the decider of whether or not I'd be accepted into a higher echelon in this ethereal and idyllic world. I talked a little about that dream in the context of my suspected experiences of angels toward the end of chapter 2. I just want to mention it again here—this time, while we're considering evidence for life after biological death. You may remember that the dream was filled with Light, and my wife and daughter were with me. What I didn't mention were the Heaven-like characteristics of every aspect of the dream. For instance, my wife, my daughter, and I were also figures of Light. In addition, the city was made up of immaculately clean houses in perfect condition, with gray-painted siding and warm tan-colored trim, vaguely reminiscent to me of Rock Island at its most beautiful, with a kind of suggestion of a neighborhood in San Francisco. The sky was a cloudless blue, and the city was in perpetual summer. Indeed, it felt heavenly. Was it what it seemed to be?

Many years earlier, when I was working as a porter-orderly in a hospital in California—I must have been twenty-one or twenty-two—doing alternative service for the government during the Vietnam War, I had a powerful dream about what I've imagined ever since was at least a partial representation of my death process. In the dream, I'm on a cot at night in an indeterminately huge one-room dormitory filled with sleepers on identical cots—like warming centers or disaster shelters, only a *lot* bigger, cavernous really, and nearly pitch-black. And it isn't a shelter; it's a prison run by my "grandmother," in which sleep is mandated and enforced.

I seem to be the only one awake of the possibly millions of people comatose in that dark vastness. I want to escape, but it's really dangerous even to move. Still, I slowly sit up, put my legs over the side of the cot, stand, and, fearfully scanning the scene, cautiously make my way to a cement staircase set sideways onto one wall, leading up, probably about fifty feet, to a landing at the top of the stairs. In the wall on the landing is a closed door. I knock, and a porter, dressed richly in something like nineteenth-century servant's livery, immediately opens the door and welcomes me in. The place—a huge banquet hall—is flaring with light from myriad crystal chandeliers hanging from the high ceiling, and down the middle of the room is a very long table, heaped with wonderful food, punch bowls, and decorations. There's a large crowd of diners, mostly standing around the room with drinks in their hands and engaged in loud and happy conversation. It seems very much like how I imagine old Christmas parties in the large and ornate banquet halls of Europe. I'm heartily welcomed in by the diners. The porter closes the door behind me. I'm safe . . . and, I think, saved.

The symbolism is obvious, right? A strong dose of Plato's cave, some Gnosticism thrown in, and the millennia-old idea of a great banquet upon first entering the Otherworld—at least for those who've escaped the tyranny of Nature. By the way, I should say that, whether these dreams (and the following) may say something about my, or *the* Afterlife, I think they're all about what I'm calling (after the Egyptians, Greeks and Romans, and many more ancient traditions) the *Antechamber* to whatever lies beyond earthly life.

Speaking of the Great Banquet in the Antechamber of the Afterlife, I had another dream recently that also featured that jubilant celebration. In this dream, I'm in a gigantic version of a colonnaded Roman garden, as far as the eye can see. Everywhere Roman dining tables and chairs and *clinas*—the couches on which wealthy Romans reclined, while reaching for rich food on heavily laden tables. Everywhere, women and men joyously feasting. But, oddly, there is a shadow—almost literally—moving through that incalculably enormous garden and its crowd of celebrants. I'm informed by higher-ups that there is a gang of thieves at the Banquet, people who shouldn't be there, stealing and eating what we might call "the Food that gives Eternal Life." It's my job to hurriedly gather a posse of undercover agents who will spread out among that impossible number of diners, find the bad actors, and throw them out of Heaven.

Thinking about the dream afterward, I have at least two major questions. First, how was it going to be remotely possible to find those bad actors in that crowd? Second, and hugely more important, is Heaven leaky around the edges? I mean, how would it be possible for those who don't belong there to get in? Maybe the Antechambers of Eternal Life, being *ante*chambers and not Heaven in its fullness, are not foolproof!

I've had a number of other dreams that I suspect are glimpses into my post mortem fate, but I'm only going to lay out one more. This is clearly an Antechamber dream. I've made it to Heaven, but as it turns out, the real thing is behind a door at the far end of the room I've just entered, fresh from my earthly death. The room is large and looks like a gigantic version of a Victorian drawing room, with lots of overstuffed furniture, elaborate little tables, ornate table and floor lamps, doilies everywhere. And (again), it's packed with people. These are not celebrating, though. They all look somewhere between lip-chewing anxious and outright terrified. There's a gray light over everything. As it happens, the furniture itself is actually made up of *people* who are so afraid to leave the room that they've shape-shifted into those overstuffed sofas and chairs, tables, lamps, and whatever else.

The word (somehow) reaches me that, with my background in psychology, my task is to "therapize" every one of these lost and anxious people, make them psychologically and spiritually healthy enough to be fit for Heaven, and exit the room through that far door. In other words, before *I* can walk through it, I have to clear the room! Who knows how many centuries of the dead have congregated here and how long it will take me to help them overcome their fears and whatever may be their cause. The task looks daunting, to say the least. And I'm not a Bodhisattva who *wants* to make sure everyone gets to nirvana before she or he takes the final step for themselves and goes *poof*. Or, if I am, I haven't seen much of that level of virtually infinite selflessness in myself so far.

My overall impression from that dream is that Heaven may not be a clean shot—at least not for me or the people in the room. And I'm reminded of Hamlet, who was thinking about committing suicide, and then was struck by the premonition that there may be more crap to deal with on the other side. If this dream, like the one I recounted just before it, is even only *symbolic* of what lies ahead for me after the demise of my biological entity, it puts a bit of a damper on my hope for a relatively smooth transition from this life to a blissful next!

OBEs and NDEs

Apparently, there's a kind of gray area between dreams of flying and out-of-body experiences (OBEs). Children and young adults seem to have the most dreams of flying. I certainly did. But in my dreams, staying up in the air got harder and harder as the years passed. At seventy-four, I never dream of flying.

Some researchers suggest that dreams in general embody an out-of-body element, almost as if imagination itself is an OBE, or a series thereof, and dream environments are actually alternative dimensions of Reality. Of course, it depends on what you mean by *actually* and *dimensions*. But there do seem to be OBEs that arise not in dream states but in the twilight area between sleeping and waking where many other psi phenomena also take place. Whatever OBEs represent and however they manifest, they do seem to me to demonstrate that, as I've mentioned here and there throughout this book, there's a lot more Psyche (and Its environments) around than most of us think. Ditto for all psi phenomena. As I've mentioned throughout the book, I've become convinced that we live and move and have our being within an all-enveloping Psychic Medium.

Based on the work primarily of Emily and Edward Kelly, along with Bruce Greyson, in *Irreducible Mind* (2007), some OBEs seem to shade off into near death experiences (NDEs), most do not.[2] I think the "near" part of this is probably extremely important. The truth is those who have NDEs *do not in fact die*. From my perspective, at most what we can say is that NDEs may be experiences of the Antechamber of the Afterlife that I proposed above. I also believe that Antechamber experiences, no matter how detailed they are for those who undergo them, are *re*-presenting symbolically a real near death, trancelike, or "swooning" environment that is not directly perceivable *as it is in itself* by the experiencer. Instead, as Jeffrey Kripal suggests in *Changed in a Flash*, it is composed of a 3-D projection of individual persons and their idiosyncratic life experiences, including the natural, cultural, ethnic, racial, and spiritual settings in which they have lived and that have made huge contributions to their individual identities.[3] This seems clear from the strikingly different descriptions of the NDE landscapes as well as significant variation in the events and characters encountered in these experiences.

As an illustration and to make a long story short, let me offer another of my "lyrical illuminations," written in 2000. It's called "Paradise Is What You Dream It."

> *It might be just this, Paradise—a wilderness of elk*
> *ranging frozen tundra;*
> *a poplar forest in a snowstorm; on an illimitable*
> *sun-savaged plain, panting zebra . . .*
> *You move from one scene to another, additioning,*
> *eventually enormously, encompassing more and*
> *more, yet never reaching Everything,*
> *until you're prepared to be it.*
> *How shall I describe these multitudinous*

dimensions, lingering, limitless,
spaces in the heart—above all, Love?
They're made of every millisecond of pleasure any
creature has ever known—grains of granite, silica,
powdered glass, joy, surprise, wonder!
O how glad, glad, glad with such a brimming
gladness have I here that I'll always smell the fresh
shavings
my grandfather planed from the wood for our new
stoop, our blue Formica table!
That I'll stride if I please with my wife and
daughter among the flowers of
Grant Park,
plunge chest-deep in the waves of the August
lake's water!
I'll be that Greatfish of the myths, dividing at my
up-rising, feeding millions!
Now see those five fire mountains floating off the
Florida Keys, blue in this mist of mingling,
sky and sea, blooming pink and green, announcing
hurricanes, gusting visibly from within!
Paradise at first, I think, is what you dream it.

Condensed and streamlined, Ibn 'Arabi said that, when we die, "the inner becomes the outer."[4] And Kripal says, "we die into our imaginations."[5] I think, in each instance, we're talking about the Antechamber.

Does the evidence of physical effects, presences, voices, apparitions, dreams, OBEs and NDEs from personal experiences—my own and others I trust—*prove* the reality of *Eternal* Life for persons? In themselves, I think they don't. Many of the psi events we looked at above were experienced within a few days of death. Some were experienced, at the most, only *months* later. From my perspective, these near- and midterm post mortem happenings, as well as OBEs and NDEs, *do* give strong evidence that the psyche can survive, even perhaps flourish, for *some* time independent of the body.

The apparently longer-term events—like Ruth's dead son blowing her hair a year after his death, my mother's parents trying to get through her bedroom door (years after they'd died), the apparition of the long-dead boy to Frank and of my great-great-great-grandmother or Sinoda's impersonation of her—certainly suggest *long*-term thriving of the psyche after biological death. Or perhaps, in Sinoda's case, the long, maybe *very* long-term thriving of psyches that might not *ever* have been incarnate, at least not in our kind of matter. Like NDEs, the dreams I reported *may* be evidence of an Antechamber to the Afterlife . . . or may be the *only* Afterlife there is, at least for persons as *individuals*. Perhaps on the other side of that door at the far side of the Victorian room is oblivion, nirvana, or a self-forgetful merging with the One?

Or not. Maybe there's more . . . *much* more. But for me, the experiences we've looked at so far don't clinch the matter. That goes for the possible reincarnation "memories" I've had too (which I'm not going to relate . . . in my case, too speculative). But if true, they would certainly tend to indicate some real *longevity* of at least *serial* psyches somehow related to a single essence, an ongoing identity that *might* itself be Immortal. Next, I want to consider the possibility that the near universality of the world's spiritual traditions about Eternal Life, past traditions and present—past traditions *within* present ones—could offer more significant evidence for the forever staying power of *persons*.

Evidence for Eternal Life from the Field of History of Religions

Here, I'm not going to do a catalogue of every tribe, nation, or culture's beliefs about the Immortality of persons. While that kind of approach can create an overwhelming sense of the probability, even certainty, of such Immortality through the sheer accumulation of the nearly universal facts of human belief, to do it right would generate thousands of pages. Also, it would tend very quickly, for me at least, to become not much more than an elaborate, boring, and largely repetitive list. Along with that, there'd be the densely cross-referenced comparisons among details and themes among these myriad spiritual traditions, both those details and themes that are highly variable and others that are pretty much common to them all. Yet, after all that, still no *proof* of Immortality. Everyone (nearly) *could* be delusional.

So, I'm not going to do all that. If *you* want to, I've included a number of books in the bibliography that will get you started on that journey (if you haven't already started). What I *do* want to do is highlight a few traditions about the Immortality of persons from different places and times, enough so that the (near) universality of those beliefs, even with their variations, becomes visible. So, I have to make huge generalizations. Because they try to radically condense complicated material, huge generalizations are not ever entirely true, but they *can* capture major ideas.

Also, while there is some degree of chronological order (not at all absolute), which might suggest a movement from what the Egyptologist Jan Assmann calls "implicit theology" to "explicit theology,"[6] I don't ever mean that explicit theology is superior to implicit. But I think it's still true that explicit theologies at least *express* a more thorough thinking through of things. I'm not even going to try to present what I think are the most sophisticated explicit theologies—Judaism, Christianity, Islam, and Hinduism. Way too much for this book. And I assume that most readers are more or less familiar with the outlines of the beliefs about Immortality and Eternal Life of these systems anyway. Finally, I chose the following examples as representative samplings, as well as for some of their features that I think are really interesting, even arresting.

By the way, I *don't* think everyone is delusional!

Shamanism

Shamanism is the earliest detectable spiritual belief system. As I see it, its main characteristics include the following.

Everything is charged with spiritual power.

The cosmos has a vertical axis at the center, which sometimes is imagined to be everywhere, that allows access to (often) multiple levels or layers of Reality. These layers, especially at their extremes, manifest Eternity.

Basically, up is Good, and down is Bad.

There are some named spiritual powers, including spirits of natural forces (like wind, fire, flowing water, and so forth), things (like mountains, rivers, particularly unusual rocks, and so on), ancestors, and frequently (but not always) an indistinct cosmic or High God.

The spiritual, or divine/Divine, is connected with the Earth plane, layer, or level by diviners, oracles, seers, medicine men or women, and healers of body and psyche, rather than by priests or priestesses. The diviners, oracles, seers, and so on, as well as ordinary people on vision quests or whatever you want to call them, enter Ecstatic States of spirit possession and/or psychic merger with spirits and ancestors. They do this to see Reality more deeply, to find protection, to seek the occultation of the individual person, and to do things "the right way." In these altered states of consciousness (often aided by sacred dances, drumming, and drugs), they experience other layers, levels, and dimensions of Reality and, in some cases at least, experience Reality as One . . . something like Pythagoras's "All."

When persons, whether human or animal, die, they go to variously conceived forms of an Eternal or at least indeterminately long Afterlife that may be located in the Sky, the Underworld, or certain geographical features—a mountain, distant islands, or at the far reaches of the compass points. Based on their earthly conduct, disincarnate persons (usually limited to humans) are judged (but not always)—the worthy going to joyful Places, the unworthy to miserable ones. Immortality is *consciously* thought of as an endless (or, again, indeterminate) number of days. But since the activities in these "Heavens" and "Hells" are imagined as endlessly repeated, I think they resemble states of mind and so, *unconsciously* (mostly), a sense of true Eternity—the Time*less* Now. As I just mentioned, this latter state of mind is often sought out in ecstatic experiences during the course of one's earthly life.

No matter how theologically sophisticated a spiritual system becomes, as in the world's present-day "great religions," shamanistic intuitions about the nature of Reality and persons and their fates are still very much present within them. Furthermore, no matter what official dogmas are promoted, many members of these religions are still thinking about Reality in shamanistic terms.

Paleolithic Peoples

First up, what scholars can gather from Paleolithic burial practices and grave goods—perhaps as well from cave and rock paintings and a few artifacts like flutes, blocks of red ochre, figurines, and the like—tend strongly to suggest that contemporary primal traditions are almost certainly outgrowths from these belief systems implied from the ancient artefacts. Looking at it the other way around, anthropologists often project back onto the Paleolithic evidence and infer it to imply at least some of the beliefs and practices of contemporary primal peoples. Here, I'm going to focus on Paleolithic burials.

Although controversy still surrounds the degree to which beliefs about human Immortality (probably in something like a shamanic context) can be understood from Paleolithic burials, in his book *The Paleolithic Origins of Human Burial* (2011), the archaeologist Paul Pettitt insists that whatever else was going on, Paleolithic peoples, both Neanderthals and early moderns, were developing an increasingly symbolic relationship between the living and the dead. While Pettitt certainly notes the evidence that suggests that cacheing (stuffing bodies into rock crevices, natural pits, holes, and so forth) predominates, he also points out that, at least by the Upper Paleolithic, some bodies were deposited in built and/or excavated spaces, often within or close to the living quarters. This, he says, demonstrates formal burial and strongly suggests a continued relationship between what we could call the ancestors and their descendants.[7] I read the idea of an ongoing relationship between the ancestors and their descendants as hinting at, but not proving, the belief that the dead continued to live. Otherwise, what kind of an ongoing relationship could they have with the living?

Australian Aboriginal People

Arguably, the Australian Aboriginal version of shamanism is the oldest one surviving and the least corrupted by an overlay or interweaving of primal and Christian ideas. In her *Shamanic Voices: A Survey of Visionary Narratives* (1979), Joan Halifax includes a number of Aboriginal accounts of shamanic journeys to other levels, or layers, of Reality. In one, she tells the story of Lizard's Son's initiation into the shamanic craft. Part of his initiation is to travel to the Sky and the Underworld, where he encounters the dead.[8]

Native Americans: The Maya

Native American affirmations of Eternal Life are, literally, all over the map. There are many variations in the accounts of the multitude of tribes, peoples, and nations that have flourished in what we call North, Central, and South America. We've already looked at the Maya (in chapter 1). Here, I just want to remind you that there were basically two Otherworlds in which the dead lived on, probably forever—the dark and frightening Underworld of Xibalba, which rotated up every day to become the night sky, and the bright realm of Metawil, a Paradise in which the royals, scribes, artists, and shamans lived forever, dancing the toe-heel strut on the surface of the Overworld Sea.

Southern Native Americans: Chavin de Huantar

In their *The Dawn of Everything: A New History of Humanity* (2021), David Graeber and David Wengrow explore a number of ancient towns and cities, looking for alternative social and political organizations to those civilizations (Egyptian, Mesopotamian, Greek, and Roman) that form the basis of Western culture. One of these is the ancient site of the pre-Inca Chavin de Huantar (which flourished between 1000 and 200 BCE) in the Andes of South America. The (presumable) shamans who officiated at Chavin left no written records to tell us what the purpose of the architecture and art may have been. But, as Graeber and Wengrow speculate, their architecture and art present a picture that strongly suggests that those who designed and administered it were in a state of altered consciousness.[9] Graeber and Wengrow lavishly document the maze of stone-walled passages, "carved with dense tangles of images," especially El Lanzón (the lance), a granite shaft or stela more than thirteen feet tall. Their conclusion is that the whole thing is hallucinogen inspired and was designed as a place in which psychospiritual journeys for those who wanted them took place.[10] In my view, whenever we're in the presence of sites like this, and/or in altered states of consciousness, what we are contacting is, indeed, other levels and layers of Reality—levels and layers of Reality that point to and, at times at least, *embody* aspects of the Eternal Life of persons. Altered states, however induced and however symbolically (rather than literally) they depict it, implicitly or explicitly, are oriented toward experiencing the essence of our identities as Immortal.

Northern Native Americans

Now, a brief flyby of North American intuitions about Immortality and Eternal Life. (It's impossible to know exactly where to place these accounts chronologically because we don't know how far back into the past they may go.) I'm guided here mainly by Gary Varner's overview *Ghosts, Spirits, and the Afterlife in Native American Folklore and Religion* (2010). Among many, perhaps most, Native American groups, the Afterlife is mainly a better version of life in this world.[11] It is reached through a series of trials—crossing a raging river or waterfall on a narrow, overturned tree trunk, climbing a ladder to the sky, or some other series of trials in which the soul is attacked by hostile spirits.[12] There is often, but not always, a judgment or sorting—bad souls slip off the tree trunk or are pushed off the ladder or are forced to take a fork in the path to the Afterlife that's clogged with thorns and briars, while the good take a road lined with roses.[13] Among the Inuit, the good migrate south, where it's warmer, and the bad are driven into the far north, where there is no escape from the cold, and nothing to eat or drink.

The goals are to be close to the Divine, either living in an idyllic village where there's perpetual dancing, gaming, ceremony, sex, and happy hunting, or to become a star. Among some tribes, there's a belief in a kind of Purgatory, where torture and fire are used to purify the soul and make it fit for Heaven.[14]

There are often portals in the landscape that allow access to the Eternity of the Otherworld.[15] Sometimes the Afterlife is layered, even in the case of Paradise.[16] Some New England tribes believe that the soul is multiple, not unlike the Egyptians, the Zoroastrians, and the Manichaeans, and that the higher personal identity stays in Heaven, while its lesser aspects incarnate. In this case, again similar to the Manichaeans, the incarnate soul can pray to its eternal essence for guidance, protection, and purification.[17] In light of some intuitions (and whole narrative scenes) I've had of what might be my own past lives and their ultimate purpose, it's really interesting to me—even, again, arresting—that some groups among the Plains Indians believe that the soul can be reincarnated until it is "finished."[18] According to Varner, the Navajo believe that in death the individual . . . without the body . . . becomes merged with the One.[19]

Africans

Although primal African beliefs about the Afterlife may often portray
a kind of folktale or fairy-tale version of It (as is true for many shamanistic groups) and the comings and goings to and from It as frequently
little more than casual, some groups have presented a deeper picture.
(Again, it's difficult to know where to place these and other African
belief systems chronologically. Nevertheless, onward!) In the Orisa spiritual tradition of the Yoruba of West Africa, as described by Philip John
Neimark in his *The Way of the Orisa* (1993), a wonderful and wonderfully succinct (I think) distinction is made between this world and the
next. The Orisa say, "The Earth is the marketplace and Heaven our
home."[20] We are incarnated in this marketplace specifically to learn
and to grow our souls—this, in the specific ways that each soul needs.
When this goal is met, we go Home. So, Earth is a temporary place of
learning, or school, and Orun—Heaven—is our permanent home. But
we will only go Home once we have learned what we were supposed to,
which may take any number of incarnations.[21] I think this is a fantastically no-nonsense way of talking about the purpose of reincarnation.
Also interesting for me is the idea that we each have a divine twin who
stays in Orun forever while we, as our current identities, are incarnating
and reincarnating[22]—as we've seen, a theme that appears in a number of
spiritual traditions from other times and places.

In his *The Hero with an African Face: Mythic Wisdom of Traditional
Africa* (1999), Clyde Ford tells a story that he says is common throughout Africa, which he calls the "failed message." The essence of the story
is that the moon tries to let people know that, while they will die as
the moon does (in its new moon phase), they will be reborn like it. But
the message is garbled by a series of messengers the moon sends, and
when it reaches humanity, only the first half of the message is delivered.
That's why people are afraid of death.[23] Another reason why people
feel discouraged about death and find it hard to envision themselves
as living Eternal Lives on its other side is that, according to the Kongo

people, Kalunga, the Infinite Sea that surrounds finite life, is both a *highway* to Mputu, the Land of the Immortal Dead, and a seemingly impossible *barrier*.[24] Ford suggests that we find the courage to take "the Middle Passage" that African slaves did (from Africa to the New World in slave-trade ships) and to strike out into Infinity to find the Place of Eternal Life, no matter the danger, fear, and discomfort.[25] He doesn't say this last bit directly. He ends with using the Middle Passage as a metaphor for the hero's journey. But where is the hero going but to the Otherworld?

Chinese

Chinese beliefs about Eternal Life and the Immortality of persons have changed significantly over the several thousand years of documented Chinese history. According to the scholar of Chinese religion Guolong Lai in his *Excavating the Afterlife: The Archaeology of Early Chinese Religion* (2015), before Buddhism arrived in China and the appearance of what he calls "religious Daoism" (Taoism) during the empire of the Eastern Han dynasty (25–220 CE), Chinese beliefs about the Afterlife went through a series of transformations from the Shang dynasty (ca. 1600–1046 BCE), through the Xi (Western) Zhou dynasty (ca. 1046–771 BCE), the Dong (Eastern) dynasty (771–251 BCE), which includes the Spring and Autumn period (ca. 771–453 BCE) and the Warring States period (ca. 453–221 BCE), to the Qin dynasty (221–206 BCE) and Han dynasty (206 BCE–220 CE).[26] Based on Lai's account, it looks to me as if all of these changes took place within a mostly shamanic belief system. The coming of Buddhism added a layer of basically suprashamanic ways of intuiting the Afterlife.

In very general terms, the Shang dynasty emphasized a Happy Afterlife in the Presence of the High God[27]—Di or Shangdi (later also called Taiyi or the Grand One).[28] The Zhou (Western and Eastern) dynasty, Spring and Autumn period, and Warring States period imagined a mostly Dark and Terrifying Afterlife and put special emphasis on the frightening and prolonged journey of the dead from this life to the Next, and the Han dynasty emphasized the soul's quest for Paradise.[29] This Han Paradise took two basic forms: one was transcendent, above the Earth plane, while the other was to be found at a distant location on the Earth.[30] As Lai says, most of the evidence for this scenario of changing views of the Afterlife comes from elite and, to some extent, "middle class" tombs, in the form of their architecture and their grave goods—both an important indicator of Afterlife beliefs.

In terms of tomb architecture, the earliest royal and semi-royal tombs were deep pits in the shape of upside-down stepped pyramids, sometimes huge, with the burial at the center, surrounded by four chambers filled with grave goods.[31] The idea seems to have been that the psyche/Psyche, still and perhaps forever connected with the body, was at the center of the universe that the tomb represented. The psyche/ Psyche was almost certainly deified and at least partially identified with the High God, Who, naturally, lived at the center of Reality.[32] These tombs, as well as the subsequent horizontally oriented versions, were alternatively thought of as the home of the deceased, a vehicle (partial chariots, most commonly wheels, are found in many tombs) for the deceased's journey from Earth to Paradise, and/or a way station in the transition from corpse to venerated ancestor. Even though the deceased's home base may have been the body in the tomb, in the Shang dynasty at least, this deified person could easily travel up and down the vertical axis of Reality, from the realm of the High God to the Earth plane.[33] By virtue of its identification and/or proximity to the High God, the deceased person became a venerated ancestor.

After the Shang (and to some extent the Zhou), things changed. Chinese society increasingly fragmented into rival warring kingdoms. For the first time, common people and peasants were drafted into the armies of the enemy kings and were slaughtered in droves.[34] Also, political assassinations and executions became commonplace.[35] In the growing atmosphere of violence and death by weapons, mostly seen as unjust, everyone, including the elites, became worried about the angry ghosts of those who'd been the victims of such violence.[36] This resulted in a view of the Afterlife as inhabited mostly by the vengeful dead.[37] Now, instead of a more or less natural transformation from a dead person to a benevolent, divinized ancestor, elaborate rituals had to be performed to make peace with the dead and help them transition through the liminal period immediately after death to the gradually gained status of (mostly) benevolent ancestors.[38] The recently dead were thought of as wandering, lost in the vastness of Reality, without a central cosmic axis to help them to orient themselves and to transform into their divinely intended identities as kind and beneficent ancestors.[39] (I should note here that in ancient Chinese religion, the venerated ancestors pretty much played the role that Saints and Angels have played in Western religions.)

Especially in the Warring States period, the difficulty the recently dead had in transitioning into powerful and good transfigured spirits became pictured as a dangerous and prolonged journey.[40] Consequently, grave goods were dominated by personal items (which would help the dead to stabilize and orient themselves to the familiar—making them feel more at home and so less anxious and angry), travel equipment (like maps and camping gear), and incantations (that would keep them safe on their arduous journey from human to divine persons).[41]

Tomb architecture changed too—from the inverted pyramidal pit to horizontal "houses," whether built above ground, dug out underground with entrance ramps, or cut into stone hillsides.[42] According to Lai, this change was, at least in part, so that offerings to the deceased could be made more directly and so, perhaps more effectively, often just outside the burial chamber.[43]

Looked at over the centuries before the coming of Buddhism, Eternal Life for Chinese souls was a kaleidoscope of Hades-like, more or less neutral, and Paradisal zones.[44] From my perspective, the essentially shamanic character of all of this is impossible to miss.

Malta

Now we go back in time several thousand years to pick up what looks like a basically nonshamanic thread in beliefs about the Eternal Life of persons—the ancient Maltese spirituality. While it's true that we can only infer such beliefs in the case of Malta, the architectural, artistic, and burial arrangements seem strongly to support the idea of a whole society oriented toward the realization of Immortality. Here, I'm relying on the Maltese archaeologist David Trump's *Malta: Prehistory and Temples* (2002). According to Trump, settlers arrived on Malta—two main islands in the middle of the Mediterranean—around 5000 BCE. The temple-building period began around 4200 BCE, climaxed around 3500 to 2500 BCE, and ended abruptly about that latter time.[45] These temples are extraordinary. For one thing, they are built of megaliths—huge stone blocks—which were dressed and raised to create massive outer walls and inner chambers. No one else on the planet was building monumental structures of stone at this time. Nor would that take place for another two thousand years.

For another thing, they were laid out, apparently intentionally, to resemble the outlines of statuettes and larger-than-life-sized statues of what is irreverently referred to as "the Fat Lady," almost certainly a cosmic Mother Goddess.[46] The form of the temples and their cavities and vaults was globular. This form was also used for the vast underground hypogea—the enormous, cavernous, sometimes finely carved mass tomb-temples.[47] Trump believes the above-ground temples were imitations of these hypogea, which in turn were representative of the inside of the Goddess—more or less Her Womb in the Earth.[48] This is his hint; I've made the idea explicit. This suggests that the dead, who were buried in these hypogea in the fetal position and smeared with red ochre (symbolic of blood and, so, of life), expected to be reborn, either into Another World or reincarnated on Earth.[49]

The Minoans

We've already looked at the Minoans of Crete in chapter 1 and explored a little their apparently hallucinogenic and ecstatic view of Nature and the Spirit or spirits behind it. We've seen how they achieved Ecstatic Altered States of Consciousness through dancing and drugs (perhaps especially opium, but also probably beer and wine). For our present purposes, I want to emphasize Rodney Castleden's belief that these Expansive States of Consciousness give us clues that in their rituals and dances the Minoans were celebrating anticipations of a Joyous post mortem Life beyond the grave.[50] According to Castelden's view, one of the most straightforward of these indications is the famous Hagia Triada sarcophagus, which he interprets (as do other scholars in the field) as depicting both a sumptuous and joyful funeral procession, the journey to the Otherworld, and the Bliss that will be experienced there.[51] He also notes that a Minoan symbol for the soul was the butterfly[52] and that the dead were frequently buried in a fetal position[53]—again, a possible indication that they expected to be reborn into the Minoan Heaven, something like the later Greek Elysium. During the Temple Period (2000–1470 BCE), there seems to be no sense of an Afterlife Judgment between the souls of the good and bad. This appears in Minoan ideas of Life after Death only with the coming of the Mycenaeans.[54]

Stonehenge

Stonehenge (at its peak about 2400 BCE) has seen increasingly sophisticated archaeological explorations on the site itself, as well as new discoveries in the area surrounding the megaliths. For example, researchers have now excavated a wooden structure of concentric circles of posts (Woodhenge) just up the River Avon that connects the two sites, which, they now know, was a marker of a village, which has been partially excavated.[55] Also, for miles around Stonehenge many graves have been discovered, many of them barrows.[56] And more graves have been discovered on the Stonehenge site itself, as well as what appears to be a ritual road leading into the megalithic circles of stones.[57] Stonehenge archaeologists have tentatively concluded that there was a ritual route of the dead and their family and friends from the Woodhenge world of the living, down the Avon to Stonehenge, where rituals designed to mark or to generate rebirth and Eternal Life took place.[58] From there, the bodies were taken out into the surrounding countryside for burial.[59] Pryor provides a wealth of detailed support for that hypothesis, along with the claim that the bluestones of the inner circle, inside the trilithons, stood for, even impersonated, certain specific venerated ancestors, probably ancient chiefs and magicians.[60]

India

Here, I'm not going to dwell on the visions of Eternal Life for persons that Hinduism and Buddhism propose. We've already looked at these to some extent in earlier discussions. So, to summarize my take on these subcontinental views: In Hinduism, the Goal is Oneness with Brahman and Its State of Consciousness and Being—*sat, chit, ananda*, as we've seen. In other words, with Infinite and Eternal All-thingness. For Buddhism, on the other hand, the Goal is something like extinguishing all traces of the person into No-thingness. The route for gaining either of these states is often a functionally infinite number of reincarnations. Most of these involve a return to the Earth plane, although there may be many stopovers in various Heavens and Hells.

The Greeks

In chapter 1, we looked briefly at several Greek likely stories about the Infinite Worth and Eternal Life of persons—the Minoan background, the Eleusinian mysteries, the Dionysian mysteries, and the Platonic and Pythagorean philosophical versions of these stories. Here, I just want to mention—again, briefly—the Orphic strain in ideas about the Afterlife in the Greek spiritual tradition. I'm using the classical scholar W. K. C. Guthrie's *Orpheus and Greek Religion*

(1952), especially chapter 5: "The Future Life as Seen by Orpheus." Controversies exist about how much of what clearly influenced the poet Pindar, the tragedians, and Platonic and Pythagorean, as well as later ascetic beliefs and practices within the Greek cultural sphere, is due to Orphism. Likewise, there are questions about whether or not there even *was* a historical person named Orpheus. All that aside, my interest is in *whatever* came to be associated with his name.

As Guthrie makes clear, several teachings were central to this tradition: (1) the Darkness of this world (often viewed as a trial, a test, and/or a purgatory . . . even a "living" death)[61] that human beings (and maybe other creatures as well) have to undergo before they can experience liberation from the (tomb of the) world and gain the status of minor Gods and Goddesses in Heaven[62]—so, reincarnation[63]; and (2) Judgment after each lifetime, which determines the quality of the next incarnation.[64] It probably goes without saying that purification from the world in preparation for transcendence of it is an extremely difficult program, but one that shows up in many spiritual traditions, as we've had a chance to see. Ideas similar to these, maybe partially experienced in some NDEs and in some of my dreams—plus Hamlet's remark!—make me wonder how straight a shot it really is from this life to Paradise on the other side. (Think of the perilous journey that a number of spiritual traditions envision.)

The Etruscans

There are important differences between early Chinese religions and the religion of the Etruscans. From my perspective, as I've just mentioned, the pre-Buddhist Chinese spiritual tradition shows the continuing predominance of a shamanic thrust (abstract Deities, veneration of ancestors, and threatening ghosts, for example), while the movement on the part of the Etruscans toward a more anthropomorphic—consequently, *personalistic*—experience of the Divine (and less focused interest in ancestors and ghosts) moves toward greater person-to-Person communion with Gods Who care. Still, there's no question that the two views of the Afterlife are strikingly similar. It's extremely unlikely that this could have been caused by what anthropologists call *cultural diffusion* and much more likely to have arisen through *independent origination*.

I want to briefly look at the Etruscan tradition and refer you back to the Chinese scheme for comparison. For the Etruscan view of the Afterlife, I'm using primarily *The Religion of the Etruscans* (2006), edited by Nancy Thomson de Grummond and Erika Simon, chapter 5: "The Grave and Beyond in Etruscan Religion," written by Ingrid Krauskopf, a contributor to the book. According to Krauskopf (in agreement with other scholars), the Etruscans believed that, at the moment of death, the soul began a long and dangerous journey to the far-off Realm of the Dead, a journey that required an overland trek and/or an oceanic voyage, both of them beset by tormenting Demons.[65] Indeed, both model ships and chariots have been found in Etruscan tombs.[66] If the Destination was reached safely, Eternal Life was pictured as an unending banquet—good food and good company. In fact, the company was all the better because formerly mortal persons, including the newly arrived deceased, had been transfigured into Gods and Goddesses, minor to be sure, but nonetheless sufficiently divine to live for all Eternity in Bliss.[67]

Along with the idea of a long and perilous journey was the seemingly incompatible belief that the soul would live happily in the tomb. Many Etruscan tombs were built to look like houses (whether constructed above ground or, more often, carved into hillsides and cliffs). They were furnished with all the utensils and personal items that the deceased would need to feel, and stay, at home.[68]

There's controversy among Etruscan scholars about whether these different visions of the Afterlife—the journey to a distant, blissful Realm of the Dead or the finding of Eternal Joy "at home" in the tomb—were opposed views of Eternal Life or whether they were believed in together.[69] The ancient Egyptians certainly had no trouble believing that the deceased person would be simultaneously present on different levels of Reality. My own experiences of physical effects, presences, voices, apparitions, and so on lead me to think that the Etruscans, who no doubt had their own experiences of such things, could also view the dead as happily operating on multiple levels at the same time.

Really fascinating to me is the evidence that the Etruscan dead, while not able to return to this world per se, nonetheless may have been able to move from the Realm of the Dead proper to that Realm's Antechamber—there, perhaps, to make contact with the living . . . *precisely by* engineering physical effects, voices, presences, and apparitions, and showing up in dreams on the other side of a barrier of some kind.[70] I wonder, too, if at least some OBEs and NDEs on the part of the living might be excursions into that Antechamber, which the Etruscans discerned.

Mesopotamia and the Semitic Peoples of the Fertile Crescent

It is sometimes mistakenly believed that the ancient Mesopotamians and the Semitic peoples of the Fertile Crescent did not believe in Eternal Life after death. In fact, they did. It's just that, for them, the Afterlife was lived out in a dreary, cold, dark Underworld with mud for food and dirty water for drink.[71] Even the great heroes, like the legendary Gilgamesh in Mesopotamia and King David in Judea, underwent that ghastly fate.

A possible exception to this version of Eternal Life after death might be depicted in the Canaanite Ba'al Cycle from Ugarit, in which the god Ba'al dies and is resurrected. If the Canaanite kings were thought to become assimilated into Ba'al after their deaths, much as ancient Egyptians believed they became one with Osiris, then a Pleasant, even Glorious, Immortality might have been applied to them.[72] Sadly, probably to nobody else. It was only with the Persian Zoroastrian conquests of these areas in the sixth century BCE that a brighter future for the deceased of the general public became envisioned.

Do any of these examples (and many others) of people's beliefs—and I would say, *behind* these *beliefs*, *actual experiences* as well as intuitions—about an Eternal Life for persons clinch the truth of the matter? I have to say no. But, from my point of view, depending on the weight you give to deep human *experiences* and the truthfulness you allow for powerful *intuitions*, not to mention your understanding of the accuracy (at least symbolic) of *imagination* plus the sheer *quantity* and *the similarities of themes* across time and space among these belief systems and *the number of people* who have held and hold them, as well as the *centrality* of these systems to their sense of the *meaningfulness* of their lives—all of these factors *do* seem to me to strongly tilt the balance toward the *probability* of Immortality of some kind or kinds.

Kheper, Neheh, Djet: Kinds of Immortality and the Dynamic that Enables Them

Once through the Antechambers of the Afterlife, human beings have imagined, intuited, experienced, felt the truth of, had revealed to them, hallucinated (not necessarily in the negative sense of the word)—whatever words you might want to use—three major *kinds* of possible Immortalities, or ways to experience Eternal Life. (I'm aware that theologians distinguish these two terms—Immortality and Eternal Life—but I don't want to go into all that, so I'm using them interchangeably.) I'm trying here a type of overarching classification of the kinds I can think of. I'm sure I've left some out. Also, based on my own intuitions and my subjective experiences of what I take to be forms of our Immortality, I'm suggesting an overarching Dynamic that *enables their realization*. I'm calling this the *Lifting-Up Dynamic*. I'm intentionally excluding possible *specific mechanisms* for the gaining of the actual condition of Eternal Life in Its several forms, because I'm less interested in *how* it's done than *that* it's done and what it might *be*, once it *is* done.

Note: The examples I've given of different specific cultural views of the Afterlife—even the Mesopotamian and Fertile Crescent Semitic ones—can, I believe, be fitted into the following classification.

There are overlaps, or meshings, in my classification of the kinds of Immortality. As an overall framework for these differing but not unrelated kinds of Immortality that I've thought of, I'm going to use the ancient Egyptian idea of three basic forms of Eternal Life—Kheper, Neheh, and Djet. I've already presented these in earlier sections of the book (see chapter 1). But here I want to expand the Egyptian versions of these forms to incorporate *other people's ideas*—including my own. So, please forgive me, ancient Egyptians—ditto for Egyptologists. But I hope at least the former group feels honored by my choice of their framework for this project.

Why am I using the Egyptian scheme as my framework? In short, because I think it's brilliant and pretty well nails (with a little expanded interpretation) the general categories into which the kinds in my scheme fall. Remember what Kheper, Neheh, and Djet were for the Egyptians who look to me like they observed Eternal Life most closely and thought about It most systematically of all other peoples in all other places and times. Briefly (with my more expansive definition), Kheper was the symbol for the Eternal Creative Unfolding of the universe—and of the Psyche of Re the Creator—and, as aspects of Him, us as well. The Egyptians had a somewhat narrower definition than mine: dawn and early morning as the sun rose—as Re was resurrected from His death during the night. As such, Jan Assmann sees Kheper as an aspect of Neheh—in effect, the same dawn of the same day, over and over again.[73] So, for him, this creative aspect of Re's life cycle was severely limited and not all that creative (since that creation was an Eternal Iteration of the same thing). But I'm breaking Kheper (the verb form) off from Neheh because, for my purposes, it initially stands better on its own as an embodiment of the idea of the continuous growth of the universe, yes, but at least as importantly, of the psyche-soul-spirit—this along a *linear* but *rising-line* trajectory. Neheh, the Eternal Return of the same, or *Cyclical* Eternity—the same "day" endlessly repeated—I'm leaving mostly intact (a few modifications). For the Egyptians, Djet-Eternity was Eternity proper—a timeless, frozen, everything-all-at-once *Eternal Now*. I'm keeping that notion here, but noting that, for me, the Eternal Now is the *unpacked* Source of both Kheper and Neheh.

So, with these things in mind, let's proceed. My first category falls under the auspices of Kheper—as noted, what I'm interpreting as Eternal Growth of the psyche/Psyche, always something new, fresh, better, and more expansive. It's what I'm calling the *Step-by-Step Kheper Model* of Eternal Life—simply *Kheper* for short. Included here are two megasystems—reincarnation, of course, but also the Islamic Sufi notion of way stations, especially as laid out by Ibn 'Arabi.[74] Ibn 'Arabi's idea seems, at least mostly, to be about a systematic growing of consciousness while still incarnate in a body in this world. This is not unlike the recommendations of Plato, the Neoplatonists, the Hermeticists, the Pythagoreans, the Plains Indians we looked at above, much of modern psychology (especially depth and transcendental), and twelve-step programs. Of course, I recommend this category for a richer and more integrated and filled out earthly life. But I suspect that it's even better suited to an Afterlife in which time (in our sense), age, and eventually declining energies are not a factor and so one in which Kheper is *limitlessly* more effective, particularly if your Goal is a Beatified Final State—Heaven, Elysium, or even oneness with (or proximity to) the One—in my belief, as you already know, the God of Love. But, if the Goal is reached, it seems to me that your state is no longer one of growth, Kheper, but Eternal *Arrival*. In other words, Djet.

In this model, there are layers and layers of spaces and times, dimensions and levels of the consciousness and being of evolving or unfolding *persons*, like Egyptian akh's, ka's, ba's, and so on and Buddhist Heavens or, more simply, the incongruences of time reported by many NDE travelers. Judgment, sifting, or life review is a necessary part of this, as it is in, for example, Jungian analysis. There is no forward movement or soul growth without an action-reflection model here. We certainly see this evaluating element in the reincarnation systems, as well as in purgatorial ideologies. However, the idea of the Last Judgment, where the soul is assigned to everlasting Bliss or Punishment without any chance to learn from its mistakes and grow, obviously is a horse of a different color. And, in my view, demonic.

In the *apocatastasis panton* systems, as well as in al-Ghazali's extra-Quranic story (see chapter 1). and Ibn 'Arabi's idea that God makes Hell feel like Paradise to its inmates[75] (which is similar to universal salvation), we see a very strong denial of the Last Judgment idea.

My own take:

While I like the way stations model better—it feels more expansive . . . you know, the sky's the limit . . . ever-growing identities in, hopefully, happier venues—I'm certainly open to the idea that some, or many, of these way stations are reached by our being recycled to earthly lives. In fact, there seems to me to be quite a lot of pretty convincing evidence for reincarnation. I myself have visions of "podding" (like whales), as Oversouls (made up of a multiplicity of "kindred spirits," or psyches) that send down underdeveloped aspects of Themselves to incarnate, and then haul them back up for integration into the Megaperson of the Oversoul of Which my own identity is a part. On the other hand, are "my" reincarnations reincarnations of *me* or *Me* (as individual and/or the Oversoul), or are they incursions of other psyches welling up from my or the Collective Psyche? Maybe yes to both questions.

Many people, maybe most, have almost certainly thought of Eternal Life as an endless succession of days or moments, similar to, or identical with, days and moments of their earthly lives—going on forever, infinite in number. Think of that, though: living something like our earthly time-bound lives—without, of course, health problems or aging and, it goes without saying, death—and never being able, even if you *want* to, to stop it . . . *ever*. This, to me, seems close to the Neheh Model of Immortality. Unlike the continuous growth of Kheper, eternal repetition finally requires coming back to, and so, being stuck in, an infinite iteration of the same.

That seems like a major drawback to me of the Neheh Model—no way to get off the train (on its circular tracks). There's another issue too: What are we actually going to *do* in this model . . . Forever? As we've seen already, this could be banqueting, hunting, dancing, sex, playing games, and other pleasant pastimes. But at what point would we get sick of it? How about compulsively reliving and reliving the same most wonderful moments of our earthly lives Forever? Even that sounds unappealing to me.

What I mean is this: if these things—the days, the moments, the activities, the events—were infinitely repeated, even with variations, the "laws" of Infinity, in this case the Infinite Form of *time*, dictate that each iteration, even those with variation (if there are such things), would be repeated an "infinite number" of times. So that each Infinity would be equal to every other—Infinity plus Infinity is . . . well . . . Infinity. Or, in this instance, Eternity. Eternity, strictly speaking, is time*less All-time*, and it *is* because (as I've already mentioned) the Infinite and the Infinitesimal are the same thing, as in All-time is equal to No-time. So, as I see it, each moment of Eternity is *ultimately* identical. It's the Eternal Now (with or without some element of duration). It's not that the banquet *lasts* forever (though it has, again, an aspect of duration). It's that there is *One Banquet Moment*—actually, Timeless/All-time Moment—that is forever, or say, Forever-*ness*. That means in the end, I think, Neheh is a form of Djet. And Djet is, finally, the *full expression* of Eternity.

Not, however, that It would necessarily be *experienced* as such, or *only* as that. As I've suggested, I think there is no reason to suppose that there isn't time-*layering* (and space-layering) as a sort of unpacking of Eternity. We see this, after all, in quantum physics (nonlocality, for example) and in relativity theory (different times at different speeds and in the presence, or absence, of gravitating objects) but also in our own *subjective experience* of time—how some hours, days, weeks, seasons, years drag and others fly by, oblivious of clock time (which is also relative). I don't see why Eternal Life should be any different. Somehow or other, as Plato said (in effect), "time is the moving image of Eternity."[76] To make the point (I hope) clearer, I would say "the moving embodiment, or explicating and unpacking of That Which is Nontemporal, at least as It is in Itself. Time is, or times are, what's 'inside' of Timelessness, or Timelessness in the mode(s) of time." Or, you could even say, "Timelessness is a mode of time." (The "equation" works both ways.)

So, I guess I'd affirm the reality, or effectiveness, of Neheh for those who'd like to experience Djet that way. And I suppose the same goes for Kheper.

By the way, notice that Neheh could be understood as its own Goal or justification (because it's endlessly circular)—but, as we've just seen, it ends up as Djet anyway. Notice also that there is, however, an element of Goal-directed Kheper as linear time *within* the cyclical time of Neheh, whether in this life or, I presume, the Next. Cycles *do* advance, at least *around* the circle, like a clock hand. And speaking of clocks, where the clock hand attaches at the center of the clock circle, there is no movement—*no time* (no time without movement, or at least any that we would recognize)—in other words, Djet. Or you could say, all time—again, Djet—comes from the center where the hand attaches and that gives the hand its linear (Kheper) movement around the circle (Neheh) (through mechanisms and/or electrical current). Without the movement-inducing timeless center, there would be no (measured) time at all. So, no Kheper or Neheh without Djet.

Anyway, there's a Dynamic that enables all of this that I find really interesting. More than interesting. I find It refreshing, exciting, and exhilarating! This Dynamic can be woven into—even *underlies*—the three Egyptian models of Eternal Life, at least as *I* think about them. I'm calling It the *Lifting Up Dynamic*. This idea was probably originally made most explicit in Hinduism. Each momentless Moment of time, whether linear (Kheper) or cyclical (Neheh) or both, is timelessly manifested and simultaneously withdrawn—each one—so that in every Moment, the universe is created and annihilated and created again. Everything and every event, every moment, is *immediately* lifted up into the Eternity from Which it descended, every one of these purified, made golden, made beautiful and absolutely Good! So that the dross of Nature is burned away or in some way transmuted, and everything that reaches, or returns to, Eternity is *transfigured* after its "tarnishing" by the world—I would even say restored to what it always *is* (in Djet).

Here, I want to bring in the Christian theologian Paul Tillich, a bit of St. Paul, and my own expanded interpretation of this process. Tillich calls his version of this "essentialization," by which he can be interpreted to mean that the negative material of one's life is stripped entirely away, not leaving much of the individual—his or her positive qualities and acts (which were meagre)—for continuance in Eternal Life. But, says Tillich, this person's poverty in terms of Goodness is augmented by her or his oneness with the Goodness of the collective human experiences of the "positive".[77] Okay, maybe. I'm going to supplement that idea with a couple of passages from St. Paul, both of which are found in I Corinthians, the first in chapter 15:35–53 and the second in I Corinthians, chapter 15:54–55. Although ambiguous (and the source of a lot of interpretation through the centuries), the first passage *does* seem to say that our finite and mortal natures must "put on" what is presumably our Immortal Natures (verse 53). It seems to me that "put on" implies a *layering* of one nature over another rather than a *separation*. In other words, *both* natures—the earthly and the Heavenly—are retained in a *composite* person/Person in Heaven. The second passage continues this idea and adds, significantly I think, the idea that biological death—perhaps psychological (or spiritual) too—is "swallowed up" in the triumph of Eternal Life (verse 54). In my view, what is "swallowed" is metabolized, in that process transformed, and made an integral part of an "essentializing" person on her or his way to a Blissful Eternal Life. That might make even the spiritually impoverished person's identity in the Afterlife full and rich!

You can see a kind of megacycle here too: the flowing out of Eternity and the return—a different kind of Neheh. You can also see a linear progression. Time *does* move forward, even if at every moment it and the creatures, moments, and events within it are lifted up and purified, a type of Kheper. And, ultimately, even though in both descent and ascent there are layers—a Neoplatonic touch—above there is Djet.

There is one more model of Eternal Life, although I hesitate to call it that, which doesn't figure, at least not in any obvious or coherent way, into my categories. I'm calling this model the *This Is It! Model*. I guess it's basically Zen. Anyway, the idea is that Nature, Its creatures, moments, and events, *are* Eternity—and there's nothing *more* . . . period. From my perspective, given Plato's dictum about time being the moving image of Eternity, they *must* be. But I would say they are an extremely fragmented and actually *interrupted* expressions of It and that there's *much* more Beyond. The *This Is It! Model* is certainly *not* the Eternal Life envisioned by the spiritual systems we've looked at or the categories and kinds of Eternal Life we've thought about here. As my friend and personal doctor said one day when we were talking about the experience of earthly life, "If this is all there is, it's . . . well . . . disappointing."

This is it? Tell that to the starving and disease-ravaged children of Gaza, Sudan, or any other such place.

I suspect that the kinds of Immortality we've been discussing are *all* true . . . and, to some extent, at our own discretion. By this I mean that within the framework of (expansively defined) Kheper, Neheh, and Djet, which I believe are set by the Creator, we are free to experience Eternal Life in any and all of these ways. As Infinitely Valued, Unique *persons* who are individualizations of *the Person*, we are free in the Afterlife to stay individuals as long as we wish—or can *stand* it. If and when we want to get off the train, if we're really ready for the leap (perhaps the culmination of Kheper), we can. Then we fall (perhaps with relief) into the Arms of God, there to be Eternally (Infinitely) Cherished as "finished," as the Plains Indians put it. And—perhaps Temporally-Timelessly—aware of it.

Three Short Reveries

Most mornings I wake up feeling excited about the day beginning to unfold with all of its potential and promise for creating and advancing my many creative projects. Like nannying our now six-month-old granddaughter, researching, writing, sculpting, teaching, talking with friends, and, when weather permits, working on our house and yard. In some modes of creativity—for example, when I help our granddaughter make one of her breakthroughs, like learning to crawl, cutting her first teeth, eating her first solid food, and so on, and I share her sense of triumph and joy, or when a sculpture has finally let me know what it wants to be, or I learn something fresh and new in my studying, or when one of my students experiences what we've been studying coming together in an *ah-ha!* moment, or the block-long buckthorn bushes are trimmed and, at fourteen feet tall, look majestic—*in all these things and more* I become lost to myself and at one with the explosion of creativity going on all around me and inside me. I feel a part of the creative advance of the world—Nature, yes, but also the Joyful Creating of a Transcendent yet Immediately Present God. And I think, "*This* is Eternal Life—whatever happens to me, whatever happens in human history, whatever others do, whatever happens to the universe." For me, this is an experience of the Lifting Up Dynamic for Kheper-Eternity.

On long, almost hourless summer afternoons, lying in the hammock hung between our gigantic ash tree and our Siberian elm, looking up into the thick canopy of green far above my head, listening to the birds calling to one another, I often fall into a sense of the Timelessness of the cycling of Nature—the foliage that returns exuberantly every spring, the generations upon generations of the squirrels and birds—I relax into Nature's over-and-over-again, get dozy, and let myself go into the miraculous embrace of the assurance that somehow this is all lifted up in a glorious paean of grounded yet transcending celebration of the Eternal Return. I feel myself in the arms of Neheh-Eternity (again, gained through the agency of the Lifting Up Dynamic).

And, sometimes, usually as a sudden rush of knowing, unbidden, unexpected, I feel this Moment—right here, right now—being drawn up instantaneously, through layers and layers of Exultation, the Darkness transmuted and joining with the Light, and set, stored, lodged with a Timeless Above-time—I think, the Mind of God, Who generates these things, remembers them, and makes them Present all-at-once . . . finished, fulfilled, and perfect. Then I feel the truth of Djet-Eternity (once more, empowered by the Lifting Up Dynamic).

In the end, I think, we have to *experience* Immortality, actually *feel* It— and trust the truth of It. Alone, evidence and pondering won't get us there. At most, they can shove us *up to the Moment* of realization but not *over* It into *Knowing*. I think *everything* is Eternal. But only those who *know* know their, and everything else's, Immortality.

7
Why Are We Here?

We are here to commune with the Infinite Person and with that Person as each other, with and within Whom we are and, to the extent that we can, to grow toward that Person's Fullness of Truth, Beauty, and Love. This communing may take many forms—inner and outer—and may involve pain as well as pleasure.

Why Questions and How Questions

Before we get to the question "Why are we here?," the first question to ask is "Why is there *anything*?"

Notice that the *why* question assumes *meaning, meaningfulness, intention*. The *how* question—"How does it come to be that?"—is neutral about meaning. It's about the mechanics of how something works or how it comes to be. Up to certain limits (like those we encounter in quantum physics), science is pretty good at answering *how* questions. Questions about *meaning* can only—and, I must add, inadequately—be answered by spirituality and religion—the deepest Heart, the closest we can get to the Core of us.

But back to: Why is there *anything*?

On one level, because the Creator wants it. But what does God want? I think, among whatever else, *Experience*—Experience of stars colliding, for example, but also the Experiences of living things up to their capacities, each according to its sensory and neuronal "design limits." Does God want to feel the Exhilaration and Joy (however transient) of the mayfly? What about the horror of being eaten whole by a crocodile? Maybe. But, then, what kind of a God is *that*?

I think we have to face the fact that, one way or another, the Creator has manifested Light and Darkness, Pleasure and Pain, Joy and Despair, Triumph and Tragedy, Life and Death. As I've said several times, it seems to me that God may have many Purposes, or Goals, for Experiencing. Unfortunately, some of These may be *awful* for us.

So, the question "Why is there anything?" involves—here we go again!—the question "Why is there Evil, even natural Evil, more urgently moral-ethical Evil?" I'm sorry that, after all our discussions about this in various places throughout this book . . . *I'm going to conclude that no one but God has the answer to this.*

On to the "Why are we here?" question.

That *why* question assumes some*one*—a *person*, because nothing except a person can ask it, and only highly sentient and aware persons. No matter what less sentient living things may (or may not) feel, only highly aware persons can feel the full force of the question, articulate it, and try to answer it.

Taking a page from the anthropic cosmological principles, it might be possible to propose that anything exists because *Sentience* was wanted—that is to say, *the Experience only sentient beings can have.*

If Nature has desires beyond, say, the clunking together of asteroids, the emergent properties of water, or the neural architecture of an ant, then clearly one of Its desires is the *Experience* of *Experiencing* Itself . . . *Experiencing.* So, how can It do that? By—at least in our case— anthropomorphizing Itself. It must be able to feel and think in order to feel (enough) and think (enough) to become aware (enough) of Itself. This requires high-order consciousness.

As I've suggested earlier, of the feelings, thoughts, and awarenesses we have, the most fulfilling of these is Love. Love only happens when sentient creatures meet . . . and so, the lyrical illumination that heads this chapter. The "Why is there *anything*?" question inevitably becomes, then, the "Why is there *us*?" question. It's just a matter of *fact*, since we alone (that we know of) can ask it, and we alone (that we know of) can answer it, even if only partially—and, as it looks to me, pretty much incoherently.

To be more specific about the *why* question, I'm going to lay out nine answers to this question, and then offer objections to and further questions about them. Both my objections and further questions surface exactly because underlying both the question and its supposed answers is the Presence of Evil—specific evils and also the general Evil that shows Itself precisely in those specific appearances of It that prompt the answers. I'll be taking into account moral-ethical Evils, but natural Evils as well, which, as I've already suggested, *become* moral-ethical Evils when Nature crosses the line from inanimate to living creatures and impacts these to their detriment. As I've previously said, as long as they stay natural Evils, they may or may not be regrettable—like flood basalts, changes in the saltiness of water, climate swings, an expanding red giant star that evaporates its planets, and so forth. But when they impact living things, especially those that can feel fear and pain, the feelings and, in more sentient creatures, the thoughts they have about their own damaged states of being and perhaps immanent demises can be catastrophic for them.

Maybe, like my proposed many Divine Purposes (most of Which we cannot fathom or probably even imagine), I suggest that there may be *many* Reasons we are here. Maybe, at least at one level, They're specific to individuals. Even here, my guess is that there may be many, or at least several, Purposes for *your* life, for *your* being . . . *you*, living *your* life specifically, and *me living mine*. All ultimately Divine Purposes, Divine Reasons.

Answers to the "Why Are We Here?" Question

Answer One: It's Just the Way It Is

Objection: This is a nonanswer and explains, or answers, nothing.

Answer Two: We Are Here to Grow Our Souls

This answer pictures the world as a school—the *World as a School Model*. While this overall answer probably applies to every high-level sentient creature (such as ourselves), there are specific tasks for growing our souls based on our individual temperaments, strengths, and weaknesses. You've already realized that I believe that, in all cases, no matter how individualized, and no matter the more specific needs of particular persons, the most legitimate and compelling overarching goal for soul growth is in the direction of *greater Humaneness*, greater, deeper, more selfless, and more inclusive Love.

Here's a list of some of the things I think we need to learn, if the *School Model* is at least partially valid (incomplete, of course). You might think about how some of these things might, or might not, apply to your own soul-growth tasks. So, we need to learn to fulfill ourselves along the lines of our natural proclivities but also, depending on whatever compelling interest may be involved, perhaps to fill out in some ways that are *not* along the lines of our usual tendencies. That's growth. Also, to reconcile with split-off aspects of our identities (for example, in Jung's terms, shadow aspects of ourselves, (in Beahrs's terms, alternative centers of consciousness within), as well as with others where this is possible. We need to develop firm boundaries while we keep open hearts. Out of self-love and strength, we need to become kinder, fairer, more loving, more humane to overcome unwarranted fears without becoming reckless, to become humble but not accept humiliation, and so on. Beyond all these, and in concert with them, we need to become wiser, perhaps to work for causes that espouse these values, to teach when called upon, to serve others' well-being, and so forth. All of this and more requires psychospiritual growth—a very good reason for being here!

Notice that all of these answers to why we are here assume that *we learn to overcome Evil in general and the specific Evils that* not *learning and* not *doing these and other good things result in.*

Objection: But what about all those people, of every age, in all times and places, who can *never* grow—who cannot, as I'm saying, fulfill *any* of the specific Purposes that are, I think, at the core of the meaningfulness of life as a person, at least a human person? I don't only mean those who've been thwarted or destroyed by the moral-ethical Evil of other persons, including those less sentient persons who are predators—literally and metaphorically—psychologically and physically? What about persons who don't have either the feeling or cognitive capacities to grow emotionally and/or intellectually? Are such arrested, thwarted, incapacitated, tortured, murdered, and so on persons just throwaways, in the same sense that not all seeds planted grow? Just collateral damage in the context of those relatively few who *do* thrive in the enterprise of learning? And what about natural Evils, which are moral-ethical Evils because they impact persons? What about bacteria and viruses? What about earthquakes?

Answer Three: We Are Here to Create

Creation at virtually every level of Reality as we know it is a major thrust of Nature and, in my belief, the *Person* behind Nature, within It, and in some sense, *as* It. It doesn't seem surprising, then, that creation—from children to symphonies, societies and spiritual systems to business ventures, from pyramids to Taj Mahals, and so on—would be a hallmark of *persons* in harmony with the ever-originating Source (Kheper again!). So the *World as an Ongoing Creative Venture Model* is another answer to the "Why are we here?" question. We are here to create. My own life has been fueled mostly by the drive to do exactly that. In creating, we can do something wonderful that feels, in part at least, like self-transcendence and, while we're doing it, a delicious and refreshing self-losing in something somehow more than ourselves, or at least other. There is a fantastic feeling of giving oneself over to the Beautiful and the True. And while flowing with the creative side of Nature, we're also going beyond It and feeling something perhaps of the Joy and Exhilaration that God feels.

Objection: But what of all those persons, from the robin couple I witnessed losing their young to excessive summer heat, to the brilliant unrecognized poet, and then on to those millions and millions whose lives are crippled, distorted, ravaged, destroyed? If we are here to create, that "we" is only really a privileged or lucky handful.

Notice that answers two and three involve striving—ideally, striving for Excellence in all that we do. Unconsciously, semiconsciously, or consciously, it seems to me that, beneath all our particular strivings for Excellence, we are striving to enter the Kingdom of Heaven. At least this is the hoped-for, or even expected, fruit of our labors. The downside is, as Jesus apparently said, that Salvation is gained one person at a time (Matthew 7:13). That may or may not be bad news for many of us. But I think that, at least ultimately, there's *no* bad news for *any* of us.

Answer Four: We Are Here to Be Sown and See What Comes Up

If this world is not an inclusive-of-all school or place to create, perhaps it is, instead, a garden or a soul nursery—the *World as a Soul-Nursery Model*—whose souls are sown like seeds. Some come up, and some shrivel or are eaten by birds.

Objection: But then we're back to Nature . . . and the Evil of Indifference. Ditto the *objections* above. This answer is, for me at least, morally-ethically abhorrent.

Answer Five: We Are Here to Realize Where We Don't Want to Be

Or is Reality, at least at this level, a prison, a reform school, or purgatory, and our lives here a sort of aversion therapy? And once we've had enough, we make a move to get out of here as fast as we can? This is, in general terms, the *World as a Prison or Purgatory Model* proposed by Platonism, Manichaeism, Hinduism, Buddhism, and a number of other philosophies and theologies. It is said that we can leave when we're ready.

Objection: But none of us is *ever* ready. No matter how many reincarnations. If the world is a prison or purgatory that we need to become reformed enough to escape, I see little evidence for such reformation actually occurring—at least not for the multitudes of persons. How does an eight-pound toddler (who should be toddling but can't) become reformed? And, on the other side of the coin, what about all the Beauty and Joy that *is* present in the world—the Beauty and Joy of being together . . . and loving each other? *The clear indications of the Infinite Worth of persons?*

Answer Six: We Are Here to Be Punished

This is the *World as Hell Model*. Reform is not the purpose of Hell. The purpose of Hell is to inflict pain.

Objection: This model is plainly and simply monstrous.

Answer Seven: We Are Here Just for the Experience, or the Journey for Its Own Sake

I've already alluded to this in the introduction to this chapter . . . but as one of God's possible Motivations, or Purposes, for creation. What about us? It does seem to me that a lot of us have powerful, beautiful, and meaningful experiences being here—not least of which is being *us* specifically. And, of course, to experience one another . . . at the high end of that, loving one another.

Objection: But vast numbers of persons (both human and other than that) look to me like their experiences here are stifled, truncated, and miserable and filled with pain and terror.

Answer Eight: We Are Here to Save the Universe

In this *Save the Universe Model*, we are here to lift the whole universe up into God through our own personal transformations. In other words, we're here to save Nature *from* Itself and *for* God. My reaction to this kind of eschatology is: What a pile of . . . .!

Objection: We can't save ourselves; we can't save our planet, either from itself or from us. How are we going to save Nature? Evil is such a powerful Presence and Force, in both Its natural and Its moral-ethical forms, that there is no possibility of Its ever being saved—certainly not by creatures like us, who are obviously swamped by It. The narcissism such an eschatology requires is itself a moral-ethical Evil of almost unimaginably vast proportions. It's clear to me that if *anyone* can save the universe, including us as a part of it, *it must be God*. And I believe He/She/It is doing exactly that—every momentless Moment—by lifting *everything* up, transformed and transfigured, into God's Self.

Answer Nine: Salvational Love

Except for the Hell Model of answer six and It's Just the Way It is Model of answer one, I *do* feel *some* truth in most of the answers I've laid out above to the "Why are we here?" question. I am deeply respectful of those philosophers, like J. G. Fichte, Friedrich Hegel, and Stanley Rosen, as well as theologians, like Nicholas of Cusa, Ibn 'Arabi, Paul Tillich, Keith Ward, C. S. Lewis (1898–1963), and a great many others, who have ruminated so sincerely and insightfully about this question (and others)—Western and Eastern, ancient, medieval, and modern. But again, as you already know, for me the most emotionally and cognitively fulfilling, the most all-embracing answer to the question of why we're here is to *meet* one another and, in that meeting, *to love* . . . one another, ourselves, and God. All of that requires *persons* and, I believe, centrally involves their *Salvation*—this, by the Person Who makes them and calls them to *commune* in the Intimate Vastness of Unlimited Love.

Objection: As with all the other objections to these answers, many, maybe most, sentient beings, even humans, fail miserably at this loving thing—again, in my view, because of the Evil inherent in being at all, especially in being a *living* creature and clearly in being a sentient one—finite, extremely complicated, and evolved to not only survive but to predate.

Still, there is nothing beyond Love, except, of course, in God . . . whatever that Beyond might be within that Infinite Person. Whatever answers God surely has, they are certainly more adequate—and infinitely so—than any of ours. They are, in any case, God's Business, to Which we are not—indeed, *cannot*—be privy. And I'm okay with that. Actually, *more* than okay.

8
My Likely Story

That exists, not as we do in the here-and-now,
but inexplicably.
This is striving toward it.
Psyche is, and, via matter, comes back online
bit by bit,
refracted through many-layered lenses, and is
spewed, distracted,
through a multitude of prisms, expanded pools
of light, however canted,
as biologic entities provide increasing
opportunities
for awakening,
remembering, and continued extension or ascent.
What was forgotten becomes increasingly
available
as more and more is made explicit.
Why the fall, the nodding off, or sudden narcolepsy
vis-à-vis presumably infinite Awareness/Being?
I have no idea. But its occurrence and the history
of recovery from this unfortunate, or fortunate,
event, as the case may be,

constitutes my working hypothesis for the history
of the cosmos and my life as I have lived it.

DOUGLAS M. GILLETTE,
AT THE THRESHOLDS OF ELYSIUM

What I Want to Say First

As I said at the beginning of our journey together through this book, *I don't know what Reality is. I don't know anyone who does.*

Nonetheless, in this last chapter, I want to lay out something of what I *think* It is. Well . . . a little more than that, because as I've presented them throughout the book, there are things I've experienced in the day-to-day as well as in the forms of psi, at the low end, and Spirit, at the high, which I *know* to be a part of Reality. I *know* them because I've lived them, or they've lived me—unasked for, unexpected, uninvited . . . but they've happened *to* me and to people I trust to tell the truth. At the very least, many of the things I've shared with you are *psychological facts.* They've happened within my psyche/Psyche . . . as everything else we can think of does. Remember solipsism, and how it can't be defeated? We just have to go on living as if it weren't the case, but with the awareness that it is!

Because of these psychological facts, I've had to acknowledge *knowledge* of them, not *speculation* about them. Other material I've presented *is* speculation. But it's speculation that, from my point of view, is closely tied (in most cases) to the actual experiences. Some of my speculation goes a little further than that. But all of that "little further" is *just* a *little* further. If I've used the speculations of others, especially scientists, philosophers, and theologians, which I have of course, it's only been because their musings have reverberated with my own, both the experiences and the speculations that I've drawn out of those experiences, those psychological facts. At no point have I used someone else's speculation in place of my own . . . slapped it over my thinking like paint on wood. Nor have I gone too far off into the weeds for the sheer fun of it. That weedy stuff *is* fun for me, but in the end, it's pretty much just intellectual entertainment. Which is not the purpose of this book.

The organization of this chapter largely follows the preceding chapters, with one exception. I start off with God, rather than introduce Him/Her/It after discussing Psyche, Nature, and Persons first, as I did in the main body of the text. The reason for that order in the main body is that I wanted to emphasize that our psychological experiences take precedence over our experiences of Nature, Personhood, and God. Psyche is first in the sense that that's what we know ourselves *to be* and to be *within*. Without psyche/Psyche we could experience no Nature, or Personhood, nor a Supracosmic Person. Solipsism again . . . sorry! As well, most persons that we know—whether incarnate, formerly incarnate, or perhaps never-been-incarnate (in our sense at least)—are, so far as we can tell, emergent from or manifested by the expressing of psyche/Psyche through the medium of matter, or Nature, and therefore, with the qualified exception of God, combinations of psyche/Psyche and matter (whatever either of these is, really) and, consequently, finite. But here I want to emphasize the absolute precedence of God (Psyche and Person) over matter, space, time, and so on as the way things *are ontologically*—to borrow the philosophical way of putting this—in terms of the logical order of Being, rather than in terms of how we experience them.

Also, for the most part, I want to start each section that follows with a statement about what I do *know*, and then follow that up with *speculation* that, again, at least from my perspective, is closely tied to those things I know I know. Again, it goes without saying, but I'll say it anyway: these are *my* psychological facts and *my* speculations—my likely story. They may not be yours. If yours are similar, I'm ecstatic! If not, then okay. Either way, what I have to say here constitutes my working hypothesis for the history of the cosmos and my life as I have lived it.

God

I know there is God. I have experienced the Presence of Who I call God as far back as I can remember, which, as I've noted several times in earlier chapters, goes deep into my toddlerhood and, with the possibility that I remember my birth night, to earliest infancy. I know, whatever else is going on with God, that *God is Good and Loving.* He certainly has been good and loving *to me. I know that God is Beautiful.* He/She/It has infused me with a powerful sense of Beauty—all the forms of external Beauty and also mansions and layers of internal Beauty . . . Beauty of soul, in myself at my best, and in others I've known, both intimately and more distantly. *I know that God is as Truthful* as He can be in His communications and interfaces with finite creatures, up to the level of their capacities. I know this has been true for me.

As I narrated in chapter 5, I am aware that the God I know is a God-*image* or, rather, the composite of several converging God-images from different cultures. These Images for me are indeed convergent, such that my God-images, and ultimately my single God-image is Self-coherent. I have experienced God as a psychological fact mostly in the form of *a Person*—One Who is my Awesome and Unaccountable Creator and, in my daily life, the Overseer of my life, my Companion, my Friend, my Validator, my Helper, my Guide, the One Who closes certain avenues (sometimes with much pain to me) and opens the ways God knows are better for me and that I actually experience as enhancing my character, my real goals, the person and acts that are the most authentic version of me. God has filled my life with Magic and Wonder, Confidence and Joy, and the Fulfillment of all the dreams I've had—the ones that genuinely pertained to me.

My own life experience has taught me that God-images *feel like* the Infinite Person interfacing with finite persons in such a way that They are both validating of those finite persons and challenging to them—challenging and luring the finite person to grow. Growth as a person *has meant to me* both establishing more firmly but also more flexibly a personal identity. As a core part of that program, it has also meant feeling, thinking, speaking, and acting increasingly in more humane ways. In other words, learning to love more fully. By extension of my own experience, I *speculate* that Personal Validation and Growth in the capacity to love (and be loved) is actually what all at least human striving is aiming at. This suggests to me that God is luring us toward more humane God-images, which, in turn, are increasingly accurate images of Him.

While I've experienced God as a Person, I have also, and with no contradiction, felt directly His/Her/Its Vastness. I have felt God shading off behind the Image I have of Him into Fathomlessness. In that sense, I have felt Her Infinity, an Infinity that, while I still feel That as a Person, It is a Person of such Magnitude that It does really begin to feel like a Thing, One that is so distant from my capacity to experience personhood that I feel deeply and truly frightened of Him. Still, I don't experience God as misrepresenting Himself when He shows Himself to me as a Person or God-image when He's really an Impersonal Thing . . . only that, for my finite intelligence and finite ways of evaluating and categorizing, I can no longer *feel* that Infinity as *Immediately* Personal, though I do experience even It as an, or the, *Infinite Person* but Indefinitely Extended. And when I feel overwhelmed by that alienness, He shows Himself smiling at me from out of the very Center of It, as if to say, "Don't be alarmed. I'm still and always *Me to you.*"

That brings me to the beginning point of *speculation*, rather than *knowing*, to *I think* rather than *I know*. As I suggested earlier (in chapter 5), what I think the followers of Eastern religions are encountering when they talk about the Void, or Pure Consciousness without Mind, is at least two things. First—the explanation I've already proposed—they're encountering Infinity and Eternity as that Void. And second, they're experiencing that fantastic and awful feeling of the Thingness of God, Which, as I just said, is really an unimaginable (literally)

Aspect of the Infinite Person. I think that these *Things*, along with Pure Consciousness without Mind, are, in a certain sense, *not* God as such but rather the *Tools* the Person that is God uses to set up the conditions for there to be finite creation at all—for there to be place, locality, space; for there to be time; and for there to be things and psyche or mind. All of these aspects of Reality (with the possible exception of mind/Mind) are, obviously, finite. And they all require an Infinite and/or Undelimitable Background. This is where the rabbit holes in chapters 2 and 3 are all going.

Another way to look at this question of the Infinite Background and the (supposedly) finite foreground is Mandelbrot's way: all finite aspects of Reality are actually Infinity (and, by extension, Eternity) reworked, we could say, into finite forms that necessarily are set off from one another by the gaps between them; gaps that are not Void, not empty, but finite things themselves. In this hypothesis, and in my interpretation of it, there is still "only" *God* (because, by definition, God's Infinity, as well as Eternity, is all there is). But because God can Infinitely and Eternally do whatever God Is or Wishes, God Self-finitizes while remaining Infinite. Yet, as in my second proposal for what Eastern mystics are encountering as the Void and, as we've already speculated, another way to think about this Void of Infinity and Eternity and the Void of Mindlessness (but as the already and fundamentally in-place requirement for the manifestation of mind/Mind) is Isaac of Luria's tsimtsum—the placeless, timeless, mindless Place within the Infinite Person, which that Person has vacated (imaginally) to make room for something "other than" Himself.

This all begs the question of exactly how we can get multiplicity/Multiplicity out of Oneness, since multiplicity, by definition, is finite, and *the* One (once again) is Infinite. So, related to the Kabbalist system, but also maybe Mandelbrot's, is the idea, most famously proposed by Fichte and Hegel, that God begins the process of manifesting multiplicity/Multiplicity by positing a Part of Himself as going over into the

Not-Me, or into Self-negation, and then affirming that His Not-Me is really Himself in a new form, one that eventually makes room for finite others. These are all, I think, about making "as if" His Infinity (and Eternity) could also be experienced as a multiplistic Reality. And, as I've said earlier, for God, "as if" is as real as His (also posited) condition of Absolute Oneness.

In my likely story this "as if" transition can be viewed (by our discursive, one-thing-after-another finite perspective) as occurring, like the evolution of the physical universe, in *layers/Layers*. We've looked at a number of layered systems—both psychic (in chapter 2) and ontological (in chapter 5)—and discovered that, as in the case of calculus, where we can create as long a string of numbers (or entities, Hypostases, and so on) as we like or are able, we can never create enough layers or numbers to ever reach Infinity. So, in the context of the layered spiritual systems we looked at (again, in chapter 5) in order to try to account for the imaginal fact that there is a disjunction between a God of Infinite Goodness and Beauty—and Infinite Personhood at all—and the created or manifested world as we know it, none of these step-down transformer models really work. But let me say that while they don't work absolutely, either for accounting for how we get from an Infinite One to the multiplicity/Multiplicity, or from Pure Good to the emergence of Evil, there is *something* about them that seems right, true—at least to me.

My own *experience* of layers/Layers like these is that there *is* a gradient of Goodness and Beauty (and Truth) that runs from the Absolute to the relative—somewhere along the line of which Evil, Ugliness, Untruth, Dissimulation, or Fragmentation make their appearance. As we've seen, David Bohm tries to account for this by saying that the implicate order is only partially expressed as the explicate. (But does he answer the question of how this comes to be or why?) The Neoplatonists (and, following in their footsteps, the Gnostics and the Kabbalists, among others) do try to account for how it comes to be but, in my view, don't answer satisfactorily the *why* question (or, in the end, even the *how* question). Where this is most important—at least to me—is when we get to the question of Evil. Following Richard Dawkins, Lyall Watson proposes that moral-ethical Evil arises at the level of "selfish" genes. Taking my cue from Robert Hazen, I've suggested that It first shows Itself maybe even at the level of RNA or DNA—in other words, in life-or-death competition and predation. In the physical universe, although nobody gets hurt until there are mechanisms for existential dread to become experienced, competition and predation do seem to represent a step down, or up, however you think about it—a layer one or more steps removed from unadulterated Goodness. Consequently, natural Evil (if there is such thing) can be seen as *inherent* to a finite world or worlds, just by virtue of their finitude—their fragmented, partial representation of original Wholeness—while moral-ethical Evil can be seen as an *emergent* factor in living systems, bound as they are to a dimension in which competition and predation are essential ingredients of the life condition itself.

Just to finish my hypothesis of a Layered God—and that would mean a *psychically* Layered God in some sense that mostly escapes me—I want to suggest that the Neoplatonic system to which I qualifiedly subscribe would line up with my notion that there is a Supracosmic Consciousness (Plotinus's One, but Conscious and Intentional) beyond but also including all the lower forms of consciousness. That would mean God, both the Knowable and the Unknowable Aspects of Him/Her/It. This would be followed by Cosmic Consciousness, Which would have both an upper Layer, equivalent to Plotinus's Intelligible Realm, and a lower, which would be more or less equivalent to Plotinus's World Soul. In my view, the upper Level grades in a granulated way (but still more or less smoothly) into the lower and has many layers of spaces and times—dimensions. Somewhere along this continuum, Jung's collective unconscious (which I would render Collective *Consciousness*) becomes distinguishable. This latter is the Background for all further levels of consciousness—that of life as a whole, all the biological categories of living things (kingdoms, phyla, classes, and so on), and, in the human case, all genders, cultures, races, nations, families, and individuals. I say this not to try to figure it all out because, as I've emphasized in various places in this book, I don't think the Neoplatonists *have* figured it all out. I say this because I have *experienced* something *like* this, *felt* It, *intuited* It *within my own psyche.* A small example of this is the mirror experience I've talked about several times—the sense of the peeling away of deeper and deeper and larger layers of Self—and also because both my psi and spiritual experiences have pointed me in that direction. Does it work? For me, *provisionally.*

God and Psyche

I want to consider this layered thing in the context of God and Psyche and psyches in a little more detail. *I know that my psyche is layered and that these layers are inhabited by a multitude of entities, some of them persons, some personish. I know* this because of, as I just indicated, the *experiences* I've had—*psychological facts*—from the day-to-day to psi to spiritual. I've certainly experienced feelings, ideas, sensations—some bodily, some emotional and/or intellectual—coming into my ego-consciousness (and going out of it!). *I know* what it's like to be beside myself, or to be suddenly and powerfully infused by breakthrough inspirations and realizations that make me feel that I have moved to a higher level of consciousness, *a larger, freer, wiser, more insightful version of me.* Through my own depth-psychological analysis and the exercises that go with that—for example, dream interpretation, active imagination dialogue, guided imagery meditation, and so on—I have communicated with some of Beahrs's mental units within me, many full-fledged alternative aspects of me, some seemingly fragmentary bits of alternative me's, and some that I could not identify as me at all. In psi and spiritual experiences, I have experienced telepathy, precognition, incipient apparitions, full-on apparitions, angelic and demonic presences, and so forth. I've also experienced the layering that I am as being lifted up, enraptured, breathless into the Ecstasy of feeling one with Pythagoras's All and, beyond that, with God, both in His Self-finitized mode and in that Utterly Undefinable More that lies behind that. Feeling *That* leads me to *believe* that at the Center of the multitude that is my individual psyche is the last and greatest of the rabbit holes, as I've mentioned above.

I know that we live *within* a Psychic Medium in Which, as it seems to me, communication among everyone—living and dead, humans, animals, plants, so-called extraterrestrials, and so forth, as well as alternative spaces and times—occurs. Called by various names—collective unconscious, Collective Consciousness, subliminal consciousness, psychic ether . . . whatever—It has powerfully impacted my life, in both small and very large ways in the form of "visitors," welcome and unwelcome—never looked for or expected but showing up in any case. *I think* this Psychic Medium accounts for my psi and my spiritual experiences. *I know that I interact with It* in *a more general way* both in the things that I've imagined sooner or later manifesting in my life and in my experienced ability to negotiate with It.

Let me tell you just a couple of stories about this negotiating thing.

I sometimes "go on strike" against the terms and conditions I'm currently living in. When I do that, it feels as if Someone—I often call it "the Universe," but I really mean God, or at least one or more of His go-betweens (like Cosmic Consciousness)—is listening and responding, almost as if when I say no, there's a deliberation on the "other side," which then offers me something different. Usually, that doesn't fill the bill, so I again say no. This back-and-forth may go on for a while, until "Someone" says, "Okay. I guess he's serious. Let's give him what he wants." Or "Let's get him on the right path, even if he doesn't understand what's happening at first." For example, when, after much struggle, I decided to go on strike against the military draft and become a conscientious objector during the Vietnam War and was resolved to visit what would soon be my new "home," Joliet Prison in Illinois, I suddenly and quite unexpectedly received a letter from my draft board granting my request. That experience redirected me back to my core enthusiasm—spirituality and, at that time, specifically Judaism. After a period of hardship doing alternative service for the government, I went to Israel to experience the Jewish (and Christian) homeland directly. That eventually led to my first master's degree from the University of Chicago (a dream I had long held).

Or when I went on strike against being a car salesman, and after a period of emotional, financial, and health hardships, I began Jungian analysis, which led me to Chicago Theological Seminary . . . which led to my second master's degree and, a few years later, collaboration with one of the professors there on what became an enormously popular book (another dream fulfilled). Or when I broke up with two women at the same time (yes, I'd been caught in the horrors of a love triangle), after a period of deep aloneness, the woman of my dreams—by now, my wife of twenty-seven years—showed up. There are many more such stories that *I've actually lived*. And through all of these and more, I *knew* I was negotiating with Something or Someone out there in the Psychic Medium in Which our individual psyches are enclosed and, I think, from Which they are expressed.

I don't know, but I strongly suspect that, among the Structures and Dynamics of this Psychic Medium, are Oversouls and Higher Selves that have larger identities than most of the persons, or person-like characters, that have shown up in my psi experiences, but smaller identities when compared with the All and, beyond that, God. I suspect this because of certain dreams and visions I've had. Along with this scenario has come the possibility (at least for speculation) of way stations and/ or reincarnations along a very long road to optimal expansion of my psyche en route perhaps to Psyche, whether Cosmic Consciousness or Supracosmic Consciousness or both.

This brings me to something else *I know*: that the Face God shows us in His/Her/Its interactions with us as individuals is Itself Multiple— and, not surprisingly, in a way that resonates with the complexity of the human psyche in general and each one of us individually. I also know this because of the many varied experiences, descriptions, and depictions of God that individuals, tribes, nations, religions, and so on have of God. It makes me wonder if the Infinite Person Herself is a Multiplicity within His/Her/Its Essence, fragments as It Self-finitizes in order to make a world of "others-than-Himself/Herself/Itself," or whether it's *we*—our own inherent diversity—that, in effect, forces God into our many different molds. *I think* that all three possibilities may be true. But going back to the (unsolved) problem of how we can get multiplicity out of oneness, I don't see how there could actually be pure Oneness if what It produces is Multiplicity/multiplicity. So, I suspect that God is simultaneously Infinite Oneness and Finite Multiplicity. From our side of the divide between the finite and the Infinite, it looks as though the Multiplicity within God is *potential* and that not all potentials become actual, at least not *here*. In other words, that a selection process has occurred within God that allows some potentials to become actual (in *our* world) and others not. But, I further speculate, that, on *God's* side of this divide, potentials are *as actual and as real* as any actualities that appear on *our* side.

I don't know, but I think that the Psyche of the Infinite Person is not only as Complex as the most complex psyches that we know directly and immediately—ours—but almost certainly infinitely more so. It does seem to me that for complex psyches to exist on *our* side of the divide, they must *be* in some way on the other. God must be at least what we are! So, if that's true, how far do our psyches accurately depict the Divine Psyche? *I know* we can experience—emotionally and cognitively—psyches of any kind or size *only* along the lines of the structures and dynamics of our own psyches. So, in that sense, as Expressions of the Infinite Psyche on a finite scale—which is necessarily diminished in its capacities, and also only partial, because it has been shaped by the survival needs of creatures that have evolved in a competitive and predatory, and relative and relational, dimension of Reality—our psyches *must* express *something but only something* of the Infinite Psyche. The competitive and predatory conditions for being in this dimension of Reality don't seem to me to apply to the Infinite Person (ultimately, there *is* only one Infinity, so there is no competition, predation, or evolution *as* It, at least in Its Essence).

Even so, *I think* there is justification for trying to see at least a little way into the Divine (or Supracosmic) Psyche—again, of course, only along the lines of the structures and dynamics of our own. Here again, I *do* think Plotinus especially is helpful. As we've talked about, just now and in earlier places in this book, Plotinus and his Platonic predecessors and subsequent followers (in somewhat different ways) suggest that there are four *somethings*—Hypostases, Aspects, Persons, Psyches, Gods?—"within" the Infinite or Supracosmic, Psyche. These are arranged in descending order from the Infinite and wholly Immaterial to the finite enmeshed in, and largely defined by, matter. As I've indicated many times throughout this book, but want to reiterate, one of my main differences with Plotinus and my solidarity with the *theistic* Neoplatonists is that, while Plotinus's One is Unconscious and *Sub*personal, my experience of the One is that It is an Infinite Person, and consequently, Infinitely Eternally *Super*conscious. As Infinitely Eternally Superconscious, He/She/It enfolds . . . Self-expresses . . . *simultaneously and spatially-temporally* . . . all of His Hypostases, Stages, or whatever you want to call them.

God and Nature

This moves us toward my likely story about Nature. I want to say a couple of preliminary things about God and matter per se before we look at God and Nature in a more general way. What I'm about to say contains elements of *I know* and *I think*. *I think* Psyche (here, the Cosmic Psyche or Cosmic Consciousness) expresses Itself through and perhaps *as* matter. To a materialist, it looks like *matter* is expressing *psyche* . . . which it is, but in my view, as *the agent or medium* of *Psyche's* expression. In my hypothesis, I'm thinking generally, but I'm really focused on the brain-mind or brain-psyche problem, the crux of the controversies in the so-called philosophy of mind enterprise. *I don't know, but I suspect* that the brain is other than the finite psyches it seems to express or, according to materialists, generate. My reasons for *thinking* this include: (1) Psyche can apparently exist separately from the brain . . . at least for a while; evidence for this is mainly from apparitions, NDEs, and OBEs. (2) The brain is *local*—it occupies space—whereas psyche is *not* spatial. (3) *If* the laws that govern matter, including the form of matter that we call space, and the math that shapes them are in some way precedent (yet not necessarily *earlier*) to matter, which they seem to be, and if they at least *look* like they are the products of Mind, they might actually *be* that. If so, they could suggest a Supramaterial Psyche (Cosmic and Supracosmic).

Okay. On to the more general problem of God and Nature.

I know there is a disjunction between the nature of Nature and the Nature of a Loving God, or even of a God Who is at least Humane and fundamentally Morally-Ethically Good. *I think* that either the world of Nature is partially split off from such a God in some inexplicable way and so is a fragmentary expression of Him, or that Nature is a direct and intended Expression of some sort of Divine Wholeness, the character of Which seems repugnant to me, falling far short, as it does, of a God of Love.

There are several ways that I can think further about this apparent disjunction. If Nature is a direct Expression of God, or even *is* God (as far as It goes), then it seems to me, God is not Someone or Something I am interested in worshiping or even having as my Companion—

certainly not as my Guide to greater Humaneness and Goodness. But it might be possible for me to *think*, "Well, although Nature is irremediably a Beautiful Terror, both a nurturer and a threat to my happiness and well-being and the happiness and well-being of others, especially those I love, there might be good and compelling Reasons why God would express Himself/Herself/Itself in this way—good and compelling for Him, maybe less good and compelling for us, at least in the short run. From my perspective, those Reasons are beyond what any finite creature can *know*.

However, that last possibility implies that there might be a *Goodness* that lies *behind* or *beyond* the bloody mayhem that Nature certainly is. But this "solution," for me, leads directly to the other possibility—that Nature is *not* an Immediate or Direct Expression of Who God is. Rather, It is the product of some at least partially alienated Aspect of God—a "Second God," a rebellious Angel or Offspring of some kind, like a Prodigal Son, or, at the very least, a partial and flawed result of God's energy running out of steam as God's Substance radiates out into No-thingness (this latter, as in Plotinus's system). One way or another, these are the major variations on Neoplatonic models. But for me, as I've already said, God is *not* like the sun and *doesn't* radiate. There's nothing other than God for Him to radiate into . . . because God is Infinite. So, no mixing of Being with Nonbeing to explain the apparent disjunction (unless you work the tsimtsum into this in a particular way). So, within this context, I'm left with the option of a split-off Aspect of the Good God that somehow achieved at least semiautonomy from Its Source (tsimtsum or not).

This is *also* a Neoplatonic idea—the World Soul, or the Psyche of Nature (Cosmic Consciousness), "falling" out of the Infinite and Eternal Goodness of God, and then remembering, however vaguely, the Fullness It once knew, but, limited by space, time, and matter, unable to regain that Fullness except by struggling, one creature, one event, one moment at a time, to imitate or recreate that Fullness as best It can under the circumstances in which It finds Itself. Unable to rejoin Unity-in-Multiplicity, It must move forward discursively, patching together an intractable multiplicity into a kind of unity—however, one that, because It is in time, can never transcend it. And transcendence is the only way back!

This is one of my working hypotheses actually, because this is what Nature, if It is a Psyche, or at least a Person*ish* Entity as a Whole, looks like to me, particularly when it comes to evolution— both overall and in terms of the development of persons. It looks to me like someone who has sustained a life-threatening trauma, is gradually coming to consciousness, and is awkwardly trying to wake up and get himself/herself around—recover her/his former full functionality. He or she stumbles around and gropes at things, catches hold, tries to steady herself/himself, and then pushes onward to the next graspable thing. I mean this physically and also psychologically. I'm well aware that this is a mythological explanation. But, as I've said before, myth sometimes is the only language we have at certain levels of dumbfoundedness to communicate a truth that, for whatever reason, can't be expressed discursively.

While, from my perspective, this hypothesis fits the phenomenology—the structures and dynamics that are presented—I'm not happy with it. It still doesn't solve the problem of how you go from Perfection-Wholeness-Goodness-Beauty . . . and Absolute Love . . . to the world as we actually experience it. Why not? Because it doesn't account for *how it is possible* for anything, maybe especially a Thing as vast and powerful or, more to the point, as *important* as Nature—the very thing that gives rise to persons—to go off the rails and, in effect, rebel against God. Or, if not rebel, then inadvertently become separated from the Wholeness of the Infinite Person. How could you *ever* be separate from Infinity? Here again, we have the issue of how the One generates the Many. But, more urgently, how the Good can give rise to Evil. Because it is really the origin of Evil—again—that we're talking about. I could suggest free will, even *within* the Divine Economy—God's Capacity, Which would be Infinite—to manifest *to* God Her Own Opposition to Herself, Her Own Imperfection, Greediness, Cruelty, Indifference, and so on. (This is similar to Fichte's and Hegel's way of trying to understand the problem.)

But then we're back to the first option, in which God is Himself Good *and* Evil—consequently, not worthy of our worship or any of the roles we assign Him that all amount to assuring our (eventual) well-being. I can imagine, though, that Evil serves some of those Purposes of God that I, and I think pretty much everyone else, can't fathom. However, at the same time, I *can* see how, at moderate levels of intensity, Evil can serve the Purpose of soul growth . . . the maturation of the person in character, strength, compassion, wisdom, and the capacity to love, in other words, Humaneness.

There is, of course, the fantastic Beauty and also the Order and Unity of Nature that It *does* achieve, however painful aspects of these might be to individuals. What accounts for these breathtaking qualities? Again, one possibility is that Nature really is a Direct Expression of the Beauty and Unity of God, albeit less full, less perfect, and fragmentary or partial. And that's it! We're just looking right at God in Her/His/Its Guise *as* Nature. Also again, the other possibility is that Nature is *not* a Direct Expression of God, and the Beauty, Order, and Unity of Nature is the result of God's shining through It so brilliantly that that Divine Shining almost succeeds in overwhelming our experience of the rest of Nature, like brilliant sunlight blasting through a latticework and blinding us. Maybe both are true: God both *is* Nature and *beyond* It. That's more or less the position of Panentheism, the other one of my primary theological stances.

Going back again to my version of theistic Neoplatonism, influenced by my take on Panentheism, it seems to me that the recognition that Reality, including Divine Reality, is Layered does not mean that

anything is less real or inferior to anything else. The various layers/
Layers, as well as their inhabitants, are all equally valued and real to
God. But some are fuller expressions of the Divine Psyche than others.
So that, as I would further differ from Plotinus and modify his hier-
archy of Hypostases: (1) all Layers or Dimensions are distinguishable
yet completely simultaneous and congruent with one another, with
no contradiction; (2) all are Infinite and Eternal in at least one of the
senses we looked at in chapter 6; and (3) all are Conscious, although
perhaps to different degrees. I do *think* that Nature is less Conscious
than the Intelligible Realm, Which is less Conscious than the One.

God and Persons

In chapter 4 I agreed with Lyall Watson and, before him, Ernst Haeckel
in stretching the idea of what qualifies as a person to include *Volvox*
and similar organisms. I even went further and suggested that *anything*
with a sense of "I," however vague and unconscious, might be considered a person. With God, of course, at the high end of such a continuum and RNA toward the lower end, that covers *all* things that could
be thought of as alive. I've gone still further and wondered with David
Chalmers if a thermostat might qualify[1] and gone further still to consider the possibility that quarks might be thought of in some sense as
persons. Beyond that—if Alfred North Whitehead is right about "occa-
sions" being "lured" toward greater things, "creative advances," he calls
them[2]—could they be considered to have an (admittedly) deeply unconscious "I-ness?"

And I've proposed that persons are of Infinite Worth and are
Immortal. What *I know* is that persons I've known and loved, humans
and animals I've been close to, yet also certain things—settings, houses,
the family car, objects I treasure—*feel to me* as if they are of Infinite
Worth—the *things* because of their association with loved *persons*. If
I feel that and if God is the Source of any and all feelings of Infinite

Valuing that we or anything else has (which I think is true), and because God *is* Infinite, and so anything He manifests, He manifests with Infinite Intention, Caring, and Concern, then *everything* is actually of Infinite Worth to Him. *I think* that, because God is the Infinite *Person*, everything He/She/It Expresses is also a person, however minimally.

Does that mean that God values a quark as much as He does a human being? It might. Is She as concerned about the death of the gnat I killed three days ago as He is about the death of my or your mother, father, spouse, child, and so on? Again, maybe. Sound crazy? Yep. But then there's Georg Cantor with his infinities, some "larger" than others.[3] So, on one level, as I suspect, *everything* is a person and of equal value— namely, Infinite. Yet on another level, some persons are more fully, complexly, and consciously persons. These are "more" Infinitely Valued by God than others that are more simply and unconsciously Infinite.

If I focus on the relationship between *psyches* and *persons*, what do I see? I guess I think that, in a general sense, psyches make up persons. In that sense, a person is the total of the structures and dynamics of a psyche. In effect, at least for simpler instances, they're the same thing. If a thermostat or a quark is a person, then it is also a psyche, however dimly in both cases. On the other hand, at least for complex psyches, I think that persons are the climax and pinnacle of such psyches, like the tips of waves on an Infinite Ocean.

As we've seen, there may be any number of persons, or person*ish* elements, within any one psyche. All contribute to the person that that psyche expresses. But, in the end, what you see is what you get. In a pragmatic sense, the person is what is presented as you or me.

I can say, "I *am* or *have* a psyche." I can say, "I *am* a person." But I *can't* say, "I *have* a person."

But there's more. All finite persons, and the psyches that make them up and give rise to them, as I've suggested, are a marriage of psyche and matter of *some* kind. This is certainly true for finite persons of *this* dimension of Reality. I think it's true for finite persons of other dimensions as well, some of which interface with ours from time to time.

In my view, where this marriage between psyche/Psyche and matter that gives rise to persons does *not* apply is in the case of God. The Infinite Person *is* the Supracosmic Psyche. In God, Psyche and Person are identical. That's how being Infinite works. In spite of Georg Cantor, at actual Infinity, there is only *one* of these. I do think that Nature is, or manifests, a Psyche or something resembling a Psyche, Which, among other things, I've called Cosmic Consciousness. But, as we all know, there are *degrees* of consciousness. I'm not sure just how conscious Nature is, or any part of It, including us. Or if It is a Person, or just Person*ish*. I suspect that the Infinite Person is present in the Psyche of Nature, as He/She/It is in all of Nature's particulars . . . including us (Panentheism again)—but, I think, unconsciously or semiconsciously. Yet, to be optimistic, rising, expanding, becoming gradually more *felt.*

Whatever the case, where the rubber hits the road *for me*, there are only two versions of persons that are of Absolute Worth—God and persons like us or very similar to us, especially those with at least *some* capacity for self-reflection. More importantly, persons who can meet . . . and love.

Which a thermostat can't.

God and Eternal Life

I know from my own experiences of the dead and from similar experiences of people whose reports I trust, that finite psyches-as-the-persons-we-knew *do* survive the death of their former bodies—at least for days, weeks, months, years, even decades . . . maybe centuries. When their apparitions manifest fully, their persons very much seem to be housed in a material medium of *some* kind that looks a lot like ours and seems to function similarly. They smile and wave if they're happy and stare blankly or even frown angrily if they're not. Often, they look as they did in their prime or, otherwise, as they did perhaps shortly before they died. I'm guessing that has something to do with what they think their viewers would be most comfortable with.

Full apparitions that express malicious or at least mischievous intentions show it in the expressions on their faces and sometimes in their overall physical appearance and behaviors, as in my example of "the Oak Park Demon" and maybe Sinoda (depending on who she really is). Some of these and other "dark" visitors, mostly unwelcome, may have never had lives in our dimension of Reality. Some almost certainly *have*. Who knows where they come from? So far as the malicious apparitions are concerned, I shudder to think what their home environments might be like. I think all of these apparitions—the happy and the less than that—can meet us, and we them, in what I've called Antechambers, places to come together between dimensions of Reality.

I suspect that some, many, most, or all of us have lived before . . . in other dimensions or environments, and perhaps, as the case may be, in this present one.

I believe that Eternity, Which, in Its pure form, is Timeless/All-times, is equally at home with being manifested as layers of times that run on different schedules from the ones we are most used to. *I think* Infinity, Which is Spaceless/All-space, is similar. After all, as Einstein discovered, space and time, while not the same thing, are inextricably bound and, therefore, manifest together.

I suspect that things along these lines are more complicated than the three forms of Eternity—and Eternal Life—of the ancient Egyptian scheme—Kheper, Neheh, and Djet—which we looked at most closely in chapter 6. Yet, *I think* that basic breakdown of the kinds, or layers, of Eternity and Eternal Life is an accurate shorthand for the framing of the types of post mortem environments in which we'll find ourselves. And *I do think* we'll find ourselves in a variety of forms and supporting mediums of Life in Eternity. Some of them may not be pleasant.

Which brings me to a very short consideration of the *un*pleasant kinds, which, hopefully, function more as reeducation centers rather than places of punishment. *I imagine* that many persons may find themselves, initially at least, in one of these. As I've mentioned, I suppose I subscribe to some combination of Tillich's essentialization and St. Paul's idea that Death (meaning, among other things, I think, Evil) is swallowed up, consequently metabolized, by Goodness, and thereby transfigured into a kind of Good that, from our vantage point, disappears over and flourishes on the other side of Nicholas of Cusa's Wall of Paradise. As I've previously noted, this is a Wall that I, for one, cannot see over. But I trust that God is simultaneously both Infinitely Loving and Infinitely Just. How He/She/It manages to bring these opposites together is God's business.

I believe that all ends well.

I like the idea of Kheper—the continuous and, in effect, endless freshness of new creative ventures, I suspect made possible by perhaps innumerable way stations of adventure and growth as persons. I also really like at least aspects of Neheh—especially forever actually reliving my most cherished moments. And, if and when I'm ready, I like the idea of stepping across the abyss calculus insists on between the "last number" and Djet-Eternity, as a memory of God's that I may share—safe in the rabbit hole at my Center, Immutable, Unassailable, Infinitely Valued . . . "forever." I feel what I take to be the reality of the Lifting Up Dynamic I mentioned in chapter 6, distributed throughout all the kinds of Eternal Life. In any case, once I'm in Djet-Eternity—or, rather *know* it, because I think we're always in It—then, if Stanley Rosen's brilliant take on Eternity and Time is right, or at least headed in the right direction, I'll be able to experience perhaps *everything*—I'd prefer everything *Good*—from my perch near, or at, the Center of *God's* Infinite Consciousness, in His Kingdom of Light, where all lives are completed, transfigured into a higher Goodness, and all the best dreams come true.

Why We're Here

I know I'm here to become a more authentic being (meaning more Humane and Loving) by *becoming* through the hardships and fulfillments that are the inherent ingredients of soul growth in this particular medium—this particular layer/Layer of the Reality that is God. *I also know* I'm here to create—even perhaps co-create with *the* Creator. *I know* I'm here to learn and teach, to raise children, and to support others in their adventures of becoming.

The Reasons *you're* here may be quite similar or quite different from mine. As I've said, *I think* God has *many* Purposes, some of Which we can *feel*, some of Which we can only guess, and probably most of Which we can't even begin to imagine. I believe They are all ultimately Good.

That's It!

That's it. That's the current version of my likely story. There may be others I haven't become conscious of yet. If you ask me if I really believe it, I'll say, "Well . . . it's something like that."

So, here I am, somewhere along the way on my adventures of becoming within an Infinite Person . . . astonished, exalted, and breathless!

Godspeed to you on yours!

Notes

A Note on the Notes

In many instances in the references, especially (but not exclusively) in books devoted to cosmology, quantum physics, and occasionally to comparative religion and philosophy, the discussions or allusions to specific subjects are widely scattered throughout the books. That's one reason for my sometimes many page references to the same subject from a single author. The other reason I've included multiple page references to the same subject in a single book is to provide as wide an angle on that particular subject as possible. A few times, I've just given up and referred you to the indices of the cited works.

....

Introduction

1. Tennyson, "The Higher Pantheism," stanza 6, in *Tennyson's Poetry*, 373.
2. Smith, *World's Religions*, 198.
3. Smith, *World's Religions*, 20–21.
4. Laughlin, *Different Universe*, 149, 152, 166, 210, 212.
5. Otto, *Idea of the Holy*.
6. Assmann, *Search for God*, 242.

7. "Aratus," Wikipedia, last edited May 2023.

8. Tegmark, *Our Mathematical Universe*, 271.

9. Tegmark, *Our Mathematical Universe*, 366.

1. Likely Stories

1. Plato, *Timaeus* 29b3–d3, in *Collected Dialogues*, 1167.

2. Hornung, *Conceptions of God*, 184–88, 190, 236–37, 252–53; Assmann, *Search for God*, 240–44.

3. Clark, *Myth and Symbol*, 35–67.

4. Assmann, *Death and Salvation*, 127, 371–74.

5. Simpson, "The Teaching for King Merikare," vv. 124–38, in *Literature of Ancient Egypt*, 164.

6. Budge, chap. 15, vv. 1–5, in *Egyptian Book of the Dead*, 246–47.

7. Assmann, *Death and Salvation*, 60, 73–77, 90, 100, 413–14.

8. Assmann, *Death and Salvation*, 87–94.

9. Assmann, *Death and Salvation*, 44–77.

10. Assmann, *Death and Salvation*, 15, 42, 88.

11. Assmann, *Death and Salvation*, 15, 42, 88; Budge, *Egyptian Book of the Dead*, lv–lxxxi; Clark, *Myth and Symbol*, 252–56.

12. Clark, *Myth and Symbol*, 143–56.

13. Bremmer, *Concept*, 54, 61.

14. Bremmer, *Concept*, 56–57.

15. Bremmer, *Concept*, 56–57, 75–76, 84.

16. Bremmer, *Concept*, 21–53, 70–71.

17. Bremmer, *Concept*, 68.

18. Castleden, *Minoans*, 124, 129, 132, 136, 192.

19. Castleden, *Minoans*, 142–43, 151.

20. Castleden, *Minoans*, 142, 169.

21. Castleden, *Minoans*, 125, 127.

22. Kerenyi, *Eleusis*, xix–xx.

23. Kerenyi, *Eleusis*, 148–50.

24. Kerenyi, *Eleusis*, 151–52, 155.

25. Kerenyi, *Eleusis*, 95, 174.

26. Kerenyi, *Eleusis*, 148.

27. Kerenyi, *Eleusis*, 151–52.

28. Kerenyi, *Eleusis*, 169–74.

29. Kerenyi, *Eleusis*, 174.

30. Kerenyi, *Eleusis*, 95, 174.

31. Luchte, *Pythagoras*, 61, 64.

32. Luchte, *Pythagoras*, 77.

33. Luchte, *Pythagoras*, 89.

34. Luchte, *Pythagoras*, 129.

35. Luchte, *Pythagoras*, 128.

36. Luchte, *Pythagoras*, 160.

37. Malandra, *Introduction to Ancient Iranian Religion*, 23.

38. Malandra, *Iranian*, 19–21.

39. Malandra, *Iranian*, 104–105.

40. Malandra, *Iranian*, 102ff.

41. Kelly, *Early Christian Doctrines*, 473–74.

42. Kelly, *Early Christian Doctrines*, 483–84.

43. Al-Ghazali, *Remembrance*, 256–58.

44. Barrow and Tipler, *Anthropic Cosmological Principle*, 15–20.

45. Barrow and Tipler, *Anthropic Cosmological Principle*, 21–22.

46. Barrow and Tipler, *Anthropic Cosmological Principle*, 22–23.

47. Barrow and Tipler, *Anthropic Cosmological Principle*, 23.

2. Psyche: The Multitude

1. Kelly et al., *Irreducible Mind*, 78.

2. Kelly et al., *Irreducible Mind*, 78.

3. Shear, *Explaining Consciousness*, 177–95, 197–215.

4. Kelly et al., *Irreducible Mind*, 78.

5. Kelly et al., *Irreducible Mind*, 66, 76.

6. Kelly et al., *Irreducible Mind*, 77, 78.

7. Kelly et al., *Irreducible Mind*, 83.

8. Kelly et al., *Irreducible Mind*, 84.

9. Jacobi, *Psychology of C. G. Jung*, 35.

10. Beahrs, *Unity and Multiplicity*, 50, 67, 68, 77, 81, 86, 103, 115, 118.

11. Beahrs, *Unity and Multiplicity*, 77–78.

12. Beahrs, *Unity and Multiplicity*, 53–68.

13. Beahrs, *Unity and Multiplicity*, 54.

14. Beahrs, *Unity and Multiplicity*, 60–68.

15. Beahrs, *Unity and Multiplicity*, 50–78, 136, 148, 161, 183–84.

16. Beahrs, *Unity and Multiplicity*, 108–9.

17. Beahrs, *Unity and Multiplicity*, 106–7, 125–30, 136, 141–63.

18. Beahrs, *Unity and Multiplicity*, 4, 20, 34–38, 60, 115, 117, 120, 134, 160, 161, 177, 184–85.

19. Beahrs, *Unity and Multiplicity*, 76.

20. Beahrs, *Unity and Multiplicity*, 126, 157–62.

21. Beahrs, *Unity and Multiplicity*, 107, 129–30, 150–57, 162–65.

22. Beahrs, *Unity and Multiplicity*, 121, 126–28, 141–50, 158.

23. Beahrs, *Unity and Multiplicity*, 108–9.

24. Beahrs, *Unity and Multiplicity*, 45.

25. Beahrs, *Unity and Multiplicity*, xv, 51.

26. Beahrs, *Unity and Multiplicity*, 83, 166–77, 178–80.

27. Jacobi, *Psychology of C. G. Jung*, 135.

28. Jacobi, *Psychology of C. G. Jung*, 61, 107ff., 127, 132.

29. Jacobi, *Psychology of C. G. Jung*, 5.

30. Jacobi, *Psychology of C. G. Jung*, 5.

31. Jacobi, *Psychology of C. G. Jung*, 8–9, 31, 81.

32. Jacobi, *Psychology of C. G. Jung*, 5–10, 30, 140.

33. Jacobi, *Psychology of C. G. Jung*, 39ff.

34. Jacobi, *Psychology of C. G. Jung*, 6, 7, 8, 21, 35, 111, 113.

35. Jacobi, *Psychology of C. G. Jung*, 36–39.

36. Jacobi, *Psychology of C. G. Jung*, 109–14.

37. Jacobi, *Psychology of C. G. Jung*, 114–24.

38. Jacobi, *Psychology of C. G. Jung*, 107, 126–32.

39. Jacobi, *Psychology of C. G. Jung*, 29–36, 29n.

40. Jacobi, *Psychology of C. G. Jung*, 5–10, 30, 140.

41. Jacobi, *Psychology of C. G. Jung*, 10n, 105–9.

42. Jacobi, *Complex, Archetype, Symbol*, 155.

43. Beahrs, *Unity and Multiplicity*, 53–68; Jacobi, *Psychology of C. G. Jung*, 55–57.

44. Beahrs, *Unity and Multiplicity*, 50–51, 53; Jacobi, *Psychology of C. G. Jung*, 38.

45. Gurney et al., *Phantasms of the Living*, 485, 527–531.

46. Private conversations with researchers J. Allen Hynek and Budd Hopkins (circa 1979); Strieber and Kripal, *Supernatural*, 58–59, 74, 190.

3. Nature: A Beautiful Terror

1. Benton, *When Life Nearly Died*, 275–76.
2. Hazen, *Story of Earth*, 144.
3. Benton, *When Life Nearly Died*, 132–35; Ward and Kirschvink, *New History of Life*, 218–24, 226–27, 237–43, 311, 352.
4. Raup, *Extinction*, 67.
5. Benton, *When Life Nearly Died*, 144–45, 174–75.
6. Ward and Kirschvink, *New History of Life*, 69, 100ff.
7. Ward and Kirschvink, *New History of Life*, 73.
8. Ward and Kirschvink, *New History of Life*, 86.
9. Ward and Kirschvink, *New History of Life*, 85, 111–16.
10. Ward and Kirschvink, *New History of Life*, 95, 116–18.
11. Ward and Kirschvink, *New History of Life*, 175.
12. Watson, *Beyond Supernature*, 172–73.
13. Watson, *Dark Nature*, xvi.
14. Hazen, *Story of Earth*, 130, 142–44.
15. Hazen, *Story of Earth*, 130.
16. Whitehead, *Process and Reality*, 16, 88, 92, 177, 206, 287, 288, 308, 339.
17. Morris, *Runes*, 96–100.
18. Watson, *Dark Nature*, 87, 261, 264, 271, 282.
19. Watson, *Dark Nature*, 243.
20. Baggott, *Quantum*, 344–45.
21. Casti, *Paradigms*, 442–67; Maudlin, *Non-Locality*, 225–29.
22. Casti, *Paradigms*, 478–79; Greene, *Elegant*, 131, 175, 419.
23. Casti, *Paradigms*, 479.
24. Watson, *Beyond Supernature*, 30.
25. Clark, *Unknown*, 194–96.
26. Baggott, *Quantum*, 34.
27. Greene, *Elegant*, 350–52.
28. Baggott, *Quantum*, 95; Hawking, *Brief History*, 129.
29. Baggott, *Quantum*, 93–95.
30. Barrow and Tipler, *Anthropic Cosmological Principle*, 375, 376, 622–23.
31. Clark, *Unknown*, 5, 6, 10, 225–26.
32. Bohm, *Wholeness*, 241–42.
33. Hawking, *Brief History*, 109–10; Laughlin, *Different Universe*, 102–14.
34. Laughlin, *Different Universe*, 121.

35. Greene, *Elegant*, 46–52.

36. Clark, *Unknown*, 258–60.

37. Baggott, *Quantum*, 21–25; Becker, *What Is Real?*, 24–25, 26, 41, 111, 152–153, 173, 240, 286; Hawking, *Brief History*, 28–30, 213.

38. Maudlin, *Non-Locality*, 41.

39. Greene, *Elegant*, 32–33.

40. Becker, *What Is Real?*, 152.

41. Malin, *Nature Loves*, 18–24.

42. Becker, *What Is Real?*, 7, 53, 113, 120–21, 174, 201, 245–48, 254, 255, 263; Greene, *Elegant*, 53–84, 87, 126, 169, 210, 289, 343, 377.

43. Baggott, *Quantum Space*, 27, 35.

44. Maudlin, *Non-Locality*, 41.

45. Bohm, *Wholeness*, 190, 200–1, 204–17, 209–13, 218–27, 223–24, 227–36, 236–40, 240–45, 247, 252–53, 257–58.

46. Maudlin, *Non-Locality*, 72.

47. Greene, *Elegant*, 130.

48. Mandelbrot, *Fractal Geometry*, 1, 25, 30–31, 32.

49. Baggott, *Higgs*, 2–4.

50. Clark, *Unknown*, 275; Greene, *Elegant*, 8–12.

51. Casti, *Paradigms*, 442–43; Malin, *Nature Loves*, 44–49.

52. Becker, *What Is Real?*, 22.

53. Becker, *What Is Real?*, 70.

54. Baggott, *Higgs*, 80–81.

55. Baggott, *Higgs*, 55.

56. Baggott, *Higgs*, 60.

57. Laughlin, *Different Universe*, 65–66.

58. Greene, *Elegant*, 112–14.

59. Baggott, *Quantum*, 56–57.

60. Baggott, *Quantum*, 56.

61. Baggott, *Quantum*, 56–57; Davies and Gribbin, *Matter Myth*, 220–21.

62. Becker, *What Is Real?*, 256; Greene, *Elegant*, 106–8.

63. Greene, *Elegant*, 106–8.

64. Becker, *What Is Real?*, 18–20.

65. Casti, *Paradigms*, 433.

66. Casti, *Paradigms*, 433.

67. Baggott, *Quantum*, 54–55.

68. Hawking, *Brief History*, 139.

69. Becker, *What Is Real?*, 67 and multiple additional references in his index; Casti, *Paradigms*, 442–43; Malin, *Nature Loves*, 1, 3, 10, 42–44, 60, 72, 145; Maudlin, *Non-Locality*, 281.

70. Becker, *What Is Real?*, multiple references in his index; Casti, *Paradigms*, 457–58; Malin, *Nature Loves*, 72, 73, 85, 261, 262.

71. Becker, *What Is Real?*, multiple references in his index; Casti, *Paradigms*, 444–46; Malin, *Nature Loves*, 216, 260–61.

72. Casti, *Paradigms*, 445.

73. Becker, *What Is Real?*, 67–69; Casti, *Paradigms*, 446–50; Malin, *Nature Loves*, 213–14, 217–18.

74. Casti, *Paradigms*, 450–53; Malin, *Nature Loves*, 261–62.

75. Becker, *What Is Real?*, 233–34; Casti, *Paradigms*, 465–67; Maudlin, *Non-Locality*, 179–81.

76. Maudlin, *Non-Locality*, 180–81.

77. Kripal, *Flip*, 161.

78. Maudlin, *Non-Locality*, 102.

79. Becker, *What Is Real?*, 124; Casti, *Paradigms*, 453–56, and multiple references throughout the book.

80. Casti, *Paradigms*, 434.

81. Becker, *What Is Real?*, 124.

82. Maudlin, *Non-Locality*, 225–29.

83. Laughlin, *Different Universe*, 149, 152, 166, 210, 212.

84. Laughlin, *Different Universe*, 49–56, 170–73.

85. Laughlin, *Different Universe*, 50–51.

86. Becker, *What Is Real?*, multiple references (see index); Bohm, *Wholeness*, basically the whole book; Casti, *Paradigms*, 461–65.

87. Bohm, *Wholeness*, 187.

88. Bohm, *Wholeness*, 193.

89. Bohm, *Wholeness*, 193.

90. Bohm, *Wholeness*, 188.

91. Bohm, *Wholeness*, 193.

92. Bohm, *Wholeness*, 189.

93. Bohm, *Wholeness*, 191.

94. Bohm, *Wholeness*, 197.

95. Bohm, *Wholeness*, 196.

96. Greene, *Elegant*, 97–103.

97. Plato, *Timaeus* 37d, in *Collected Dialogues*, 1167.

98. Becker, *What Is Real?*, 54–60, 164–65.

99. Becker, *What Is Real?*, 149–53.

100. Becker, *What Is Real?*, 204–7.

101. Becker, *What Is Real?*, 215–18.

102. Maudlin, *Non-Locality*, 21–28, 51, 72, 111, 185.

103. Rosen, *Metaphysics*, 22–27.

104. Rosen, *Metaphysics*, 31–34.

105. Rosen, *Metaphysics*, 85–87.

106. Greene, *Elegant*, 424.

107. Greene, *Elegant*, 364–70, 385–86.

108. Baggott, *Quantum*, 70–71.

109. Baggot, *Quantum*, 70–71; Bohm, *Wholeness*, 106; Hawking, *Brief History*, 173; Laughlin, *Different Universe*, 146, 154–55.

110. Clegg, *Infinity*, 124.

111. Maudlin, *Non-Locality*, 109–10, 197–98.

112. Clegg, *Infinity*, 137, 157–59, 160–61, 169, 174–80, 182–187, 189–90, 199, 200.

113. Tegmark, *Our Mathematical Universe*, 252.

114. Tegmark, *Our Mathematical Universe*, 259.

115. Kripal, *Flip*, 161.

116. Lonergan, *Insight*, 117–21.

117. Lonergan, *Insight*, 50–56, 631, 632.

118. Gould, *Book of Life*, 1–21.

119. Barrow and Tipler, *Anthropic Cosmological Principle*, 647–55.

120. Barrow and Tipler, *Anthropic Cosmological Principle*, 524–41; Hazen, *Story of Earth*, 80–82.

121. Morris, *Runes*, 6–7.

122. Luchte, *Pythagoras*, 44.

123. Greene, *Elegant*, 127–31.

124. Plotinus, *Enneads*, 151–52, 213, 217–28; Stamatellos, *Plotinus and the Presocratics*, 93, 116–17, 119–23, 132.

125. Dawkins, *Greatest Show*, 364–65.

4. Persons: Presence Fully Visited

1. Chalmers, *Conscious Mind*, 293.

2. Morris, *Runes*, 237.

3. Watson, *Beyond Supernature*, 40–42.

4. Watson, *Beyond Supernature*, 40–42.

5. Fichte, part one in *Science of Knowledge*, 93–138, but really the whole book.

6. Descartes, *Meditations on First Philosophy*, 18, 92.

7. Gillette, *Thresholds of Elysium*, 201.

5. Divine Self-Disclosures:
Unsettling and Ecstatic Intimacies

1. Tolkien, *Tree and Leaf*, 72.

2. Amos 5: 21–24.

3. Micah 6:8.

4. Gillette, *Thresholds of Elysium*, 28, 79.

5. Schlitt, *Divine Subjectivity*, xvii–xix, 38, 41, 44, 46–48, 54, 101, 129.

6. Chittick, *Self-Disclosure*, IV 231.31, 169.

7. Nicholas of Cusa, *Selected Spiritual Writings*, 254.

8. Mandelbrot, *Fractal Geometry*, 1, 25, 30–31, 32.

9. Shear, *Inner Dimension*, 99–100, 104–5, 107, 116–17, 172–73, 222–24.

10. Chittick, *Imaginal Worlds*, 59–60, 88.

11. Chittick, *Imaginal Worlds*, 59–60.

12. Shear, *Inner Dimension*, 36.

13. Wilber, *No Boundary*, 3–4, 76, 126, 128, 158.

14. Scholem, *Major Trends in Jewish Mysticism*, 258–68.

15. Scholem, *Major Trends in Jewish Mysticism*, 260–64.

16. Scholem, *Major Trends in Jewish Mysticism*, 261.

17. Scholem, *Major Trends in Jewish Mysticism*, 262.

18. Scholem, *Major Trends in Jewish Mysticism*, 263.

19. Plotinus, *Enneads*, xxi, 354, 379.

20. Plotinus, *Enneads*, 361, 382; see also *Enneads* VI.2, VI.7.3, in Stamatellos, *Plotinus and the Presocratics*, 1, 25.

21. Plotinus, *Enneads*, 379, 338–90; see also *Enneads* VI.7, VI.8, VI.9, in Stamatellos, 25, 26.

22. Plotinus, *Enneads*, xxxi.

23. Plotinus, *Enneads*, xxxiii.

24. Plotinus, *Enneads*, xxxi, 36.

25. Plotinus, *Enneads*, 371.

26. Plotinus, *Enneads*, xcv, xxxiii.

27. Plotinus, *Enneads*, 372, 375–78.

28. Plotinus, *Enneads*, xxxiii–xxxiv.

29. Plotinus, *Enneads*, xxxviii, 94.

30. Plotinus, *Enneads*, xcii, 58.

31. Plotinus, *Enneads*, xxxviii.

32. Plotinus, *Enneads*, xcvii, 227–28; Wagner, *Neoplatonism*, 72, 296–301, see especially *Enneads* II.1, III.7, III.2.1, III.8, VI.4.27.23–25, pp. 301, 286.

33. Plotinus, *Enneads*, 93, 347; see also *Enneads* III.2.1, in Wagner, 289–90.

34. Scholem, *Major Trends in Jewish Mysticism*, 216.

35. Scholem, *Major Trends in Jewish Mysticism*, 214, 217–18.

36. Scholem, *Major Trends in Jewish Mysticism*, 216.

37. Scholem, *Major Trends in Jewish Mysticism*, 219.

38. Scholem, *Major Trends in Jewish Mysticism*, 236–37.

39. Scholem, *Major Trends in Jewish Mysticism*, 218–20.

40. Scholem, *Major Trends in Jewish Mysticism*, 219–20.

41. Scholem, *Major Trends in Jewish Mysticism*, 237.

42. Scholem, *Major Trends in Jewish Mysticism*, 238–39.

43. Scholem, *Major Trends in Jewish Mysticism*, 238.

44. Grant, *Gnosticism*, 34ff.; Robinson, *Nag Hammadi*, 8–10.

45. Robinson, *Nag Hammadi*, 4.

46. Grant, *Gnosticism*, 19, 21, 22, 23, 25; Robinson, *Nag Hammadi*, 194, 304, 334.

47. Robinson, *Nag Hammadi*; see especially, "The Gospel of Truth," 37–55; "The Tripartite Tractate," 54–97; "On the Origin of the World," 160–79; "Zostrianos," 368–93.

48. Grant, *Gnosticism*, 15–26, 87–88, 169; Robinson, *Nag Hammadi*, 6.

49. Malandra, *Introduction to Ancient Iranian Religion*, 16–17.

50. Malandra, *Introduction to Ancient Iranian Religion*, 4–26.

51. Malandra, *Introduction to Ancient Iranian Religion*, 19–20.

52. Chittick, *Sufi Path*, 211; Chittick, *Imaginal Worlds*, 78, 142–44, 167–68; Chittick, *Self-Disclosure*, 100, 155, 173–76, 178, 181–84, 225, 254, 255, 299.

53. McGuire, *Collected Works*, 107–200, especially 169–78.

54. Jung, *Portable Jung*, 526, 527, 534, 538, 540, 549.

55. Basham, *Wonder That Was India*, 251.

56. Basham, *Wonder That Was India*, 257.

57. Basham, *Wonder That Was India*, 339.
58. Basham, *Wonder That Was India*, 284.
59. Wilson, *World Scripture*, 113.
60. Smith, *World's Religions*, 214–18.
61. Chittick, *Self-Disclosure*, 169.

6. The Immortality of Persons

1. Gurney et al., *Phantasms of the Living*, 483, 527–31.
2. Kelly, *Irreducible Mind*, 367–405.
3. Krohn and Kripal, *Changed in a Flash*, 131, 152, 190–91, 223, 277–78, 190–91, 280–81.
4. Chittick, *Imaginal Worlds*, 104–8.
5. Krohn and Kripal, *Changed in a Flash*, 175.
6. Assmann, *Search for God*, 10.
7. Pettitt, *Paleolithic Origins*, 265.
8. Halifax, *Shamanic Voices*, 52–54.
9. Graeber and Wengrow, *Dawn of Everything*, 389.
10. Graeber and Wengrow, *Dawn of Everything*, 388–89.
11. Varner, *Ghosts, Spirits and the Afterlife*, 61.
12. Varner, *Ghosts, Spirits and the Afterlife*, 61.
13. Varner, *Ghosts, Spirits and the Afterlife*, 63–64.
14. Varner, *Ghosts, Spirits and the Afterlife*, 61.
15. Varner, *Ghosts, Spirits and the Afterlife*, 69.
16. Varner, *Ghosts, Spirits and the Afterlife*, 69.
17. Varner, *Ghosts, Spirits and the Afterlife*, 78.
18. Varner, *Ghosts, Spirits and the Afterlife*, 77–78.
19. Varner, *Ghosts, Spirits and the Afterlife*, 67.
20. Neimark, *Way of the Orisa*, 44.
21. Neimark, *Way of the Orisa*, 45.
22. Neimark, *Way of the Orisa*, 45.
23. Ford, *Hero with an African Face*, 193–194.
24. Ford, *Hero with an African Face*, 195.
25. Ford, *Hero with an African Face*, 199.
26. Lai, *Excavating the Afterlife*, xi, 32–50.
27. Lai, *Excavating the Afterlife*, 60–61.
28. Lai, *Excavating the Afterlife*, 34–35.

29. Lai, *Excavating the Afterlife*, 131–33.

30. Lai, *Excavating the Afterlife*, 156, 187.

31. Lai, *Excavating the Afterlife*, 2–6, 77–80.

32. Lai, *Excavating the Afterlife*, 1–2, 97, 120.

33. Lai, *Excavating the Afterlife*, 62.

34. Lai, *Excavating the Afterlife*, 46–48.

35. Lai, *Excavating the Afterlife*, 36–43.

36. Lai, *Excavating the Afterlife*, 28–29, 36–39.

37. Lai, *Excavating the Afterlife*, 31, 120.

38. Lai, *Excavating the Afterlife*, 93, 115, 117–20.

39. Lai, *Excavating the Afterlife*, 119, 120.

40. Lai, *Excavating the Afterlife*, 131–34, 161, 191.

41. Lai, *Excavating the Afterlife*, 51, 80, 89, 174.

42. Lai, *Excavating the Afterlife*, 80–97.

43. Lai, *Excavating the Afterlife*, 93–97.

44. Lai, *Excavating the Afterlife*, 162–65, 187.

45. Trump, *Malta*, 10–11, 45.

46. Trump, *Malta*, 88.

47. Trump, *Malta*, 87.

48. Trump, *Malta*, 115.

49. Trump, *Malta*, 45, 117.

50. Castleden, *Minoans*, 152.

51. Castleden, *Minoans*, 157.

52. Castleden, *Minoans*, 152.

53. Castleden, *Minoans*, 153.

54. Castleden, *Minoans*, 152.

55. Pryor, *Stonehenge*, 101–4.

56. Pryor, *Stonehenge*, 103.

57. Pryor, *Stonehenge*, 126.

58. Pryor, *Stonehenge*, 101–4, 126.

59. Pryor, *Stonehenge*, 103.

60. Pryor, *Stonehenge*, 126–28.

61. Guthrie, *Orpheus*, 156–87.

62. Guthrie, *Orpheus*, 169, 172–75.

63. Guthrie, *Orpheus*, 167–75.

64. Guthrie, *Orpheus*, 156–68.

65. Grummond and Smith, *The Religion of the Etruscans*, 66–69.

66. Grummond, *The Religion of the Etruscans*, 78.

67. Grummond, *The Religion of the Etruscans*, 69–70.

68. Grummond, *The Religion of the Etruscans*, 71–73.

69. Grummond, *The Religion of the Etruscans*, 72–73.

70. Grummond, *The Religion of the Etruscans*, 75.

71. Jacobsen, *Treasures of Darkness*, 52, 67, 212.

72. Smith, *Origins of Biblical*, 9, 98–100.

73. Assmann, *Death and Salvation*, 372.

74. Chittick, *Self-Disclosure*, 114, 154, 178, 290.

75. Chittick, *Imaginal Worlds*, 116–19.

76. Plato, *Timaeus* 37d, in *Collected Dialogues*, 1167.

77. Tillich, *Systematic Theology*, vol. 3, 406-409.

8. My Likely Story

1. Chalmers, *Conscious Mind*, 281, 293–99, 301.

2. Whitehead, *Process*, 21, 28, 35, 88, 128, 189, 222, 227, 346, 349.

3. Clegg, *Infinity*, 137, 157–59, 160–69, 174–80, 182–87, 189–90.

Bibliography

Al-Ghazali, Abu Hami Muhammad. *The Remembrance of Death and the Afterlife: Book XL of the Revival of the Religious Sciences*. Translated by Thomas J. Winter. Cambridge, UK: Islamic Texts Society, 1995.

Assmann, Jan. *Death and Salvation in Ancient Egypt*. Ithaca, NY: Cornell University Press, 2005.

———. *The Mind of Egypt: History and Meaning in the Time of the Pharaohs*. New York: Henry Holt and Company, 2002.

———. *The Search for God in Ancient Egypt*. Ithaca, NY: Cornell University Press, 2001.

Baggott, Jim. *Higgs: The Invention and Discovery of the "God Particle."* Oxford, UK: Oxford University Press, 2012.

———. *Quantum Space: Loop Quantum Gravity and the Search for the Structure of Space, Time, and the Universe*. Oxford, UK: Oxford University Press, 2018.

Barrow, John D., and Frank J. Tipler. *The Anthropic Cosmological Principle*. Oxford, UK: Oxford University Press, 1986.

Basham, Arthur L. *The Wonder That Was India*. New York: Grove Press, Inc., 1959.

Beahrs, John O. *Unity and Multiplicity: Multilevel Consciousness of Self in Hypnosis, Psychiatric Disorder and Mental Health*. New York: Brunner/Mazel, 1982.

Becker, Adam. *What Is Real? The Unfinished Quest for the Meaning of Quantum Physics*. New York.: Basic Books, 2018.

Benton, Michael J. *When Life Nearly Died: The Greatest Mass Extinction of All Time*. London: Thames and Hudson, 2015.

Berkeley, George. *A Treatise Concerning the Principles of Human Knowledge.* Edited by Jonathan Dancy. Oxford, UK: Oxford University Press, 1998.

Bohm, David. *Wholeness and the Implicate Order.* London: Routledge, 1980.

Brannen, Peter. *The Ends of the World: Volcanic Apocalypses, Lethal Oceans, and Our Quest to Understand Earth's Past Mass Extinctions.* New York: HarperCollinsPublishers, 2017.

Bremmer, Jan N. *The Early Greek Concept of the Soul.* Princeton, NJ: Princeton University Press, 1983.

Budge, E. A. Wallis, trans. *The Egyptian Book of the Dead: (The Papyrus of Ani) Egyptian Text Transliteration and Translation.* New York: Dover, 1967.

Carroll, Sean. *The Big Picture: On the Origins of Life, Meaning, and the Universe Itself.* New York: Dutton, 2016.

Casti, John L. *Paradigms Lost: Images of Man in the Mirror of Science.* New York: William Morrow and Company, 1989.

Castleden, Rodney. *Minoans: Life in Bronze Age Crete.* London: Routledge, 1990.

Chaisson, Eric J. *Cosmic Evolution: The Rise of Complexity in Nature.* Cambridge, MA: Harvard University Press, 2001.

Chalmers, David J. *The Conscious Mind: In Search of a Fundamental Theory.* Oxford, UK: Oxford University Press, 1996.

Chittick, William C. *Imaginal Worlds: Ibn al-'Arabi and the Problem of Religious Diversity.* Albany, NY: State University of New York Press, 1994.

——. *The Self-Disclosure of God: Principles of Ibn al-'Arabi's Cosmology.* Albany, NY: State University of New York Press, 1998.

——. *The Sufi Path of Knowledge: Ibn al-'Arabi's Metaphysics of Imagination.* Albany, NY: State University of New York Press, 1989.

Clark, Stewart. *The Unknown Universe: A New Exploration of Time, Space, and Modern Cosmology.* New York: Pegasus Books, 2016.

Clayton, Philip, and Arthur Peacocke, eds. *In Whom We Live and Move and Have Our Being: Panentheistic Reflections on God's Presence in a Scientific World.* Grand Rapids, MI: William B. Eerdmans, 2004.

Clegg, Brian. *Infinity: The Quest to Think the Unthinkable.* New York: Carroll and Graf, 2003.

Davies, Paul, and John Gribbin. *The Matter Myth: Dramatic Discoveries that*

Challenge Our Understanding of Physical Reality. New York: Simon and Schuster, 2007.

Descartes, René. *Meditations on First Philosophy: With Selections from the Objections and Replies*. Translated by Michael Moriarty. Oxford, UK: Oxford University Press, 2008.

Evans, Hillary. *Sliders: The Enigma of Streetlight Interference*. San Antonio, TX: Anomalist Books, 2010.

Fichte, J. G. *The Science of Knowledge*. Edited and Translated by Peter Heath and John Lachs. Cambridge, UK: Cambridge University Press, 1982.

Ford, Clyde W. *The Hero with an African Face: Mythic Wisdom of Traditional Africa*. New York: Bantam Books, 1999.

Fowden, Garth. *The Egyptian Hermes: A Historical Approach to the Late Pagan Mind*. Princeton, NJ: Princeton University Press, 1986.

Gillette, Douglas M. *The Shaman's Secret: The Lost Resurrection Teachings of the Ancient Maya*. New York: Bantam Books, 1997.

———. *At the Thresholds of Elysium*. Palatine, IL: DouglasGilletteCreations, 2016.

Gould, Stephen Jay, ed. *The Book of Life: An Illustrated History of the Evolution of Life on Earth*. New York: W. W. Norton, 2001.

Graeber, David, and David Wengrow. *The Dawn of Everything: A New History of Humanity*. New York: Straus and Giroux, 2021.

Grant, Robert M. *Gnosticism and Early Christianity*. New York: Harper and Row, 1966.

Greene, Brian. *The Elegant Universe: Superstrings, Hidden Dimensions, and the Quest for the Ultimate Theory*. New York: W. W. Norton, 2003.

Grimal, Nicolas. *A History of Ancient Egypt*. Oxford, UK: Basil Blackwell, 1994.

Grummond, Nancy Thomson de, and Erika Simon, eds. *The Religion of the Etruscans*. Austin: University of Texas Press, 2006.

Gurney, E., F. W. H. Myers, and F. Podmore. *Phantasms of the Living*. Vol. 1. London: Tribner, 1886.

Guthrie, William K. C. *Orpheus and Greek Religion*. Princeton, NJ: Princeton University Press, 1993.

Halifax, Joan. *Shamanic Voices: A Survey of Visionary Narratives*. New York: E. P. Dutton, 1979.

Hawking, Stephen. *A Brief History of Time*. New York: Bantam Books, 2017.

Hazen, Robert M. *The Story of Earth: The First 4.5 Billion Years, from Stardust to Living Planet*. New York: Penguin Books, 2012.

Hegel, Georg Wilhelm Friedrich. *Hegel's Phenomenology of Spirit*. Translated by A. V. Miller. Text analysis and foreword by J. N. Findlay. Oxford, UK: Oxford University Press, 1977.

Heinberg, Richard. *Memories and Visions of Paradise: Exploring the Myth of a Lost Golden Age*. Los Angeles: Jeremy P. Tarcher, 1989.

Hornung, Erik. *Conceptions of God in Ancient Egypt: The One and the Many*. Ithaca, NY: Cornell University Press, 1982.

Hume, David. *A Treatise of Human Nature*. London: Penguin, 1985.

Izutsu, Toshihiko. *Creation and the Timeless Order of Things: Essays in Islamic Mystical Philosophy*. Ashland, OR: White Cloud Press, 1994.

Jacobi, Jolande. *Complex, Archetype, Symbol in the Psychology of C. G. Jung*. Princeton, NJ: Princeton University Press, 1959.

———. *The Psychology of C. G. Jung: An Introduction with Illustrations*. London: Yale University Press, 1973

Jacobsen, Thorkild. *The Treasures of Darkness: A History of Mesopotamian Religion*. London: Yale University Press, 1976.

Jung, Carl. *The Portable Jung*. Edited by Joseph Campbell. New York: Viking Press, 1971.

Kelly, Edward F., Emily Williams Kelly, Adam Crabtree, Alan Gauld, Michael Grosso, and Bruce Greyson. *Irreducible Mind: Toward a Psychology for the 21st Century*. New York: Rowman and Littlefield, 2007.

Kelly, John N. D. *Early Christian Doctrines*. New York: Harper and Row, 1978.

Kerenyi, Carl. *Eleusis: Archetypal Image of Mother and Daughter*. Princeton, NJ: Princeton University Press, 1967.

Klein, Richard G. *The Human Career: Human Biological and Cultural Origins, Third Edition*. Chicago: University of Chicago Press, 2009.

Kripal, Jeffrey J. *The Flip: Epiphanies of Mind and the Future of Knowledge*. New York: Bellevue Literary Press, 2019.

Krohn, Elizabeth G., and Jeffrey J. Kripal. *Changed in a Flash: One Woman's Near-Death Experience and Why a Scholar Thinks It Empowers Us All*. Berkeley, CA: North Atlantic Books, 2018.

Lai, Guolong. *Excavating the Afterlife: The Archaeology of Early Chinese Religion*. Seattle, WA: University of Washington Press, 2015.

Laughlin, Robert B. *A Different Universe: Reinventing Physics from the Bottom Down*. New York: Basic Books, 2005.

Lewis, Clive S. *The Great Divorce*. New York: HarperCollins, 1973.

Lonergan, Bernard. *Collected Works of Bernard Lonergan: Insight*. Toronto, Canada: University of Toronto Press, 1957.

Luchte, James. *Pythagoras and the Doctrine of Transmigration: Wandering Souls*. Martin: University of Tennessee, 2009.

Malandra, William W. *An Introduction to Ancient Iranian Religion: Readings from the Avesta and the Achaemenid Inscriptions*. Minneapolis: University of Minnesota Press, 1983.

Malin, Shimon. *Nature Loves to Hide: Quantum Physics and the Nature of Reality, a Western Perspective*. Oxford, UK: Oxford University Press, 2001.

Mandelbrot, Benoit B. *The Fractal Geometry of Nature*. Battleboro, VT: Echo Point Books, 2022.

Maudlin, Tim. *Quantum Non-Locality and Relativity: Metaphysical Intimations of Modern Physics*. Oxford, UK: John Wiley, 2011.

McGinn, Colin. *The Problem of Consciousness*. Oxford, UK: Blackwell, 1991.

Morowitz, Harold J. *The Emergence of Everything: How the World Became Complex*. Oxford, UK: Oxford University Press, 2002.

Morris, Simon Conway. *The Runes of Evolution: How the Universe Became Self-Aware*. West Conshohocken, PA: Templeton Press, 2015.

Myers, Frederic W. H. *Human Personality and Its Survival of Bodily Death*. Mineola, TX: Dover, 1961.

Neimark, Philip John. *The Way of the Orisa: Empowering Your Life through the Ancient African Religion of Ifa*. New York: HarperOne, 1993.

Nicholas of Cusa. *Nicholas of Cusa: Selected Spiritual Writings*. Translated by H. Lawrence Bond. New York: Paulist Press, 1997.

Nicholson, Shirley, ed. *Shamanism*. Wheaton, IL: Theosophical Publishing House, 1987

O'Meara, Dominic, ed. *Neoplatonism and Christian Thought*. Albany, NY: State University of New York Press, 1982.

Otto, Rudolf. *The Idea of the Holy*. Oxford, UK: Oxford University Press, 1958.

Pettitt, Paul. *The Paleolithic Origins of Human Burial*. London: Routledge, 2010.

Plato. *The Collected Dialogues*. Edited by Edith Hamilton and Huntington Cairns. Princeton, NJ: Princeton University Press, 1989.

Plotinus. *The Enneads*. Translated by Stephen MacKenna. London, UK: Penguin Books, 1991.

Pryor, Francis. *Stonehenge: The Story of a Sacred Landscape*. New York: Pegasus Books, 2017.

Radin, Dean. *The Conscious Universe: The Scientific Truth of Psychic Phenomena*. New York: HarperCollins, 1997.

Raup, David M. *Extinction: Bad Genes or Bad Luck?* New York: W. W. Norton, 1991.

Reich, David. *Who We Are and How We Got Here: Ancient DNA and the New Science of the Human Past*. New York: Vintage Books, 2018.

Robinson, James M., ed. *The Nag Hammadi Library*. San Francisco, CA: Harper and Row, 1981.

Rosen, Stanley. *Metaphysics in Ordinary Language*. South Bend, IN: St. Augustine's Press, 2010.

Rundle Clark, Robert T. *Myth and Symbol in Ancient Egypt*. London, UK: Thames and Hudson Ltd., 1959.

Schlitt, Dale M. *Divine Subjectivity: Understanding Hegel's Philosophy of Religion*. Scranton, PA: University of Scranton Press, 2009.

Schneider, Tammi J. *An Introduction to Ancient Mesopotamian Religion*. Grand Rapids, MI: William B. Eerdmans, 2011.

Scholem, Gershom G. *Major Trends in Jewish Mysticism*. New York: Schocken Books, 1946.

Scott, Walter, ed. *Hermetica: The Ancient Greek and Latin Writings Which Contain Religious or Philosophic Teachings Ascribed to Hermes Trismegistus*. Boston: Shambhala Publications, 1982.

Shear, Jonathan, ed. *Explaining Consciousness: The Hard Problem*. Cambridge, MA: MIT Press, 1995.

———. *The Inner Dimension: Philosophy and the Experience of Consciousness, 2nd Edition*. London: Harmonia Books, 1990.

Sheldrake, Rupert. *Morphic Resonance: The Nature of Formative Causation*. Rochester, VT: Park Street Press, 2009.

———. *Morphic Resonance and the Presence of the Past: The Memory of Nature*. Rochester, VT: Park Street Press, 2012.

Simpson, William Kelly. *The Literature of Ancient Egypt: An Anthology of Stories, Instructions, Stelae, Autobiographies, and Poetry, Third Edition*. London: Yale University Press, 2003.

Sing, Simon. *Big Bang: The Origin of the Universe*. New York: HarperCollins, 2004.

Smith, Huston. *The World's Religions: Our Great Wisdom Traditions*. San Francisco, CA: HarperSanFrancisco, 1991.

Smith, Mark S. *The Origins of Biblical Monotheism: Israel's Polytheistic*

Background and the Ugaritic Texts. Oxford, UK: Oxford University Press, 2001.

Stamatellos, Giannis. *Plotinus and the Presocratics: A Philosophical Study of Presocratic Influences in Plotinus' Enneads.* Albany, NY: State University of New York Press, 2007.

Stang, Charles M. *Our Divine Double.* Cambridge, MA: Harvard University Press, 2016.

Strieber, Whitley, and Jeffrey J. Kripal. *The Supernatural: Why the Unexplained Is Real.* New York: Penguin-Random House, 2016.

Talbot, Michael. *The Holographic Universe.* New York: HarperCollins, 1991.

Tennyson, Alfred. *Tennyson's Poetry.* Edited by Robert W. Hill. New York: W. W. Norton, 1971.

Tegmark, Max. *Our Mathematical Universe: My Quest for the Ultimate Nature of Reality.* New York: Vintage Books, 2014.

Thomas, Winton D., ed. *Documents from Old Testament Times.* New York: Harper and Brothers, 1958.

Tillich, Paul. *Systematic Theology.* 3 vols. Chicago: University of Chicago Press, 1951–1976.

Tolkien, John R. R. *Tree and Leaf.* Dublin, Ireland: HarperCollins, 1998.

Trump, David H. *Malta: Prehistory and Temples.* Santa Venera, Malta: Midsea Books, 2004.

Varner, Gary R. *Ghosts, Spirits and the Afterlife in Native American Folklore and Religion: Case Studies in Religion: Native American Traditions.* Raleigh, NC: Oakchylde Books, Lulu Press, 2010.

Wagner, Michael F., ed. *Neoplatonism and Nature: Studies in Plotinus' Enneads.* Albany, NY: State University of New York Press, 2002.

Wansbrough, Henry. *The New Jerusalem Bible: Reader's Edition.* New York: Doubleday, 1990.

Ward, Peter, and Joe Kirschvink. *A New History of Life: The Radical New Discoveries about the Origins and Evolution of Life on Earth.* New York: Bloomsbury, 2015.

Wargo, Eric. *Time Loops: Precognition, Retrocausation, and the Unconscious.* San Antonio, TX: Anomalist Books, 2018.

Watson, Lyall. *Beyond Supernature: A New Natural History of the Supernatural.* New York: Bantam Books, 1987.

———. *Dark Nature: A Natural History of Evil.* New York: HarperCollins, 1995.

Whitehead, Alfred North. *Process and Reality*. New York: Free Press, 1978.

Wilber, Ken. *No Boundary: Eastern and Western Approaches to Personal Growth*. Boston, MA: Shambhala, 1979.

Wilson, Andrew, ed. *World Scripture: A Comparative Anthology of Sacred Texts*. New York: Paragon House, 1991.

Wright, Edward J. *The Early History of Heaven*. Oxford, UK: Oxford University Press, 2000.

Index

Other Books by Douglas M. Gillette

At the Thresholds of Elysium
Lyrical Illuminations for Lifting Spirit into Bliss

The Shaman's Secret
The Lost Resurrection Teachings of the Ancient Maya

Primal Love
Reclaiming Our Instincts for Lasting Passion

The Lover Within
Accessing the Lover in the Male Psyche
coauthored with Robert Moore

The Magician Within
Accessing the Shaman in the Male Psyche
coauthored with Robert Moore

The Warrior Within
Accessing the Knight in the Male Psyche
coauthored with Robert Moore

The King Within
Accessing the King in the Male Psyche
coauthored with Robert Moore

King, Warrior, Magician, Lover
Rediscovering the Archetypes of the Mature Masculine
coauthored with Robert Moore

To find books on mysticism and spirituality as well as other
related topics published by Inner Traditions, go to
www.InnerTraditions.com